PRAISE FOR

Veronica's Diary III
Awakening the Woman Within

"In a world where so much of what is watched or read has been designed to manipulate, influence, or distort the truth, the third book in the Veronica's Diary series, *Awakening the Woman Within*, is refreshingly authentic."

—Jean Sheldon, Author, *The Woman in the Wing.*

"This is not a catalog of daily events; it is the story of a woman's remarkable character as she explores a new freedom in her third stage of life. Her blithe spirit invites us to travel with her through the ups and downs that eventually lead her to the study of chiropractic medicine."

—Alice Lynn, Author, *Scattered Pieces.*

"A brilliantly written masterpiece that touches the most fundamental chords of what it means to be human. Never have I read such a colorful and entertaining recount of someone's life."
—Susan D. Kalior, Author, *The Other Side of Life: The Eleven Gem Odyssey of Death.*

Library of Congress Control Number: 2010921972
ISBN 9780982648438
First Edition
Veronica Esagui, DC

Editors: Chory Ferguson, Maria E. Chitsaz

Book Cover and Graphics Designer: Jean Sheldon

Illustrations: Derrick Freeland

PAPYRUS
PRESS, LLC

21860 Willamette Drive, West Linn, OR 97068

To order additional copies of this book

www.veronicaesagui.net

Printed in the United States of America

To my friends, Dr. Peruzzi, Dr. Holdman,
Dr. Clari Fearman, Fay Zealand, Terri Flannigan,
and Mr. and Mrs. Ounuma

Author's notes

The people and the stories portrayed in this book are all true as to my recollection when I began writing my diary in Portuguese, Saturday, April 26, 1986 in Howell, New Jersey. Upon translating my diary to English I have kept it as it was written, but I have changed some individuals' names to protect their privacy.

12/3/15

To Andy,
May your journey
take you where your
dreams are. Love, your friend
Veronica

Mix your hopes and dreams with hard work, blend them
well with lots of passion and persistence, and your wishes
will come true.

—Veronica Esagui, DC

Contents

Illustrations

~ Chapter One ~

It's Show Time!

1988

Lakewood, New Jersey
USA

Spring of 1988

My nickname, Ronnie, is a result of the Americanization process. Veronica, my real name, has been enclosed in the "Ronnie" casing since arriving in the U.S. in 1962.

I don't know much about geisha girls, but I believe that term is a sound description of my persona when I got married to Al, twenty-six years ago. While growing up in Portugal, I was taught that the husband was number-one, and without him I was nothing. But after getting married, I learned that Nelly, my mother–in–law, as the mother of number-one—was even more significant than Al was. After I gave birth to Ralph, everything was still fine and dandy—until his brother Steve was born. Steve didn't have a fighting chance when it came to being treated fairly, either by his father, or his grandmother. They had both wanted my second child to be a girl!

I can't believe that I am writing about this after so many years. I can see now that the past is very hard to get rid of, because I am still holding certain resentments. Perhaps these thoughts came about because I got a letter from Mama this week, where she went on bragging, "Verónica, I am so proud of you! You went from your white school uniform to the white wedding gown, never touched by a man."

I didn't know whether to cry or laugh when I read her statement. She had given me no choice when she pre-arranged my marriage to her nephew. Doesn't she understand that I got married with my eyes closed, and without any choice in the matter? Doesn't she realize that what she did was wrong?

Al and I have nothing in common. This is not a marriage; it's more like being chained to a sinking ship! When I get home after work, he is already watching television and eating peanuts and that is where he remains for the rest of the evening, after I serve him dinner on a TV tray. It doesn't matter if it's summer or winter, the heat inside our apartment is always beyond anything I can stand, and to make matters worse, it doesn't matter how clean I leave the kitchen, when I get home I am guaranteed to have a mess waiting for me. The only subject he talks about with a certain amount of passion is re-telling me the news he heard on television or read in the paper. I could care less about the news! I've given up bringing any creative thoughts to our conversations because he will make fun of me by saying something stupid or annoying. I have no one else to talk to. I don't recognize Al any longer as the man I married. He has become a stranger. At the end of a day's work, I have no motivation to go home.

Mama never recovered from the motorcycle accident she suffered so many years ago. As she has gotten older, her body pain has also gotten worse. None of our family doctors can come up with a good explanation because all the lab tests come back negative for anything specific, so they figure it's all in her head. They keep her well supplied with narcotics which, for the most part, don't even help her. Her days of being active and having a normal life have turned into staying home and being dependent on a caregiver. She no longer paints either; her creativity is limited to only one form of expression: writing poetry. It makes me sad to know that Mama is living like a little bird inside a gilded cage, never to fly free again for the rest of her life. She is always on my mind. She is still living in Portugal with Papa and I know that most likely she won't be visiting anytime soon. She no longer travels because she also has a heart condition. All I can do is share the best part of my world through the letters we exchange every week.

For quite a while now I have been trying to figure a way to describe to Mama, the Simy Dinner Theatre, which I am, the founder and producer. After much thought I decided that I would try my best to carry her here through visualization and even though I've never done this, it's worth trying. I wrote:

> Dear Mama,
> Please have someone read this special letter to you. Close your eyes and follow me to the theatre I've named after you, but you have not seen until now.
> We enter the Kobe Japanese Restaurant through wide glass double doors. To your right is the red-lacquered checkroom, where you leave your coat in the care of a young American girl dressed in a Japanese kimono. She welcomes you with a smile, and hands you a small, numbered ticket that you must return to get your coat back before you leave the Restaurant at the end of the evening. As you turn to your left, you admire the large moon-shaped glass window that takes the full length of

the wall. Below that large window you can't help noticing the upright fish—an unusual, four-foot-tall, dark brown ceramic fish, except for the scales, which have a hint of dark green. You wonder if it is a replica of some rare type of sturgeon. He proudly displays his prominent male genitals, which is acceptable since he is wearing a silly hat and has a jolly fish face. He stands among various types of live plants and some bamboo shoots, which are cleverly growing by a river-rock path that is set along the wall. Some people entering the restaurant, obviously for the first time, remark that they have never seen a fish like that and they smile.

From the lobby where we stand, you notice that the glass-like gray marble floors are partially covered with a red carpet that runs up the Brazilian-wood steps on your left to the second floor. The stylish staircase, also with red-lacquered handrails on both sides, leads to your theatre, The Simy Dinner Theatre, on the second floor.

The steps to your right go down to the restaurant below. You can't help noticing to your immediate right a small red-lacquered shelf where Mrs. Ounuma displays her pride and joy, an arrangement of huge maroon silk flowers.

We are still standing in the lobby, and looking up you can't help noticing the luxurious, bigger-than-life, red and white Japanese silk kimono, with fancy peacocks embroidered in gold, that hangs like a drape from the second floor ceiling.

I understand that you are anxious to go upstairs to see your theatre, but Mr. and Mrs. Ounuma, the restaurant's owners, are at the bottom of the steps and can't wait to meet you. I will hold your arm as we walk down the six steps below us. Don't expect Mr. and Mrs. Ounuma to hug or shake your hand. Their culture dictates that they bow instead. Of course you feel very special, and you bow back to them. Mrs. Ounuma apologizes as she leaves to do her usual errands in the kitchen, and Mr. Ounuma starts taking customers to their tables. I will be glad to show you around.

Jerry, the Japanese bartender behind the small bar on your right, is Americanized, and shakes your hand and tells you how delighted he is to meet you. He asks you to sit at one of the comfortable bar stools and hands you a tall delicious strawberry smoothie decorated with a little colorful paper umbrella inserted into a chunk of freshly cut sweet pineapple and a strawberry. If you like, you can keep the little umbrella as a souvenir. I then ask Jerry to show you some of his artwork. At first he acts shy, but then he quickly whips out his portfolio from behind the bar with some originals of his exquisite black and white detailed drawings. Jerry is a very accomplished artist, and I just know that someday he will be very famous.

C'mon, let's say goodbye to Jerry and sit down at the sushi bar. You can take your drink with you. Yes, the sushi bar is big and it takes the full length of the wall to your right. The sushi chef is very proud of his creations, which are considered sushi masterpieces by his clientele. You will notice that people eating sushi leave $20 and an occasional $50 in the glass tip jar. That's a true sign of how much they appreciate the chef's undivided attention to every detail he puts into their meal. I know that you have never had sushi, but you love fish, and you are always ready to try something new. What better opportunity then to try a Ronnie Roll? A year ago, my favorite sushi chef at Kobe created, especially for me, the Ronnie Roll. He makes them with extra avocado pieces, and one whole sliced shrimp, little crunchy fish eggs on the inside as well as on the outside of the rice and also around the seaweed.

He tops it off with some crispy fresh greens for color. With a Ronnie Roll, I am guaranteed to find fish eggs between my teeth even an hour later after I eat.

Wait! Hold on! That round green paste on your plate is not pistachio candy! It's wasabi, Japanese horseradish! Trust me, it's not made for human consumption by itself, it has to be mixed with soy sauce, or added to the sushi in the proper amount. The first time I had sushi and I saw that tiny green ball of soft wasabi on my plate, I thought it was a mint type of dessert, for after the meal. You want to know what happened when I inadvertently wound up with a mouthful of pure wasabi? The best way to describe the effects of swallowing a chunk of pure wasabi would be to say that I was lucky that my eyeballs didn't fly out of their sockets.

There were lots and lots of tears! I know it feels good to laugh about it now! But I should have a t-shirt made that says, "I survived swallowing a chunk of wasabi."

Now, let me take you through the two large dining areas and into the Hibachi rooms. Yes, I love the view from the dining room too, and you are not imagining it if you think it looks like the river is very close to the low windows. Mr. Ounuma personally planted the beautiful bamboo trees along the building in an attempt to retain the land that the river hasn't already washed off. Twice last year the river came into the restaurant and went as far as the kitchen. A lot of water damage happened to the building because of that. But Mr. and Mrs. Ounuma are hard-working people, and they are not going to allow something like a river overflowing to destroy everything they've worked so hard for. Mr. Ounuma has been saving money so that he can purchase a special outdoor water pump to prevent it from happening again.

As we enter the hibachi room, you'll notice that there are six hibachi tables in the room. They work like grills and up to ten people can sit comfortably around one of them, while the chef performs the cooking in front of the diners. You've never had hibachi? Mama mia, you have got to experience this. Let's share a meal. What would you like; chicken, lobster, steak, or shrimp? Okay, if that's your choice, shrimp it is. Jack, is our hibachi chef tonight. Wow, you are right; the way he throws those knives in the air and moves the fresh veggies and shrimp around is like being at the circus. What a show! Oops, one of the shrimp just flew onto your plate. Jack is giving you an extra shrimp because you are my mom.

Isn't it fun to see your food being prepared? Can you taste the delicious flavor of the fresh shrimp? What about the fluffy rice with those sweet peas and small bite-size carrots? Here, have some of my fresh bean sprouts. I am glad that you like them too. They are supposed to be very healthy for you.

The show upstairs will start in a half-hour. But don't worry; I already have a table reserved just for you.

I am glad you like the way the restaurant is decorated. Did you notice that the dining room tables are covered with colorful silk tablecloths depicting fine Japanese artwork? Well, I hate to tell you this, but some customers loved the tablecloths so much that they were stealing them. Mr. and Mrs. Ounuma were forced to cover the tables with a heavy glass top. Still, once in a while, a tablecloth will disappear right from under their noses, which means the crooked customer had the nerve to pull the large tablecloth from under the glass, and most likely hid it under their coat on the way out of the restaurant.

Isn't it pretty to see the bamboo growing in large containers and used as partitions between the two large regular dining rooms? Mrs. Ounuma also has a gift for making original arrangements of dried flowers mixed with wheat and other items like nuts and dried corn. They are tastefully arranged and displayed throughout the restaurant in low ceramic pots.

C'mon, let's take the steps up to your theatre, The Simy Dinner Theatre. We finally reach the theatre atrium upstairs where there's a long table covered with a white tablecloth and on it is a large glass bowl with fresh rose petals, once again one of Mrs. Ounuma's artistic touches. Along the wall behind the table there are about a dozen 12"x14" black and white pictures of some of the actors and actresses that have performed in your theatre. Tracey, my theatre associate and best friend, is busy seated behind the table collecting the tickets from our patrons. She comes over and gives you a hug and tells you that she is glad to meet you. In theatre we always hug each other; it's part of being in touch with our own emotions, and it shows that we really care for that person. Just then, Michael, who is also my theatre partner and best friend, comes out of the theatre and shakes your hand. Then he says, "what the heck", and gives you a hug too.

Of course you like them both. Was that a wink telling me that you approve of my theatre partners? I am very lucky indeed. You stop for a moment at the red-lacquered double doors that open into the theatre, and you remain there taking in the overall view of the seated audience and the stage along the back wall. There are about twenty small tables covered with light brown tablecloths, and you notice that everyone is dressed in their finest. These are people looking forward to a fun night of entertainment. This month's show is a musical comedy.

For this kind of musical, I always paint the set black to give the illusion of infinity. Michael taught me that.

Wait until the stage lights go on; you are going to be captivated by the performers. Let's sit and enjoy.

Michael is running the stage lights. Shhhhhh, the lights are dimming in the room. I'll be right back. I have to make an announcement on stage.

"Ladies and gentleman; welcome to The Simy Dinner Theatre, and the company's original production of 'That's Entertainment.' It's show time!"

When Mama writes to me a letter it can be as much as twelve hand-written pages. When she got my letter of five pages she was impressed.

She wrote back, "Thank you for taking me to the Simy Theatre, I felt like I was there walking beside you. You are the best daughter a mother can wish for."

I hope that once in a while Mama will read my letter and let her imagination carry her to a world where she is without pain. For those minutes that she is with me, she will be happy.

I perceive a subtle sadness in Michael's face. We've known each other for four years, both as my friend and as my theatre partner. Working together all these years has taught me to read his eyes. Since he is shy and too busy to have a girlfriend, I decided to do something nice for him. I played matchmaker by telling Denise, the stage manager — who is single and nineteen years old — that he likes her, and then I told Michael that Denise likes him.

He asked, "Do you really want me to go out with her?"

Without blinking an eye, I said, "Yes, I do. Everybody needs someone special in their lives, and she really likes you, so why not?"

Now I know that I really care for Michael because I went out of my way to bring some happiness into his personal life.

They went out Friday night after the show, and I am keeping my fingers crossed that it will go well between the two of them. They are both young and it is spring. Love is in the air.

Saturday night Steve came to see one of our shows at the Simy Dinner Theatre and started talking to Denise. When the play was over, Michael looked for Denise since they had a second date set up for that night, but found out that Denise had left with Steve. Of course Michael was upset and told me what he thought of Denise as a person and that I was never again to play matchmaker, because he was capable of getting his own girlfriend without my help. I apologized and he forgave me because he knew I meant well.

Steve can't help it if the girls are drawn to him like bees to flowers. He has told me several times, "Mom, if a girl is not attracted to me it's because she is a lesbian."

My simplest stage design this year was for the comedy production of "Don't Drink the Water." I was very proud of it because the feeling of being inside an embassy was clearly conveyed to the audience, by the actors who made it come alive with their performances.

The stage sets get great reviews, but the truth is that without the human touch and the heartbeat of a cast, the stage would be an empty space without a soul. A few years back I tried working with a professional set designer for a couple of months, but he was a very sensitive guy who couldn't stand for actors to use his set. That didn't make much sense to me, and since I don't like dealing with unhappy people I told him he was better off not working with us any longer. Since that happened, I've taken it upon myself to be the set designer for all my productions. I'm having a great time doing it too.

Tracey, my theatre partner, gets the biggest kick when one of our theatre patrons, upon getting upstairs, looks at her and screams, "Oh my God! I can't believe it! It's Estelle Getty from the Golden Girls!"

Since this happens quite often, Tracey decided to play a prank. When it happened again last weekend she said to the glazed-eyed woman, "Yes I am. Would you like my autograph?"

We were laughing as Tracey finally confessed to the disappointed fan that she was not Estelle.

Ralph, our son, gave Al and me a tour at Bell Labs and the white-room where he works. Afterwards he invited us to his apartment for dinner. We are both very proud of Ralph. Our son has survived the crazy younger days of youth and he is now a working, mature, talented, smart and kind young man.

He cooked a delicious meal of fresh veggies and chicken in a large wok. Ralph is not only smart but he is also a very good cook.

I had never seen a wok being used for cooking at home, only at the Kobe Japanese Restaurant where Katie, the restaurant manager and hostess, sometimes prepares lunch just for the two of us, when we are alone at the restaurant. After heating the oil in the wok, she adds thinly sliced onions and shredded cabbage. When they are tender she throws in some previously boiled ramen noodles, a little soy sauce and fresh ginger. It's simple, quick and delicious. What Ralph made for us was more like a feast of colors.

Jerry, the Kobe restaurant bartender, told me there are two juried art shows going on next Saturday, and he wished he could enter both but can only attend one. I offered to help him out by representing him at one of the art festivals.

Jerry won first prize at both art competitions. To express his gratitude, he offered to take me out for dinner. I thanked him for his offer and told him that I would rather have a copy of one of his art works; my very favorite, a black and white, in-depth drawing of a street in Chicago.

I feel like I made out like a bandit. I had the Chicago print Jerry gave me framed and hung it over our couch in the living room.

Jacob, one of the young boys that used to be part of the cast when I put on theatrical productions at the high schools, became a highway patrolman two years ago. Time is going fast, that's for sure.

Every once in awhile Jacob comes into our store, the Howell Music Center, to talk about the good old days. He came by yesterday, and told me that a few days ago he had helped a very attractive lady when her car broke down on Route 9. When she asked him if he liked chocolate cookies, of course he said yes. The next morning at the police precinct, he received a box of chocolate cookies and a little note with her phone number. They are going out for dinner tomorrow night, and he admitted to being a bit nervous because she is a medical doctor. He wanted my advice.

Jacob is the kind of a guy that I see getting married to a country girl, the type that is happy staying home cooking, cleaning, and having his children. He is not the academic type or a suave, sophisticated Don Juan. I love Jacob very dearly, but I don't see a woman of the world falling in love with him. He is very handsome in his police uniform, and I have a gut-feeling that's all she saw.

I told him just to be himself and to enjoy the company and the dinner. If it's meant to be, it will be.

Jerry is not only a great artist, but he also has a great sense of humor. He says that because he is Japanese he can't tell the difference between one white customer or another because they all look the same. He wasn't happy just giving me a poster-copy of his artwork, so I finally accepted his invitation to have lunch with him at the Kobe, and he paid for my Ronnie Roll and seaweed salad. Jerry had noodle soup and had me laughing because he ate the noodles while making loud slurping sounds, which he said made the soup a lot more fun to eat. He said when he is with me he is comfortable eating noodles that way, because we are friends. But, if he were to take a girl out, it would not be romantic for him to eat that way.

I tried to convince him to ask Yoko on a date. She is one of the single waitresses, and is very pretty. He said, "They are all very nice until you have to live with them, and then the truth comes out."

I don't believe that Jerry will ever get married. He sounds like he had a bad experience in the romance department and now he doesn't trust anyone.

Al is all upset because he took our son Steve to the diner down the road for lunch and, according to him, Steve ordered a huge breakfast and when he was done eating it he ordered a huge lunch. Al said it was disgusting to see Steve eat like a pig. I'm not a psychologist, but I personally think that Steve was trying to show off to his father how much he could eat. It probably has something to do with when he was a child and he was only allowed to eat one small portion. Al would yell at Steve if he went for a second serving.

Michael and I were alone at The Simy Dinner Theatre putting a new set on stage when we heard a loud banging on the large glass door of the restaurant downstairs. The Kobe restaurant was closed. There were four enraged old men screaming their heads off outside. "It's bad enough that we have a Japanese restaurant in our town, but if that is not enough of an insult, those Japs have the audacity to put our American Flag upside down!"

Thank God that Mr. Ounuma was not there or he would have been lynched. Michael and I tried to calm them down by telling them that it was an innocent mistake. Considering that the Japanese flag is a red ball, whoever had put up the two flags, simply didn't look up!

Oh, no; they were going to close us down for insulting them as World War II veterans and on and on they went, saying that they were going to let the township know about it and nobody, neither family nor friends, would ever set foot in our Jap restaurant.

It was a lost argument; they were still in the war zone and the Japanese restaurant was at fault for the war itself. Michael brought the flag down and put it up the way it was supposed to be. But it was too late. The damage had been done.

Jacob's romance with the woman doctor didn't last long. After they went out on a second date she called him on the phone and told him that it wasn't going to work out between the two of them. He is such a sweetheart. I told him that for everyone there is someone out there; he just needs to be patient and the right woman will come along before he even blinks an eye. I believe in that.

Al and I got a real surprise gift for our wedding anniversary. I sure didn't expect it. I knew that Ralph was up to something when he called at four in the morning and told us not to ask any questions, and to just get our coats on and bring our video camera.

A long, shiny, black limousine was waiting for Al and me, and Ralph was sitting inside of it, with a mischievous smile. The limousine drove us to an open field where we soon found out what was going on. A large white van pulled in front of us, and from the back of the van a huge flat balloon was pulled out, which would soon become a hot air balloon!

I have never told anyone this, because I thought it was impossible to ever happen to me, but since reading the book "Around the World in 80 Days" when I was a kid, I have always dreamed about doing an air balloon expedition of some kind. I was so excited that I didn't even give a second thought to safety matters. I gladly jumped inside the basket, holding on tight to my video camera, and proceeded to try

Up, Up and Away!

to motivate Al to get into the basket with me. He was not as eager as I was. It didn't take long for Ralph to convince his father. Whatever Ralph tells Al, it automatically becomes "God's spoken word."

With the video turned on, I only had one mission in mind: to capture the take-off and what would follow next. Except for the "burner" above our heads, it felt as if I was floating in outer space. I was in heaven. After a few moments, sanity started to settle in my brain and I became aware that we were quite high from the hard earth below us. I took a swift look around and didn't see anything even close to a parachute. I decided to trust God, and Bob, our pilot, and to stop worrying about a body splatter injury followed by instant death.

Over the fields we went, and everything was going well according to Bob. Suddenly we started losing altitude, and we were so close to the ground that two golfers playing in the field below showed some concern by yelling, "Are you having problems staying up? Are you trying to land?"

"Oh no," said our calm pilot to the golfers, "we are just losing altitude, but we'll soon be up on course."

La di da, like who cares, this is fun, la di da, I was singing inside my head and smiling, with my video camera still on. Up we went again and then down we went and down we went, doing a fairly rough landing on what looked like a potato farm. I was laughing as we hit the ground but I didn't let go of my camera and kept it going, capturing every detail of our exciting crash.

The "potato" farmer came out of his house in pajamas with a shotgun pointed at us and screamed at the top of his lungs, "You bastards! I am going to kill you all for waking up my baby with all that racket. You fucking idiots and your hot air balloons! Get the hell off my property!"

Up we went again, high enough to get over his fence and off his property but not too much further. We landed gently in the middle of the highway in front of us. Luckily it was early in the morning, which is most likely why there was no traffic coming our way. The van had been following our trip along the road and was waiting for us. We all celebrated on the side of the road with a glass of champagne. What an adventure! I will never forget it.

Summer of 1988

Someone from the township called me to say that they are going to close our theatre because the curtains, set, and stage are not fireproof. They gave me one month to take care of the problem.

I looked into the cost of fireproofing everything and it would cost a fortune. We have three exits upstairs; what more do they want? Considering the size of the theatre, if there is a fire, we have more than enough exits and we are more than safe. This kind of request from the township is totally unreasonable. I have a gut-feeling that the old war veterans may be behind this whole thing.

We are in serious danger of losing the theatre and every-thing we worked so hard for. Losing my theatre will be like losing a child. Neither Michael nor Tracey has an easy solu-tion for the dilemma we are in, and I really don't know what to do about it either.

I have been staying awake thinking about how we can save the theatre. Last night I decided to follow my father's advice. I went to sleep knowing that in the morning, I would find the answer to my problem.

Papa is right. When I woke up I had an idea that sounded pretty good. Keeping my fingers crossed, I called the township to tell them that the stage, curtains, walls, and everything else had been fireproofed just as they had requested. They said they would be sending over an inspector.

"Everything has been fireproofed? You used flame retardant material for the curtains?" asked the so-called inspector as he walked around the stage not even realizing that we don't have curtains.

It's a dinner theatre, for goodness sake! We have no curtains! Inspector, my foot! What was he going to do, start a fire on the stage to see if it burned?

I called his bluff, "Yes, of course the curtains and everything else have been treated. By the way, would you like two complimentary tickets to our next production?"

"That's very kind of you. Would you mind giving me another extra ticket so I can bring my mother also?"

We passed the inspection!

Tracey and I celebrated that night, going around saying, "It's a miracle! It's a miracle!"

People wanted to know what the miracle was about, but Michael told us not to divulge the details of the miracle as it could come back to bite us. So we said it was a personal joke that we couldn't share and we stopped spreading the news.

We've had some very good productions through the years, but some are more unforgettable than others, like "Same Time Next Year." I remember that one especially because Barbara Schiavone got the heel of her right shoe caught in one of the cracks on the stage floor and went flying across the stage to finally land flat on her face. The audience believed that she was supposed to fall in that manner and at that specific moment. She ad-libbed like a pro, and not a sign of pain was seen on her face as she gracefully got up with the help of her co-star. This was the show that made us aware we needed to restore the stage floor, and also bring it up higher by two more feet for a better view all around.

"Fools" was a real fairy tale of joyfulness. We were sold out every night. One of the performances brought a standing ovation as the bench where seven actors were seated — broke. It was hilarious to see everyone sliding down to one side and still remain in character. The response of the audience was pure amusement since it was a comedy.

We also had a great time doing "1959 Pink Thunderbird," and that show went without any irregularities that I can remember except that it went extra smooth in the full extent of the word.

"Love, Sex, and the IRS" brought in full houses every weekend. People wanted to see what sex had to do with love and the IRS. But one of the actors was not reliable, and Debbie, the stage manager, found a syringe and a couple of needles backstage —which cleared the mystery of why he would hid backstage besides arriving late most of the time. Debbie told me that heroin was being used. One night it didn't seem that he was going to show up at all. The audience had finished their dinner and was ready to enjoy the show. I sat thinking and thinking, and finally I came up with what I believed to be the only solution that was going to save our necks. I convinced Tracey to run over to the Strand Theatre in Lakewood where I'd heard Mr. Van Zandt, the playwright of our play, just happened to be directing. I figured he might be gracious enough to come over and cover for the missing actor. Meanwhile, thanks to Mr. Ounuma, we kept the audience busy with some complimentary plum wine. They didn't seem to mind waiting. At the Strand Theatre they wouldn't even allow Tracey backstage and she never got to see Mr. Van Zandt. He was too busy directing his own production. To our relief, the actor finally showed up, about twenty minutes late. Our show went on after I announced to the audience that we had been delayed due to a traffic jam that had made one of our actors arrive late. After the run of the show was over, he knew better than to audition again with us. I hope he is still alive and doing well though. He was actually a very nice person.

"Alone Together" was one of those solid comedies that people just love watching over and over again. Kind of like a really good book that you have to read over and over.

I recall, "Play it Again Sam" because, for the first time in the history of our dinner theatre, the director helped me build the stage and even took it upon himself to bring in all the props — which made Tracey, our prop queen, very happy too.

I will always remember "Barefoot in the Park" because of the "snow." We all went berserk after each performance trying to clean the stage floor covered with Styrofoam pieces that had a definitive mind of their own. Some of the tiny pieces would cling to us, as if they were needy, while others played the game of catch me if you can. Tracey agreed that she had made a big mistake when she brought in the white foam particles to be used as snow.

"Shredded tissue paper is the answer," Michael told us.

He also showed me how to make thunder sounds by shaking a metal sheet behind the stage. He is truly a wealth of theatrical knowledge.

I had a very sad, or maybe I should say humiliating, experience when I was having lunch at Kobe.

A short, heavy set guy seated next to me at the sushi bar and exclaimed, "Ronnie, remember me? I used to live in the corner house from where you lived, in Freehold. Remember Martha? I'm Robert, her son!"

I had to take his word that it was Robert. He looked like an out-of-shape middle-aged man. But then again, Robert had never been in good shape even when he was a teenager. He told me that his mother had died from cancer five years before and that he had been married twice so far.

I recognized Robert's face when he said, "I used to have a crush on you when I was a kid. I still fantasize about you, in that small silver bikini you used to wear while sun-tanning in your backyard by your pool." He smiled that same gross smile he used to have every time he saw me shopping in Shop Rite. He would come from behind me and pinch my bottom. He was only fourteen then, but he was already sexually overbearing.

Oh, how I hated him then, and now even more. He wouldn't stop bragging. "I used to climb your fence and just sit there between the bushes watching you sleep on the hammock. You were a sight to behold."

What a freak! I got up and said, "That's a terrible thing for you to tell me, after all these years. I always thought that I was in the privacy of my own backyard. In other words, you were a peeping tom; and you are proud of that? Goodbye!"

I ran upstairs to the theatre and I sat in the dark room. I felt ashamed of myself for not having the guts to punch him until he was unconscious.

Autumn of 1988

After "Blithe Spirit" we did "Crimes of the Heart," and that is a show that I will never forget. It was a very intense experience to say the least when Anthony, the director of "Crimes of the Heart," didn't make it to the opening night. It was really odd that I happened to glance at the newspaper about a week before opening night, and just like that, I read that he had died from AIDS. I had never met anyone with AIDS before, but at the time I had thought he looked quite sick and frail, and his dark skin blotches made me ask a friend of his if Anthony had skin cancer. She said yes, in a matter of fact way, and walked away into the theatre, as she was co-directing with Anthony.

I realize now that neither she nor her husband, who was helping to build the set, wanted the other actors or crew to know about Anthony's illness. They were probably afraid that we would not want to work with him. The cast and crew, including myself, were upset that we were not told the truth;

after all, the AIDS virus is something very new to us and we don't know much about it except that it kills. We were scared that we might have caught it just from being in the same room with him.

I called Francis who is an expert on AIDS and she told me that it could only be transmitted through body fluids like intercourse. You don't catch AIDS from shaking hands or hugging. I trust Francis. She is still looking for a building in Newark where she can offer care for parents and their children with AIDS.

Michael came to Kobe to set up the stage lights for the next production. I sat in the lobby and listened to Melissa, the stage manager, telling me all about her boyfriend. When Melissa talks, all I have to do is nod every so often. I did that until her voice became more and more distant and my spirit left and carried me away. I imagined a misty warm rain falling softly upon Michael and me like a magnetic field that drew us higher and higher into the sky. Holding hands as we hovered over the mountains ahead, we smiled at each other as we contemplated how beautiful the earth looked from above. Just then, reality started approaching and everything was gone except for Melissa's voice bringing me back, and I said the first thing that came to my mind, "Melissa, sometimes I need to dance and jump and sing and scream for no reason. Do you ever feel that way?"

"You are the most understanding person I ever met, that's why I love talking to you." And she gave me a hug.

If I could pick a place to escape to, I would choose the fishing village of Eiriceira, in Portugal. I would live in a very small house, and as close as possible to the ocean. I would never wear shoes. The warm and soft sand would be more than enough to cover my feet when I would take a walk to my old favorite place by the rocks. I would sit and watch the ocean waves hitting the rocks around me. I would sit there all day until the sun went down. Then I would go back to my little house, cover myself with a lot of blankets, and sleep. In the morning, I would get up early enough to catch the sunrise and sit again in the spot where I sat the day before, watching the ocean waves hit the rocks that surround me and wait peacefully for the sunset. This scenario gives me great spiritual comfort.

Al is free of thoughts like these. He lives in a simple world. When he lies down at night, he is fast asleep. I stay awake, dreaming impossible dreams for as long as I can until I no longer know if I am awake or sleeping.

My friend, Francis, and her husband are still working as hard as ever trying to help children born from mothers with AIDS. A week doesn't go by that we don't talk on the phone and sometimes she will stop by my music store and we get a chance to chat. She came by this morning and I gave her a tour of our new and definitely bigger, Howell Music Center. We've moved from the center of the mall to the corner of the mall facing the highway. Our store is about five times bigger than the old one.

We sat on one of the benches just talking about family and life in general as we always do. I let out my fears about Steve going out with every girl he meets. I am afraid he might catch some deadly venereal disease. I told her that I don't know what Steve has that drives women wild.

"You don't see it because you are his mother. He projects a natural sexual energy in the way he walks and talks. Women are attracted to those types of signals. Look at that woman he is talking to. I bet she will buy anything he wants to sell her."

Francis was right. Mrs. Sanders comes into the Howell Music Center every week to buy drumsticks or drum heads, and if Steve is not in she walks out. Lately, she has been calling the store and asks to have Steve deliver the merchandise to her house. Steve leaves the store with the items during his lunch break. "I'll be back in about two hours or so." Then, he winks at me.

Mrs. Sanders lives up the street from our music store, about a five-minute walk. Her three little boys — four, five, and six years old — walk on their own to our mall. That's how close they live. I am worried that one day her husband will come home early and, upon finding his wife and Steve together, might kill them both. I will then have to adopt the three little kids and the baby she is now expecting.

I have been studying how audiences react to comedy for quite a while. When someone laughs out loud, it's almost like permission has been granted for everyone else to express his or her reaction. Most of the time we have very responsive audiences, but once in awhile we get a stiff-upper-lip bunch, and if a nuclear bomb were to drop among them we would most likely get no response. Ready to fix the problem, I started practicing the art of laughing a few weeks ago. It hasn't been easy for me to develop a loud, pleasant, contagious laugh. I have a low voice and laughing heartily is not natural for me to do.

This weekend I figured I had nothing to lose and began laughing right after the first punch line. Miracle of miracles, the audience relaxed and started responding. Laughing is definitely contagious.

Our music store continues to do well in the new location. I have Steve going to the mall down the road once a week to pass out fliers about our store specials. We have named this type of advertisement hand-to-hand combat, because the results are immediate, with calls for music lessons, and parents coming in to buy reeds, music books, and other items on sale. With Christmas almost at our doorstep, sales are already climbing steadily. Thank God for Christmas and Hanukah, two excellent holidays for retail people like us.

An out-of-the-ordinary couple came to see our show at the theatre. Barney and his wife Patricia would like to work with me as part of the stage crew. This is what I call a miracle since they also work for the Spring Lake Theatre and therefore they have a lot of theatre experience. Patricia would like to direct one of our shows in the near future. Neither one of them seems to work for a living; they must be financially comfortable. Barney used to be a veterinarian but had to quit his practice because he was allergic to animals. Now that's what I call a career tragedy.

We were having Christmas dinner at home when someone knocked at the front door. A woman in her early thirties introduced herself as Sylvia and asked me if Ralph was home. Because of the look on her face, I intuitively asked her to wait outside, and closed the door.

Ralph said that Sylvia was a mental case and I was to tell her that he was not in and she was to leave the premises. I opened the door again and told her that Ralph was not there. She started to cry and asked me to at least accept the Christmas gift she had brought for him since I was Ralph's mom. She put a paper shopping bag in my hands, hugged me, and left.

Ralph told me that he met Sylvia at a bar. They saw each other one more time and then he realized it wasn't going to work out. Since then she follows him everywhere with her car.

I couldn't help feeling sorry for Sylvia. Love can be so devastating. Inside the paper bag there was a really beautiful, beat-up, bluish ceramic bowl. I decided to keep the bowl as a memory of what it means not to be loved back — and also because I love ceramics.

For the New Year's show we did an original musical comedy, "The Best of Burlesque." Everybody was in agreement that Sam, our featured star performer, not only played a glittering, incredibly beautiful Joan Rivers, but he was actually even funnier. Two weeks before the show opened he invited us all to his favorite gay club in Asbury Park to help promote it. Tracey was out of town for the weekend with her family.

Sam put on a mini performance from "The Best of Burlesque" at his club, and then the other members of the cast and I passed the advertising fliers around the tables. It was dark and musty inside the club. I noticed that the air was thick, as if brought in as foreign matter. The people inside were mostly men, talking, drinking, and being social. I was there for about an hour when I started to feel nauseous with a pounding headache to boot. I had not eaten or drunk anything, so I knew it wasn't from something ingested. I went home feeling sick to my stomach and my head felt like a ton of bricks — just like I feel after I have to go into the chicken coop I rent where I store my stage props.

I've let Tracey know how lucky she was that she didn't go with us, as she might have gotten sick too. I told Barney about it and he said that I'm definitely allergic to mildew, and most likely the club had mildew inside since it is an old decaying building. It makes sense. I need to start looking for a better place to store the stage props.

Winter of 1989

Al, Ralph, and Steve were having Hibachi at the Kobe with me when Sylvia, the woman that has been following Ralph around, came over to our table, opened a small jewelry box, and put it next to him. She then walked to the corner of the room and stood there, staring at us. It was a man's diamond

ring. Ralph got up and tried to give the ring back but she refused to take it. He returned to our table and she stood against
the wall staring at us while we were having dinner. Ralph got
up once again and asked Mr. Ounuma to tell Sylvia to leave
the restaurant or the police would have to be called in to take
her away. She left and we thought everything was back to
normal, until we walked out of the restaurant.

Sylvia was standing in the middle of the parking lot under
one of the streetlights. I saw her looking at us, and then she
dropped to the ground as if she had passed out. I was ready
to run up to her when Ralph grabbed my arm and said, "No
mom, this is what I have been telling you that she does. She
gets out of her car and then drops to the ground. Don't pay
any attention and don't even look in her direction. She will
get up when we leave."

When we got into our car, I looked back as we left the
parking lot and she was getting up. Poor woman, I thought,
Ralph is right, she is out of her mind.

Marcy, the stage manager, and I were seated in the theatre
lobby waiting for the crowd to arrive and, as always, we get
there about one hour before things start to happen. We have
a lot of fun talking and joking around. But when she starts
making remarks about religion or race that I feel are offensive,
I get disturbed. I decided that she needed to become aware of
the consequences of prejudice.

Very nicely I asked her, "You told me that your daughter
is married to a Jew. Are you happy about their marriage?"

"Oh, yes; and he is wonderful! The best husband and father
anyone can wish for."

"I believe you, but do you realize that your grandchildren
are half Jewish? If you were all living in Germany during
Hitler's time, your grandchildren and your son-in-law would

have been put in a concentration camp and most likely killed in a gas chamber, just because of their religion."

"Ronnie, that's a terrible thing to tell me, but you are right." She became very quiet after that.

I believe that Marcy will never bring up the subject of religion again, and I hope some enlightenment has reached her from our little talk. She is a true friend and a really good person, but she is a lot like Al. They both grew up in a time when discrimination must have been part of their upbringing, and, since neither one of them has ever had any personal experience losing someone close to them because of religion or skin color, I can understand how they might be detached. Still, it doesn't make it right, and I don't feel like listening to either one of them.

This morning we received a small UPS package at our music store, addressed to Ralph. When Ralph came by the store, he opened the package. It was a unique and colorful book showing the creation of a baby from inception through its growth in the mother's womb. Inside was a letter from Sylvia accusing Ralph of having abandoned her after he had gotten her pregnant, and a prescription note with a doctor's name, stating that she was pregnant.

Ralph called the doctor's office and they told him that Sylvia must have stolen the prescription pad. According to the doctor she was a patient, but she was not pregnant.

This whole thing reminds me of the movie "Fatal Attraction." Thank God that the law is on Ralph's side; he is going to put a stop to Sylvia stalking him or she will go to jail.

Barbara Shiavonne is not only a great actress but she is also my number one director. On her recommendation I've been running our stage productions for a month and a half instead of just a month. I really like her suggestion because the work that is involved in changing the sets is very intense and physically demanding. The more I can draw out between shows, the less I have to work. Lately, Michael only comes in when I call him to help me with something that I can't do on my own. He is very busy working nights, and has started taking classes at the community college. Barney has become my right-hand, helping me with stage work. I purposely have the production's closing on Saturday night so that I can dedicate all day Sunday to putting up the next set. The director and the actors for the following show are very appreciative of this because it gives everyone a chance to rehearse and to get used to the new set from Monday through Thursday, before opening night on Friday.

After taking the set down on closing night, every part of my body is hurting, even the hair on my head hurts if that is even possible for anyone to imagine. I never get home before two in the morning because after the last show Mr. Ounuma likes to treat the cast and crew to a Hibachi dinner. I won't leave the theatre until I bring the set down that same night. If I call Michael, he will help me bring the set down and put the new one up, but I try not to take advantage of him unless I'm really in a bind. I love the work I do. Tracey comes to the theatre to drop off the props, and if she is free she will offer to help paint the set. She told me she has a very large family that needs her, and the grandchildren like to spend time with her too. She doesn't have the same freedom I have, to spend so many hours at the theatre.

Al rarely helps, which is good because when he does, he makes a mess painting and does what I call a half-assed job. He is also very impatient, so I rarely ask for his help. He comes to the opening night to see the show, and then he doesn't return until the next production's opening night. Barney has been helping me put the sets up, and if he is not available I can always find high school kids that are glad to work for a few extra bucks.

I took advantage of being alone at the music store to play on my guitar, one of Mama's songs that she wrote when she was a young girl. I sang the melody with the lyrics she wrote in Portuguese, "Like Jesus, his eyes are kind and affectionate. Like Jesus, he speaks softly and caring."

I was thinking about Michael when I sang Mama's love song.

I don't know if I understand completely how I feel about Michael. I am confused because I am content just being in his company and I value his friendship, yet he can be talking innocently about the weather and the sound of his voice is enough to make me sigh. He doesn't have a clue about how I feel about him and he never will.

~ *Chapter Two* ~

Returning to Egypt

Spring of 1989

I got a call from the Omnichord Company that supplies us
with electronic harpsichords. Our music store had reached the
highest selling number of Omnichords ever sold throughout
the US. They wanted to know what we did to sell so many
Omnichords, and if we have some kind of advertising trick.
They were very impressed with our selling skills.

I told them that we rarely sell any Omnichords at the
Howell Music Center. The majority gets sold at the Collingswood Flea Market, where we've had Ronnie's Music Den
since 1979. We do very well there because of the large traffic of teenagers walking around. I play Freebird by Lynyrd
Skynyrd on the Omnichord, loud enough to attract a crowd
around me. Then I stop playing and ask how many would like
to play Freebird this easily at home. It's a tune that everybody
wishes they could play themselves.

There are no secret methods to selling the Omnichords;
plainly said. They are easy to play and they sell at a reasonable
price. In my opinion the electronic Omnichords are a good
flea market musical item, that's all.

I went to see a Rheumatologist in Red Bank, which is where a lot of doctors have their office, most likely because the hospital is so close by. I wanted to know why the bones in my legs hurt so much. The pain is not constant but when it does it is very excruciating and it can last for days. Dr. Swanson asked me if I smoke, drink coffee, or alcohol, and when I said no to all the above, he was surprised.

He diagnosed me with the same ailment that my Uncle Augusto, who is a medical doctor in Portugal, had told me when I was a child. I have Rheumatoid Arthritis. Dr. Swanson said that the only thing he could do for me was to give me some injections to help with the pain.

I didn't make an appointment to return to his office for the shots, instead I have been taking into account what he asked; whether I drank coffee, alcohol or smoked. Obviously he thought that I might be putting something into my body that's affecting my health. I'm wondering if there's something in my regular diet that's affecting my bones.

"Have you seen the way our director Suzanne treats Mark, her husband?" Tracey asked me. Then, she went on, "She is very rude to him. Poor man, he was busy working on the stage and Suzanne got herself some sushi from the restaurant downstairs and didn't even offer him any. He asked her to give him a few pieces of sushi because he was hungry and she told him point-blank that she wasn't sharing her food with him. If he wanted to eat he would have to go downstairs and get his own food. She treats him like shit!"

Tracey is a very good wife, and she is proud of the way she takes care of Sam, her husband. She told me that if she knows that she is going to be at the theatre in the evening, or busy with other activities, she always leaves Sam's dinner ready to eat. All he has to do is warm it up in the microwave.

I have been charting everything I eat and drink. It turned out that two days after I ate a couple of chocolate bars, both my legs were hurting badly. That was a really bad finding, since I love chocolate!

I stopped eating chocolate for two weeks and the pain went away. Then, just to make sure it wasn't coincidence, I went to the German deli on Route 9 and bought every single chocolate I could get my hands on.

Only God knows how much pain I've had in the last three days. I am an adult and I've cried out loud with tears rolling down my face because my legs, and even my hips, hurt badly. I couldn't go to work that way, so I rented six romantic movies and stayed home for the day. When Al got home in the evening, I had not cleaned the house and I had not cooked or eaten all day. I spent the day laying on the couch in the living room, rubbing my painful legs, crying, and watching romantic movies one after another. I will never eat chocolate again.

We are short one actor, and Patricia wants me to ask Michael to play Clifford Anderson in "Death Trap."

I told her, "It's true that he is always ready to help us in any situation, but I can't ask him to help us every single time we are in trouble. Besides that, Michael is busy working at night and going to school in the daytime and I don't have the courage to bother him."

Barney said, "Michael would jump off a building if you were to ask him to do it. He is in love with you."

I remarked back as quickly as possible, "He loves everybody. You are confusing his kindness with love."

Barney winked back at me saying, "Trust me when I tell you that he only has eyes for you. Besides, we need him to play the part, and if you ask him he will do it."

Barney and Patricia left the theatre and I sat in the darkness holding my hands to my head, thinking, this is impossible, this is impossible, it can't be true.

I finally called Michael and asked him if he could be in "Death Trap." He told me that he had signed up for too many classes in college and was not doing well. He was dropping out of school for now and would be glad to help us out.

Michael is working nights, coming to rehearsals before going to work, and repairing his old house in his spare time. I don't know when he sleeps. Since I live very close to him, from time to time I pick him up for rehearsals. Sometimes he is so tired that he falls asleep while I drive. I slow down and take my time getting to the theatre. But instead of going directly to the Kobe I drive around Lakewood, and what would take me fifteen minutes to get to the restaurant can take me half an hour or more. When we finally arrive at Kobe, I park the van but leave the engine running and I wait until he wakes up. He doesn't know that I know that he loves me.

I have not seen Michael this week. His mom called me to say that Michael is very sick with fever and with what looks like chickenpox. He is staying with a friend. I gave his mom my chicken soup recipe.

I saw the movie "Cocoon." The story is about some very old people that regain their health by swimming in a pool. The pool has special powers because of the cocoons at the bottom of the pool that are from outer space. I liked the story and it made an impression in my mind. I don't see anything wrong with getting old as long as we grow old with dignity. Getting old can be one miserable health disaster after another. Both my parents are a good example of what happens with old age.

If it's not the heart, it's the circulation, and if it's not the hearing, it's the eyes! Everything breaks down and goes haywire! What's the end? Death! I am not afraid of dying; I just hope I drop dead when the time comes.

Michael is back. He told me that he was very lucky to have a friend who is also a nurse, and she took care of him while he was sick. I didn't say anything, but I don't see what the big deal is about being sick with the chickenpox, everybody gets it. Men are definitely little babies when it comes to getting sick.

Al makes fun of me because I always look at my tab before I pay the restaurant bill. He just gives the waiter the charge card. I proved him wrong when we got someone else's bill for lunch today. It was from the table with the four drinking businessmen.

I have also learned to always look at the food before putting it into my mouth, principally if it's asparagus soup. We were at the German restaurant in Lakewood, which is Al's favorite restaurant, and luckily I happened to look at my spoonful of asparagus. It had a blonde cockroach in it; most likely killed by boiling.

A hair in the food makes me stop eating and get something else, but a cockroach puts a damper on my appetite. The waitress wanted to bring me another cup of soup, but I figured that from the same cooking pot it was a good chance that others may have fallen in. I didn't have lunch, but Al did. I am sure he will return to the restaurant again. I am not going to be so eager.

A miracle happened today. Upon finishing putting the new set up for the next production, Michael and I sat across from each other at one of the small tables by the stage while quenching our thirst with some water from the bar behind us. We talked for a while about life in general and then we both reached for each other's hands. It was an instinctive move on both our parts as he told me he had been in love with me for a long, long time and whenever possible he would find an excuse to come by and help with the stage work so that he could see me. I confessed that I felt the same way and we talked about our feelings for each other and how we could only be friends. Time went by quickly and it was getting late. As we were leaving the restaurant and locking the door downstairs, Al was just pulling into the parking lot with his car and didn't see us. Even though we'd done nothing wrong except for holding hands, we were both relieved that Al didn't see us together.

I couldn't sleep at all last night. If Al had arrived a few minutes earlier and seen Michael and I sitting in the darkness of the theatre, it would not have looked right. It would have been difficult for anyone to believe we were innocent. Al could have jumped to the wrong conclusion and killed us both for nothing. With all of that in my mind, I felt that Michael and I had to stop working together. So I called him this morning on the phone and asked him to meet me at the Kobe.

Michael understood once I explained to him that I didn't want to hurt Al in any way, and he said he felt the same. I also told him that it would be healthier if he were seeing someone single and closer to his age. He said he loved me and he would always love me. Since it was going to be goodbye forever, we hugged each other very tight for a little while, and he said, "I love the way my arms go around you. We fit each other like two puzzle pieces."

As he was getting in his car he turned to me and said, "If you ever need me for anything whatsoever, call me."

I got into my car and drove up and down Route 9 listening to the music tape he gave me a few years ago, but I didn't cry.

It's been the longest two days of my life since Michael and I said goodbye to each other. I feel like I am brain-dead from lack of sleep. Eight hours of sleep is essential for me to be able to think clearly the next day.

Finally, I came up with a solution for our dilemma. I called Michael on the phone and asked him to meet me at the Kobe. When I pulled into the Kobe parking lot he was already there. The restaurant was still closed. I opened the front door and locked it and we both ran upstairs and sat by our favorite table.

I told him we don't have to stop seeing each other! We are friends! We can see each other as friends! I am always hugging everybody so why not hug him. I love him, he loves me, but as long as we stay friends nobody will get hurt and nobody has to know how we feel about each other; after all, friends love each other. I hug the cast and all my friends, does that mean that I am in love with them? No, so why should I not hug the person I love the most?

He agreed with me and we hugged each other and left the Kobe feeling perfectly happy, knowing that our relationship was back to normal.

Michael called this afternoon to ask me if I was free to go grocery shopping with him.

We met at his house and his mom gave us a long grocery list. It felt like she was purposely giving us the alibi to be with each other. She looks happy when she sees Michael and me together. We held hands while he was driving and we stopped for lunch at a diner in Belmar. While in the diner we talked about our lives. I told him about my mother and how she had protected me while growing up from dating anyone and how my mom and her sister had pre-arranged my marriage to Al. I also told Michael my most intimate secret. When I turned fifteen years old I had purposely locked my spirit within and built a wall around it so that no one could ever hurt me. In those days I knew that I would never be free to fall in love, and that was how I had protected myself from reaching out and getting hurt. He said he understood, and I felt at that moment that I finally had found my soul mate. Of course we will never be together as a couple in a physical manner, because we are like two ships in the night, but our souls are definitely intertwined.

If it's wrong for me to love Michael I'd rather die than never know what love is. If holding hands and hugging is bad, then I am bad and I accept my punishment. Also, I no longer want to look half my age like everybody thinks I am. Since we got together at the diner I look forward to beginning to grow old like everybody else. I've chosen that hour at the diner with Michael as the moment I became a woman. I've broken down the walls that covered me all these years. I am no longer afraid to face anything in life because I have awakened the woman within and now I know what love is.

Friday evening, when Michael came to the theatre, we hugged each other without any worries of what anyone might think. We said good-bye at the end of the evening and made plans to drive into the countryside on Sunday after the show.

Al only comes to see the shows on opening night, but Sunday he decided to show up again for no reason and Michael and I couldn't go for a drive afterwards. When Al got home he went straight to the couch to watch television and munch on salted cashews and peanuts. I went to bed and cried.

I got up Monday morning and drove to New York City. I found a quiet spot on the steps of one of their public libraries where a stone lion seemed to invite me to use his protective surroundings. Using a pencil to write on my empty paper pretzel bag, I scribbled what was on my mind.

When you hug me I can hear your heartbeat,
as time stands still for me.
Tick tock, tick tock.

In your arms I feel like a snowball
melting in the heat of the desert.
In your arms I feel like a water spring
gently sliding into the valley below.
But no matter how much I drink from it,
I never have enough to be satisfied.
You are the air I breathe.
You are the space that surrounds me.

I carried the paper bag throughout the rest of the day, and before I left to go back to New Jersey I threw it into a trashcan.

Saturday night I got to the theatre about two hours early. One never knows when something may have to be taken care of. Since everything was fine, Michael and I sat at the bar talking to each other. Then he asked me to remain calm but he had something important to tell me that was actually going to make our lives easier. He had started dating a girl who had been introduced to him a while before. She's a nurse, and when he was sick with the chickenpox he stayed in her apartment and she had nursed him back to health.

I was laughing inside my head and thinking, this is a joke! I slowed down my breathing and put on my public- relations-smiling-face of complete agreement with whatever he was saying being absolutely wonderful news.

"She is a very nice girl. A bit on the heavy side, and doesn't even come close to being as pretty as you," he assured me.

That statement made me mad, but I wasn't going to show emotion of any kind. He went on, saying that he was dating her on purpose, so that people would not know that he loved me. In other words he was using her as a cover up.

I have heard some very good excuses, but this one was an Academy Award winner. But because I am no different than Ralph or Steve's ex-girlfriends, and because when you are in love you are a fool and will do anything, absolutely anything stupid for the one you believe you are in love with, I went along with his story and even congratulated him for being so smart.

Then he asked me if I would consider going with him to the Renaissance Fair in North Jersey. We could spend the day there. Of course I said yes. I have been in theatre long enough now that I can express and act in the happiest, most pleasant manner and yet be dying inside. I learn from everything I do, I even expect it. It's called the school of life and, like Aunt Heydee used to say to me, "You can either take it or leave it."

I take it now, but when necessary I will leave it.

The trip to the Renaissance Fair was a fun-filled, pleasant experience, as I had convinced myself that it was fine for us to be alone together. We are true friends and that is why he has another woman on the side waiting for him when he comes home, just like Al is waiting for me when I get home. Michael and I are friends! We are only friends! Through the day I kept repeating those words in my head over and over again.

At the Fair there was a small lake with some rocks spread out into the water. Michael walked on top of the rocks and stood looking out and then called out for me to join him.

I stayed on the shoreline thinking, if he comes to me and takes me by the hand to walk on the rocks with him our future will be together, but if he doesn't then sooner or later we will go our own way.

He didn't come to get me, and I took that as an omen. Before we left the Fair, he bought me an expensive round silver medallion necklace with a printed fairy. On the back of the medallion it was inscribed, "Long life, and may all your dreams come true."

Okay, I said to myself, I have been a good wife and did my very best as a mother, so now I deserve what I am hoping for. My dream is to disappear. I am not happy.

Michael's friend Morph is a great cartoonist. Morph got his nickname because he drinks to the point of almost blacking out. I saw some of his creative sketches and I immediately commissioned him to paint the Howell Music Center's outside wall that's facing Route 9. He is going to draw some ideas together and show them to me before he gets started. I would like the wall to have caricatures of a rock band playing their instruments. This way, people traveling on the highway couldn't miss our music store.

Last night Michael picked me up to see "Little Shop of Horrors." I thought it was a silly story, but I was too embarrassed to say that I didn't understand why so many people make such a fuss about it.

After the show Michael asked me if I would like to see where he works, and he drove over to the factory. The building was closed and the parking lot was badly lit. We stayed in the car talking about how we felt about each other and how our lives together can never come to a reality. He mentioned that philosophy was just a bunch of words that have no conclusive meaning, not even to the philosophers themselves, and that was the reason they are constantly debating. I don't agree with that. I love philosophy, but I agreed with him just because I felt I was better off not voicing my opinion, as it wasn't important enough to have a discussion about it. Silence was lingering and it felt awkward to talk when we both knew that silence was what we needed to hear.

"It's going to sound silly, but will you sit on my lap?" he asked.

I did and we couldn't be any closer physically to each other than at that moment. We kissed on the lips for the first time, and it was as passionate as I always had imagined between two lovers. We held each other for a few minutes in silence and kissed again, and then I moved back to my seat, knowing in my heart that it was as far as we would be going.

He had a solemn look on his face when he turned to me and asked, "Ronnie, swear to me that if you die before I do, you will wait for me in the next life."

That statement took me by surprise, since death was the furthest thought in my head, but I answered, "Okay, I promise."

He seemed to be depressed instead of feeling joyous, and for the first time in my life I came to the realization that I am an odd ball when it comes to being happy at the wrong time.

I instinctively turned the radio on.

But he turned it off, saying, "Ronnie, if you don't mind, rock-and-roll music is not quite proper at this moment. We have just kissed, and…this is very serious, what we have done."

A heavy feeling of sadness came over me like deadly fumes from toxic waste. I didn't feel it was appropriate to talk about death, just like he didn't feel it was appropriate to listen to music.

He was right; we had just committed a sin. Kissing each other was an immoral act, even though he was the one that asked me to sit on his lap and brought his lips close to mine. We were both feeling uncomfortable as he drove me home. "I don't want to stop seeing you. I love you," he said.

"I do too." I put my head on his shoulder as we had arrived at my apartment complex. We hugged momentarily and as I was saying goodnight he said, "I'll see you tomorrow night at the Kobe?"

"I'll be there," I replied.

Michael and I get to Kobe very early, so that we can hug and kiss, and then talk until Tracey, the cast, and the stage crew arrives. During the week Michael and I still take rides into the countryside, hang out with Morph, go for pizza, sometimes see a movie, or go on errands for his mom.

"Same Time, Next Year" was repeated this year as per popular demand, and Barbara Schiavone once again was a shining star, not only with her performance but also as a director. Many people probably thought it was just a light silly romantic comedy that had nothing to do with real life. But it couldn't be any closer to the truth.

Cousin Suzanne has been divorced for many years but once a year she flies to the same hotel in Florida. Once a year she meets with her lover, a married man she met and fell in love many years ago.

Summer of 1989

I was at the Howell Music Center when Steve called me from the hospital.

Al and he were delivering a piano. He was driving the store van and Al was sitting in the back "watching" the piano in case it moved. Of course, if that were to happen Al would be holding it back with his hands! I have told them over and over again that it's dangerous to transport a piano without it being securely tied with heavy rope to hooks inside the van.

I learned that with my first piano delivery. I was driving the van on a roundabout and the piano went along with the turn and fell backwards. Luckily when that happened no one was in the back "watching" the piano.

This time the piano didn't turn over but weighing close to a ton, it slipped rapidly towards one of Al's leg, crushing it into the van's wall.

Al was still in surgery when I got to the hospital. They told me that his leg had fractured in numerous places and his foot was dangling, so they had to insert special screws to hold the bones together. The next day when I saw Al he was still under the effects of morphine.

Al has been home for two weeks now, lying on the couch watching television. As always when I get home, I serve him dinner and he watches one television show after another. He doesn't read books, only the newspaper's front page. Sometimes I will sit through one movie with him and then I go to bed.

It's not just because of his leg that we hardly see each other; our lives went in two different directions many years ago.

During the week I'm at the Howell Music Center with Steve, and in the evening, I'm at the Simy Dinner Theatre for rehearsals. On weekends I work in Collingswood Flea Market at Ronnie's Music Den, and at the theatre for the evening shows. If I'm done working for the evening, by eleven, I'll drive to the shore and park somewhere where I wait until it's late enough, that when I get home Al is already sleeping. Thank God he never asks me where I've been.

Al is doing well even though his leg is still in a cast. He started working at Collingswood Flea Market. Even though he can stand up with the help of his crutches, he can't walk for too long. He encouraged me to go on vacation by myself. I liked the idea.

Michael called to say he misses me. I asked him if he had any suggestions where I should go on vacation. He recommended Cape Cod, and said he wished he could do the same, but he couldn't take any days off from work.

Over the weekend I made a large dish of lasagna, boiled some calf tongues, made a Moroccan stew of meat and potatoes with oregano, the way Al likes, and put everything into individual containers and into the freezer like Tracey does for her husband. Al won't have to cook while I am gone. I made sure everything was taken care of at the theatre and planned my getaway for Monday morning.

I took all my Lynyrd Skynyrd and Eric Clapton cassette tapes and drove north in the Howell Music Center's van towards my final destination, Cape Cod.

I drove without stopping through New York, Connecticut, and finally Massachusetts. Singing along with "Sweet Home Alabama," I found my gas gauge hinting that I'd better stop very soon for gasoline. I was in North Falmouth. I sat in my van waiting to be served by the gas station attendant with a white turban on his head and a painted dot on his forehead. He kept smiling at me but he would not come out of his glass cubicle.

I finally went up to his glass window, "Hello, can I have some gas?"

"How much do you want?"

"I need a full tank."

He asked me to pay ahead, and I gave him $20. And then I went back into the van and waited to be served. I didn't quite understand why he was ignoring me and went back to his glass window.

"Excuse me, but I gave you $20. Aren't you going to put gas in my van?"

"In Massachusetts you get to pump the gas yourself." And he smiled.

I smiled back trying not to show any fear. There had to be a good reason why in New Jersey only the gas station attendant is allowed to put gas in a car. So I decided to wait for a customer to show up, and soon enough a car came by and I told the driver that I was from New Jersey and had no idea on how to put gas in my van.

I did a good job playing the damsel in distress because he stood by my side guiding me with each important step. First I pulled the latch by the trunk release. Then I opened the gas tank and put the cap down where I could see it. I removed the nozzle from the pump and put it in the tank. I learned that 87 regular was my fuel grade. I kept a tight grip on the gas nozzle. The nozzle handle returned to the off position meaning it was done. I put the nozzle back in the hoister.

I pumped my own gas! It was an exhilarating experience! I felt like I had achieved a masters' degree in mechanics.

It was about eight in the evening when I found a hotel in Falmouth. For forty dollars per night they gave me what they called "the captain's quarters." It was a white cottage set away from the main hotel at the very top of the hill. The view of the surrounding gardens made me ecstatic; it was perfect. I was in "The Ghost and Mrs. Muir" set.

There was a small restaurant just around the corner from where I was staying. Oddly enough it felt wonderful to have dinner alone and to walk through the small town without any responsibilities or thoughts about anyone else. I was sure that my sea captain would be visiting me that night, and the passion of love would be as natural as the butterflies upon the garden below.

I woke up the next morning fully energized. Now I knew how Aunt Heydee must have felt when traveling on her own all over the world. I was inebriated with my freedom. After grabbing a couple of muffins and a small container of milk from the free buffet breakfast at the hotel, I went driving around the countryside with no particular destination in mind.

I happened to drive into a field where a gathering of Indian tribes was taking place. They were having their annual powwow. The weather was pure sunshine splendid, with a slight breeze moving slowly and keeping me comfortably cool. I spent a couple of hours lying on the grass with my pocketbook and a light jacket under my neck for a pillow, listening to their drums and folk music. I enjoyed looking at their traditional clothing, the dances, and eating the corn and rice. I had never seen real Indians before. My wish to someday see a real American Indian had come true and I was glad to be on my own because I didn't have to rush or worry about someone else not wanting to be there. Later in the day I bought some Indian pottery and returned to my hotel room where I got dressed to go dancing in one of the many night-clubs around. I called Al to see how things were and I told him about my plans. He said I would be a jerk if I didn't go out dancing and have fun.

It was about ten at night, and the nightclub was full of people a lot younger than me. The music was up beat and loud. I went in with a single goal in mind, find the dance floor. I danced and danced in the middle of a bunch of people that seemed, for the most part, to be dancing by themselves. When the band stopped for a break, I left and went back to my van to look for another club. Once again I walked in as if I knew everybody there and nobody bothered with me. I was invisible. I danced until I was out of breath and once I had enough, I figured it was about time to go back to my captain's room. I wanted to get up early and take a drive to Provincetown, famous for whale watching.

The whale watching boat had a love-boat atmosphere of people hugging and kissing their same sex partners. Kissing between two men or two women was happening in a matter of fact way. I have a lot of gay male actors in the theatre, but I can't even recall any of them being with their partner at any of our shows. I had never seen anything like that so close to me, but everybody seemed to be relaxed about it. After trying not to stare at a couple of lovebirds, I decided it wasn't any of my business. My main interest was to see the whales, and there they were, those awesome huge creatures were playing with us by diving under our boat and coming up on the other side. I could swear that the whales were laughing as they sprayed us. It was a divine feeling of sea creatures and people laughing with each other. Joyful emotion was running rampant as everyone on board kept running from one side to the other of the boat and we witnessed one family of whales showing off their offspring as they would jump out of the water and fall back in with a huge splash.

The so-called Portuguese soup they served onboard was so bad that I spit out the spoonful of sour veggies. I tried without success to return the cup of soup, since I had paid the outrageous price of five dollars. I told them that when Portuguese soup is sour it means it's spoiled, and they said their Portuguese soup was supposed to taste sour.

Once the boat got back to the dock I went looking for a place to have dinner. I was walking around when I saw a long line of people trying to get into a seafood restaurant, and I figured it had to be good. The lobster stew was awesome indeed.

It was still early in the evening so I took a walk around the town. I found Provincetown to be a fun and artistic town with shops that had unique gifts and lots of original jewelry. While walking on Main Street, I came across a theatre. It didn't matter to me what the play was, I thought it would be fun to see a theatrical production that I had had nothing to do with. After being seated, I looked around and noticed that I was the only woman in the audience. The audience was men; men of all ages. Some of them were very handsome. It wasn't until the play started that I realized that it was about gay issues and that I was in a gay theatre. I was finally going to learn more about a subject matter that had been taboo all my life. There was no air conditioner inside the theatre and it felt very hot and musty. I don't know if that was the reason, but within half an hour into the first act I started sneezing. I pressed my nose up with one of my fingers trying to stop the affliction. I tried to hold my breath, but nothing helped.

I got the usual "God bless you!" from the crowd.

But after sneezing more than a couple of times the silence around told me I was annoying everyone. I can't help myself if I am like my father who used to be booed out of the movie theatres in Lisbon, Portugal when he was having a sneezing fit. After something like twelve sneezes I got up and left, most likely to everyone's relief. I will never know the end of the play. The only thing prevailing in my mind as I was driving back to my captain's quarters was that I probably had caught AIDS from one of them. What if Francis was wrong about catching AIDS from body fluids only and my running nose was the beginning of my deadly symptoms?

To my surprise, when I woke up the next morning I was cured.

I took the ferryboat to Martha's Vineyard, the island where one of the Kennedys' girlfriends had drowned.

I soon learned that the cute little gingerbread-like homes on the island were not open for tourists. I found out that they were private homes when I opened the front door to one particularly pretty pink house and a big dog came running down the steps barking at me. Thank God I closed the front door in time not to become dog food as the owner yelled at me for being nosey.

If I had learned to ride a bike when I was a kid I could have rented a motorbike to ride around the island. Instead, I had to depend on their bus service and I felt I missed seeing a lot more.

The next morning the girl at the hotel's front desk highly recommended that I go see a musical show at a theatre that was only an hour drive from the hotel. When I got there I almost died; it was "The Pirates of Penzance," the most awful musical show I've ever seen. That was the musical that

Tracey and I had seen at the Strand Theatre in Lakewood. We had been so bored that we kept counting the painted bricks on the stage wall so we wouldn't fall asleep. I told the ticket lady my disappointment after having driven an hour to get there.

It felt like déjà vu when she said, "You get your ticket and see the show. If you don't like it I will personally refund your money in full."

I loved the show! I laughed with tears and my feet kept dancing along with the music. I came to the conclusion that a production is dependent on its director and actors, and this was one of the best musicals I had ever seen — besides my own productions of course. I went back to the ticket booth and thanked the woman for encouraging me to stay. Wow, what a fun show! The only problem I had was finding my way back to the main highway. Finally out of desperation I followed a car that seemed to know where it was going and it worked. I got the idea from reading Douglas Adams, "Dirk Gently's Holistic Detective Agency."

I went back to New Jersey after having breakfast the following morning. My captain's cabin went up to $80 per night because it was the Fourth of July weekend.

Driving home I was smiling and thinking about the pirates on stage, the way they were jumping up and down singing and dancing as if they had springs in their boots. When I went back stage I found out that they were jumping on trampolines cleverly hidden behind the stage set of cut out cardboard pieces that were painted to look like ocean waves.

I truly loved the time I had alone. Funny, but I didn't think about Michael except for when I bought him a kaleidoscope at Martha's Vineyard, and I didn't think about Al either except when I bought him the Indian pottery. I will never forget this trip. I feel so blessed. Thank you God; for everything and most of all, thank you for allowing me to enjoy this incredible vacation by myself. I feel brand new, as if reborn.

When I got back home Al wanted to spend a day in Atlantic City, but his leg was still in a cast so I told him that if we could rent a wheelchair at one of the casinos I didn't mind pushing it.

It's too bad that the old pier is gone, because that was the best part of going to Atlantic City. Every summer I used to take the kids and Nelly to Atlantic City at least three or four times. We always went to the pier amusement park and spent the day watching the amateur musical shows and finished the day waiting patiently to see the horse with the pretty girl jumping off the pier and into the water below. One day the whole pier burned down, interestingly enough, just prior to the casinos taking over the boardwalk. Then the casino owners had another pier built but no more fun shows, no more horse jumping off the pier, only stores with expensive junk. Like the song says, "Nothing lasts forever but the earth and sky."

I pushed Al's wheelchair up the ramp and into the new pier mall and once we were finished looking around, I proceeded to bring him down the ramp. I didn't count on gravity or the weight of the wheelchair with him seated. I tried to hold the chair back from sliding out of my hands but I couldn't hold it and had to let go.

He screamed, "Not so fast, Ronnie."

The wheelchair picked up speed and went rolling down the ramp like a bullet into the boardwalk's crowd. I ran after him, and he was lucky that the wheelchair didn't turn over or hit some innocent bystander. I thought it was funny once I realized he was fine. Al was very upset with me, as if it was my fault that I was born a weakling.

Michael called me and asked me to meet him at the park in Lakewood. He kissed me as if I had returned from the dead and made me swear never to leave again for so many days. I gave him the kaleidoscope and we sat at the park bench kissing. I didn't say anything but I was glad that he had missed me.

Then he told me that his "girlfriend" had moved in to live with him and his mother, and it was a good arrangement because she is helping to pay part of the monthly mortgage and the bills. They owe too much and are not doing well financially. He also complained that he feels trapped in this arrangement and he is not happy.

I was thinking, oh what a pity! He loves me but he is stuck by his own choice with someone else just for the money. Well, that's life. I could not care less that he is not attracted to her.

Like he always says, we are an odd couple because of our age difference. We are one of a kind. We are special. We are unique. I'm tired of hearing that. It's not my fault that he was born later than me. I agreed politely with him, "Yes, we are odd."

Then we kissed and hugged again and as always I came home depressed.

I am sure there's no medicine or cure for what I have. It's called, being in love.

Steve wanted to talk about his new girlfriend and felt we should take a drive away from the store and Al. We took a ride to Freehold the back way. We talked about his ex-girlfriends, dating, marriage, and life. He said his dad and I were a rare case, all these years still married to each other. He didn't know of any couple that was married for so long and still happy with each other.

I decided to tell Steve the truth about the relationship between his father and me.

"Dad may be happy, but I am not. The last fifteen years we have been growing apart."

"I understand how Dad can be hard to live with, but where are you going to find a better man than him? As a matter of fact, where is he going to find a better wife than you? Mom, if you get into a relationship with another man, at your age, it will only be for one thing, sex! How long do you think that will last?"

I didn't answer. I immediately got a feeling that he knew more about my situation than I gave him credit for, and he got me thinking. Al does love me, so why do I need anything else out of life and feel so incomplete in our marriage? The answer is simple: because our marriage is missing romance, passion, mutual interest in thoughts and beliefs, and most important the physical and emotional chemistry that comes from being true soul mates. At the same time, I have to honestly ask myself if what I feel for Michael is real love or infatuation since I never had a boyfriend before I got married. Perhaps I would not be in this predicament today if I had not missed the link between being a girl and becoming a woman.

Steve was wrong when he said that sex is the only reason a man would go out with me. Michael and I love each other, and we have never had sex.

Some shows are well worth doing over and over again, like in the case of "Murder at the Howard Johnson's." Neither the audiences nor I get tired of it. The director, Bill Daniels is not only a great director, but he is also a fantastic actor. If he were a movie actor I have no question that he would be a superstar. Barbara Schiavone is in the same category, as well as Katie Grau. I guess I could just keep adding names to this list since I am working with some very talented people. But I'm also learning that no matter how talented a person is it all depends on whether or not they are lucky enough to meet someone who has the pull to get them to the top.

A good example was when, many years ago, I met the parents of one of Ralph's schoolmates at Valley Forge Academy. Paul's parents invited Al and me to their home, which was truly a beautiful mansion. Paul's mom was a movie star and his dad was an agent in the entertainment world. Paul's father found out that I played guitar and he asked me to play something on his acoustic guitar. I played a classical piece that I had composed and both he and his wife reacted as if that was the best melody they had ever heard. He asked me to send him a tape with my composition, and then he assured me that it would be out in the musical market as soon as he got it. The whole idea scared me at the time and I never sent him the tape. I do realize now that opportunity had knocked at my door to have my song published, but at that time I didn't feel I could handle it.

The Asbury Park Press went on and on about our production "The Gin Game," and I knew I had reached my goal in set designing when Mr. Ounuma asked me where I had purchased the outside porch siding. I told him that I made it by following Michael's instructions. First I cut long strips from the piano cardboard boxes I had collected from my store, and then overlaid the strips by stapling them one by one like siding. Afterwards, I painted them gray and then I rubbed newspapers over the surface while it was still drying. That's how I got that outside weathered beat-up look. Mr. Ounuma couldn't believe it and had to go up on the stage to touch the cardboard siding.

"Bus Stop" was another great show this year. I can't even think of anything more fulfilling than producing theatre. Everybody leaves the Kobe with a smile of satisfaction on their faces.

"The Nerd" was partially directed. Kind of an inside joke since the director hardly came to rehearsals. It was only because of a strong cast that never gave up and was able to basically direct themselves that we pulled it off. The show received critical acclaim. The very young Ann Marie Alliano may be a child actress, but she kept everyone inspired to stick together and have fun with the show instead of getting all stressed out.

Autumn of 1989

I love driving into New York City every chance I get. I rarely take the bus, I'd rather drive my van because it is a commercial vehicle and I can park anywhere for about an hour in front of a store as long as there is a sign that says "Parking for Deliveries." I was driving around when I saw a store with a sign that said, "Witchcraft and Vessels." It was too much for me to go by and not investigate.

I parked the van right in front of the shop and went in. It was quite dark inside except for the light that followed me in, as I opened the front door. There were lots of old books, and dried herbs in metal containers and in burlap bags in the crowded narrow store. A short, skinny, young man with a very pale complexion dressed all in black ignored me as I went by him. He looked like a wizard of some kind as he silently walked away like a slithering shadow. Just then, three businessmen entered the store. From the way they were dressed in dark blue suits, white starched shirts, ties, and each carrying an attaché case, there was no doubt in my mind that they were businessmen on their lunch break. They were laughing and joking around and as they went by me I followed them through the narrow and disorganized aisles covered with what seemed to be very old books on witchcraft. I could tell that they were looking for the same thing as I was; the secrecy of something that was probably concealed from us mere mortals. I began talking to them and we found out that we had the same idea; finding the genuine dark world of the occult.

"Look, that little guy that works here just came out from behind that filing cabinet, maybe it's a door to a dungeon." I said to them enthusiastically.

They followed me as I pulled on the tall wood cabinet with books. It opened to another room. The three of them became quiet and then one of them said, "Oh, oh!"

I needed them for protection in case it was indeed an entrance to a real dungeon, so I said, "It looks like we found a secret passage. Would you like to check it out with me?"

Their answer was, "Yeah! Sure, why not?"

They followed right behind me as I entered slowly into the backroom calling out, "Is anybody here?"

I was waiting for bloodthirsty bats to strike at us and kept my hands in front of me in case I had to fight for my life.

It was a storage room! We walked through it, and then, quite disappointed but in some way relieved that we were alive — at least that's how I felt — we got out of the store laughing, a bit nervous from what we had just done and not being caught. They all took turns shaking my hand and said thank you for the great time. I was smiling when one of them said, "You are an amazing woman."

We waved goodbye and I drove the van home, back to New Jersey.

I don't know why I told Al what happened. He got angry with me and said I was a nut and could have been killed by the three so-called businessmen. I should know better than to tell Al anything, but sometimes I forget that he is a party pooper. Michael, who is my soul mate, will be amused when he hears about it.

Except for some extravagant lighting that Michael needs to do at the Kobe, I have been running the stage lights myself. This week Michael set the lighting control panel behind the

The Secret Door

bar. That way, I am out of the patrons' view and it looks more professional.

We found a small park by Ocean County College and we meet there whenever we can both get away. We walk around talking and sit on one of the wood benches kissing and hugging each other without worrying about being seen together.

I've heard that in some religions, like in India, they believe in reincarnation. Of course, I know that I am the result of my parents' union, but am I also the result of reincarnation? Is that possible? I need to find out. Maybe my present situation is a repetition of my previous life and I can make some changes for the better so that I don't have to return again.

The last few nights I barely slept. I've been trying to keep my eyes open while letting my spirit wander through the ages of time. Last night I saw myself as a child in a place I felt comfortable enough to call home. Almost as if transported in time I was suddenly standing among papyrus grass that towered over me. I could see the same terrain on the other side of the river. I felt the warm muddy waters on my feet as I walked towards my two brothers and sat next to them to play with the mud. We spent most of those sunny warm days playing by the river, and running in and out of our hut a few steps away. Then one day for no reason the river began to dry. We were barely surviving. Food was scarce. My father was not in condition to do physical labor. His legs were covered with sores and he used a stick to hold himself up. I couldn't remember my mother's face. Perhaps she had died when I was too young to remember her.

I don't believe that I actually slept while all of this was happening. It all started while my eyes were opened and I recall closing them and then moving into a different dimension. In the morning I opened my eyes as I became aware of myself in bed. Maybe it was a dream after all, but I do remember being awake through the whole thing.

I can't wait to go to bed tonight and experience my other life, which has become very vivid to me since last night.

I found myself sitting by the river as my right hand held the wet clay. My two older brothers are no longer around, they have been sent by our father to help build the pyramids. My father is the only family I have left, and he can't really take care of me because of his age and health. His only recourse was to sell me to Senetenpu, the temple woman on the hill. She gave him a few large coins and a basket of grain. I was never to see my brothers or him again. I was trying to hold off my tears as I was very scared of my new surroundings until Senetenpu, said, "You are so pretty. Will you be my friend?" And she held my hand. She was a very beautiful lady, draped in blue and gold cloth. I was entranced by the aroma of her perfume and admired her beautiful dress and I couldn't help but smile back at her. Two young women came into the marbled floored room and took me to a small pool of water and there they scrubbed me down with soap and rubbed me with scented oils afterwards.

I was Senetenpu's companion. I got to do errands for her, and a few times I was present at her bath and they even let me pour rose water over her shoulders. Afterwards I watched as the other girls massaged her body with oils and herbs and then styled her dark wavy long hair.

Senetenpu oversees the temple where men come to be washed and entertained and then taken to private rooms for further body care. I was like a pet to the girls or perhaps more like a daughter to them. Senetenpu herself took me under her wing of protection and taught me to read and write, and after a year I was able to read to her some of her favorite poetry books.

As Senetenpu's favorite I had special privileges and was allowed to sleep at the bottom of her bed. Her bedroom was my favorite room in the temple because the wide windows opened to a humongous veranda where I sat daily between two marble statues while enjoying the view of the city surrounded by the fields in the distance. Her windows were always open and the soft see-through blue curtains with gold trim (blue was Senetenpu's favorite color) were my favorite place to play as the breeze would make them brush against my face.

One day Senetenpu walked into her bedroom unexpectedly and caught me using her lipstick and rouge. I told her I wanted to look pretty like her. She was not angry with me. She gently took the make-up from my hand.

"You don't need all this junk on your pretty face," she said, wiping my face with one of her makeup removal creams. She added, "Besides, these things were made to attract men, and at your age you should enjoy my love instead."

She laid me down next to her on the large bed and she kissed and hugged me tenderly and she told me that from that day on I could sleep next to her as the daughter she never had. It was like that for the next two years. I read all the books I could get my hands on. She taught me to sew and took great pride in letting me ride with her in her private carriage. Those were the simple happy days of my young life.

Each night I go back in time all occurrences start from the very beginning exactly as they happened the previous nights, and then the chapters keep adding up.

We were told that the Romans were taking over the villages as they rode towards our town. Senetenpu had my hair cut short and she dressed me as a slave boy.

When I asked her why she was doing that, she said, "So that you stay a virgin." Then she added, "I don't know why men have to be so cruel, but they like to burn and kill and make people suffer."

And that's what they did to us that night. They laughed as they ransacked and torched our temple. When Senetenpu tried to hold on to her favorite vase, a knife was thrown at her back killing her. Some of the girls got their clothes ripped off and the soldiers were on top of them taking their turn at hurting them, some got beaten and others taken away as prisoners. I quickly hid inside one of the wooden cabinets in the kitchen. I could hear the girls screaming and the chaos surrounding me when suddenly, to my horror, someone opened the cabinet door and a large hand came in my direction. A Roman soldier was grabbing me by the hair. Oddly enough his eyes showed no anger, instead they seemed to be asking me forgiveness when he said, "Boy, you don't have to hide."

I don't remember what happened afterwards. I must have fainted since everything went black, and the next time I became aware of my surroundings I was laying on a fur rug inside a tent. I got up and was ready to run away when I noticed the same Roman soldier standing in the corner and beginning to take his breastplate off.

"Boy, I see that you are feeling better. I could use some help here," He said while signaling me with a hand to approach him.

His name was Damasus and I realized that he thought I was a boy. That thought gave me reassurance that I was protected in that manner, and it was to my benefit that I should allow him to continue believing it. I helped him to undress and I found out that men have a different anatomy from women. I gave him a massage like I used to give Senetenpu — when she was tired from running the Temple, which was a lot of responsibility and work — I noticed that his skin was not as soft and white as hers and his hands were big and calloused. Afterwards he fell asleep just like Senetenpu used to. I felt content that I had done a good job and laid on the floor next to his bed waiting for his orders.

In the next few months I learned that Damasus' position in this miserable war was not to fight, but to stay busy as a carpenter and toolmaker among many other things, like fixing the chariots' wheels, and maintaining the weapons by fixing broken ones, and making new ones. Because I had nowhere else to go, there was no reason to run away. Even though I was legally his slave, he didn't address me like the other Roman soldiers did their slaves. He treated me as if I was his younger brother and as such I began to be an important part of his work. I became his assistant.

Once my breasts started to develop, I bound them with a cloth around my chest to keep them from being noticeable. Then the dreadful day came when I found blood coming out of my vagina. I immediately inserted a thick piece of cloth inside my pants. I had no idea of what was wrong with me and believed that I was going to die. At supper I drank a few cups of wine along with Damasus. The wine loosened my tongue and got me to go into an elaborate philosophical explanation of what death meant to me. Finally, after trying to finish my fourth cup of wine, I confessed to him that I was bleeding to death. Damasus picked me up like a rag doll as I was too dizzy from the wine to stand up on my own, and he carried me into his tent where he took my clothes off. In the three years that I was his companion he never suspected that I wasn't what I appeared to be. He was very angry at first, but right then he realized it wasn't my fault, but that the whole thing was part of the circumstances involving us. He didn't like war either, as a matter of fact, and if he had his wish, he would be home instead, working at his craft making furniture. This was just a way of making a living so that he could send his meager pay to his parents. He explained that my bleeding meant that I was a woman, which is what women do once a month. They bleed.

The next day, I couldn't wait to go to sleep. After serving Al's dinner, I told him that I was very tired and I was going to bed early. To my relief he stayed up watching television. I couldn't wait to go back to Damasus' side. I closed my eyes and waited.

Against my will Damasus took me to his parent's house where I became their servant. The months went by without seeing him and one day he came by briefly only to be gone for the next four years. I didn't think I would ever see him again. Then one day he showed up again; the Roman world had spread too far and the conquerors were returning home. Damasus father had died a few months before he came home, and his sister had gotten married and moved to Rome. Finances were not going well. Damasus took me along to meet his clients at different towns, and when we would get back he would have me assist him like in the old days. But our relationship was no longer the same. I was no longer a little boy but what I believed to be a nice looking eighteen-year-old girl in love with her master. I could feel his masculine presence taking over my senses and I noticed that he was not relaxed either when we worked together.

One morning I was holding a piece of wood to be used as a spike in one of the carriages we were working on when I dropped it by accident and it fell on one of his feet. I fell to my knees crying and saying that I was sorry I had hurt him. He lifted me in his arms and said, "The only pain I feel is in my heart, from not knowing if you love me."

I was the happiest woman alive, because he loved me as much as I loved him. From that day on we were lovers and we saw each other every night. A couple of months passed by and his mother invited a well-respected family from our town for dinner. With them came their daughter-ready for marriage.

He was laughing as he told me that night, "No wonder she is still single. She is not only ugly but she is larger than a sac of flour."

But life works in mysterious ways, and a few weeks later he said, "You are the one I will always love, but since my father died, as you know, we are in a lot of debt and we are going to lose our house and property if I don't marry Demetria. We need the dowry coming from her mother. When my mother first suggested this I was completely against it, but now I realize that I am acting out of selfishness. Don't worry. I am not leaving you. You are staying with us."

I would have given my life for Damasus if that were what he wanted from me. His marriage was a farce, a contract of convenience, and in the middle of the night he would leave Demetria and spend part of the night in my bed. Sometimes we would talk about our lives together, but of course it was just a fantasy, a total impossibility.

Demetria hated me right from the first day she saw me and made my life miserable, ordering me to do the most menial tasks that the other servants were not asked to do. I was washing the floors when she went by and kicked the bucket of water with her feet. Then she picked the bucket and hit me over the head with it. I put my hands up to protect myself and I thought I had passed out but instead I found myself back here and in my bed.

I'm not sure if I should pursue my so-called past life any further. It has changed a lot in the last few nights, but at the same time my curiosity has convinced me that I must see the whole thing through. I decided to go back tonight.

Damasus became involved in politics, and one day when he went to Rome for a few days, Demetria took advantage of his absence and hired two men to take me away from the village and do whatever they wanted with me.

The two men came into my bedroom, in the middle of the night, and after tying my hands and feet and gagging me so that I wouldn't scream, they put me in the bottom of a carriage. It was futile to escape. I was afraid they were going to kill me, so I decided to cooperate and see where they were taking me. I could always run away later when they were no longer around. Once I was behaving and had earned their trust, they admitted that it would be a waste to kill me when they could make a lot of money selling me to a certain wealthy man in Egypt who was looking for a bride. It was a long trip and they went out of their way to keep me fed and clean. I had become their precious cargo.

I knew I was back in my country when I recognized my own old village. When we got to our destination they took me to a bathhouse and had me washed and dressed by a friendly lady that seemed to be part of their clan. Then they took me to meet my future husband.

I expected an old man or someone mean and cruel that would beat me without mercy, but instead he was pleasantly handsome, about twenty years older than me, and he was the town's mayor. Amir asked me to sit next to him. He had been looking for someone like me to be his wife. It was important to him that I was young and could give him the children he longed to have. I must admit that I was happy to see that someone liked me enough to marry me. If the man I loved could get married to someone else for money, I could do the same for the adulation I could feel in Amir's eyes. At my reach were all the promises of wealth that make life so much better to be enjoyed. I was not asked to love him. I felt safe. Everyone that had meant something in my life had been taken away. I decided to devote myself to Amir. I was nursing my firstborn when upon closing my eyes, I found myself back once again in my bed. Is this a dream or am I really traveling back in time?

I can't wait to go to bed tonight and find out what happened to Amir and me. Did we live happily ever after? When I was a kid, and still living in Portugal, Aunt Heydee had done some investigating concerning our family tree, and she told us that she had found out that the Esagui's had come originally from Egypt and then went to Morocco as perfume merchants. That's probably my ancestral connection to Egypt. It makes sense.

Once again I lay in bed, closed my eyes, and rapidly went back to where I had been for the last few nights.

Amir was loved and respected by everyone for his wisdom in politics and most of all for his close counseling position with the Pharaoh. I kept busy overseeing my two son's education, the two houses we owned and the people that worked for us. I became involved with the community by helping those less fortunate than us. Once a week I would take a walk through our poorest neighborhoods to drop off clothing and food. Then, one morning when I was leaving one of the mud huts,

I saw a beggar sitting at the corner of the street. I stopped next to him and noticed that he was a foreigner from the way he was dressed.

I asked him, "Are you looking for work?"

He looked up and reacted as if he was seeing a ghost as he spoke my name. The beggar was Damasus.

Damasus' eyes had not changed. I asked him to follow me, and when I got home I sent him to the bathhouse with a set of clean clothes. Afterwards, he was brought to my receiving room. We stood apart, looking at each other, and then I motioned for him to follow me.

We took the marble steps that lead to the garden behind the house and walked silently for a while. We sat at one of the benches by the pond and then he held my hands in his and told me how he felt upon returning from Rome to find me gone. His wife told him that I had run away, but he knew that I would never have done such a thing. He knew she hated me and there had to be foul play. Somehow his mother had managed to find out that I was alive and had been sold as a bride in Egypt. It wasn't until last year when his mother was dying that she confessed to him that Demetria had paid two unscrupulous men to have me taken away. He immediately left home.

All this time Damasus had been traveling from town to town, hoping to find me. We kissed passionately and I knew I had never stopped loving him. We would never be apart again. Taking my carriage, we drove down to the river, the same river my two older brothers and I used to make mud pies as children. The old hut was still there, empty like a ghost from the past. We swore our love for each other and in that hut we made love, realizing that without each other we would never be happy again.

How Amir found out about my infidelity I had no idea. The day I didn't meet Damasus at the hut was the day I was to be punished for my sin according to the laws of the time. I was not afraid of dying, what was bothering me mostly was that I couldn't die in Damasus arms. Two soldiers escorted me outside and there I stood next to the water hole surrounded by an angry crowd.

One of them yelled out, "Whore!" The stones flew from all directions.

My sons were not present. I had done wrong and they were never going to forgive me. I thought I saw Amir standing at one of the windows of our house and I could have sworn that I saw him crying. As the stones kept hitting me, the world around me seemed to slow down and then stopped rotating and all the pain was gone. For a long time I felt myself being part of a peaceful and silent space.

I waited and waited, and suddenly I was back in my bed in the present time. I felt relieved to be back. I was alive and I pondered for a while how real my other life seemed to be.

I definitely do not want to be reincarnated again if that's what happened. I can't even imagine having to live, over and over again. I mean, how many times does it take to finally learn a lesson, if that is the purpose of reincarnation? It sounds more like punishment to me, more like what the Catholics refer to as Purgatory.

I hope that my other life was just a figment of my imagination. Besides, I don't believe in reincarnation!

I received a manuscript in the mail from a local writer who wants me to produce his "original music parody" as he calls it. It is a boring story about high school students, and I can't see the humor or the purpose for anyone wanting to see it on stage. I have been a nervous wreck trying to figure out how to tell the poor man, without hurting his feelings, that I can't use his script. Al is no help, he was laughing after saying, "Send it back to the writer, and tell him it sucks."

Al is no good at giving advice.

I decided not to write to Mr. Thompson, the writer, and instead I called him on the phone and told him his writing was nice but needed a little more of something else to make it even better.

Mr. Thompson came to our music store, and I encouraged him to take a writing class at Brookdale College like I had done a few years ago which had helped me a lot with creative writing. He said he would get back to me after he worked on his play a little more. I am hoping he doesn't come back.

For as long as I can remember I have known that I project a "goody two shoes" image. I'm certain that this whole concept has been created by people's own perception of what they want to believe. They always apologize if, by accident, they say the four-letter word. I always try my very best to make them feel comfortable about their verbal communication by saying, "My ears are not pure. I have heard those words before, and I have used them myself several times when a bad driver crosses in front of me, illegally."

They say surprised, "You? You, say those words? You are so sweet all the time. I can't even imagine you doing such a thing."

I believe my slight foreign accent is what gives me a saintly figure. But I am not as innocent as I look. No one tells me dirty jokes except for Tracey, who keeps me in stitches laughing when we get together. Sam, her husband, has a good sense of humor and doesn't mind her wildness, but Al had a fit a year ago when I came home all keyed up to share a few jokes I had heard from Tracey. Al was so upset that I decided never again to tell jokes in front of him. That event was a traumatic repeat of what happened to me at a young age when my father cut me off from expressing my stand-up comedian streak by lecturing me how a proper young lady doesn't tell jokes that might be considered risqué.

Once Al reinforced my father's philosophy, my humiliating childhood experience became too vivid for me to discard and now I can't even repeat a joke without totally screwing up the punch line.

It took awhile to get Morph committed to painting the outside wall of our music store but he finally did it.

The full-wall painting of a rock band in caricature format is both amusing and colorful, and it has proven to be a very effective form of advertisement. No one can drive by Howell Music Center without taking a second glance.

How time flies! Ralph and Steve are doing well in their own way. Ralph is still working at Bell Labs; he has his own apartment and is very happy. Steve and his new girlfriend are sharing a very nice home not too far from our music store. The only problem is that Steve is not as mature as I would like him to be. It must be hereditary, from me.

I call my parents every Sunday because I can afford it, and no matter what, I owe them my life. But when I talk to Mama it is an emotional trauma to my psyche. I keep on trying to create a bond between us but it's not working. I have come to the conclusion that I will never understand her. We are from two different worlds and we will remain that way. Papa rarely comes to the phone; he says he'd rather write a letter. I know the reason he says that. It's because Papa is very insecure about his voice which, a few times, was mistaken by someone on the other line for a female. Papa had to have throat surgery when he was about five years old because he was born with a defective voicebox. All his life he has been aware of his voice being "different" from everybody else. He thinks he has a high-pitched tone on the phone, but I don't agree, and I've never had any trouble recognizing Papa's low tenor voice.

After I talk to Mama, I feel depressed and without energy, like a dead battery. I am going to cut down my phone calls to Portugal to once a month.

Blood still runs cold in my veins whenever I have to be assertive or experience confrontation. I don't want to hurt someone's feelings and I worry that they may stop liking me. I'm also scared of speaking up. If I were a man I would say that I don't have the balls. Susan Miller, one of the directors, called me up on the phone at two in the morning, waking me up from a deep sleep, to yell at me because Tracey had not brought such and such prop, and she'd just about had it with her.

Like a sheep I said, "I'm sorry, Susan. You are right and I will talk to Tracey tomorrow. Sorry about all this."

She kept yelling, and I kept apologizing as if it was my fault, and finally she hung up.

I went back to bed and lay there wide-eyed, staring at the shadows on the bedroom walls. Rolling from one side to the other unable to sleep, feeling used and abused, I finally took a look at the alarm clock; it was three thirty in the morning! Then, like a lightening bolt, I remembered one of Aunt Heydee's favorite stories:

Once upon a time there was a married couple that lay in bed and couldn't sleep. The husband kept his wife awake telling her over and over again, "What am I going to do? I owe 500 escudos to my neighbor across the street, and I won't have the money tomorrow like I promised him! I can't sleep!"

"Stop worrying about it," lamented his sleepy wife. "You can't draw water from a stone! Just talk to him tomorrow."

"No, you don't understand. He is going to be angry if I don't pay him. I won't have the money until next week! What am I going to do?"

Finally his wife proposed to him, "Look, good man of mine, it's three in the morning! I need to sleep, and so do you!

Just open our bedroom window, (the houses in the small village where they lived, were very close to each other, one good reason why they didn't need a telephone to communicate) and after you call his name out loud, let him know that you can't pay him tomorrow. He will have to get paid next week when you have the money and that's all there is to it."

The husband got up from bed opened the bedroom window, and at the top of his lungs yelled out, "Hey, João! Hey João, wake up! I got something to tell you!"

João came to the window half asleep and asked, "What the heck are you screaming about at this forsaken hour of the night?"

Mario yelled back, "Hey, João, guess what, I don't have the money to pay you tomorrow morning. I'll pay you the money back next week... if I have it. Good night!"

Mario closed his bedroom window, and went back to bed where he fell asleep like a rock next to his wife who was already snoring.

The moral of the story, as Aunt Heydee would say, is that one should never hold anything back that will take away a good night's sleep. Yeah, how dare Susan take away my sleep to complain about stupid props in the middle of the night? Her phone call had been an inconsiderate and selfish act!

I dialed her number back. It took a while to answer. She was obviously sleeping.

"Hello...? Who is this?" her bass-like muffled sleepy-voice answered the phone as if she was still in a dream stage.

After I finished telling her Aunt Heydee's story I added, "Don't you ever call me again in the middle of the night! Good night!"

I lay down with a smile on my face, empty of anger, and fell asleep like a rock next to Al — who sleeps through anything.

Michael's mom and I were in her kitchen having our usual woman-to-woman talk.

To my surprise she confided, "Ronnie, I have to tell you this. When Michael brought Joanne home so I could meet her, I almost passed out. Michael has always liked petite women, and if they are wearing a mini skirt he will go nuts over it. This girl was a complete surprise to me. I mean, don't take me wrong, she is very nice, and she took care of Michael a while back when he was sick, but they are not made for each other."

Then she looked around the kitchen to make sure we were still alone. Michael was downstairs in the cellar working on a wood panel for the next set, and she whispered to me, "I think he started going out with her because he felt he owed it to her since she took care of him when he was sick. Now she is living with us and she helps us financially but I don't think that things are working out between the two of them."

I didn't say anything. I have never met Joanne but I feel sorry for her.

A Chinese restaurant opened next to our music store. They serve buffet-style lunch. Al loves the food there. I don't want him to know that I am not eating, so I put some broccoli on my plate and eat one piece and then I complain of stomach-ache, that way I won't have to eat at all. I am living on water.

I've figured that if I stop eating I will be so small and skinny that when Michael hugs me I will disappear into him.

Our winter show is set to kick off our fifth season with a re-peat of our first smash hit production "Plaza Suite," by Neil Simon. As always, with Barbara directing and starring in it it's going to be great. If I were a lazy producer I would run this show all year long.

Everybody makes fun of me because I won't give up on the idea that someday, very soon I hope, there will be peace on earth. On November ninth to be exact, the Berlin Wall came down. This means one less separation between mankind!

Little by little my wish will come true. I am no fool, I know it's going to take time, but with each step forward, we get closer to having a perfect world.

Two large straw fans hid Sherri's body in "The Best of Broadway." Her skin-colored body suit gave the impression that she was naked as she danced to a very sultry popular sax tune. One musical scene after another of dancing and singing with professional singers and dancers brought a few emotional moments to my memory bank of the days when I used to produce musicals with young people that had never been on stage and yet they were the best one can ever imagine. But those days are now gone, and when people are paying a good price for their ticket, they expect their money's worth.

I can honestly say that our clientele is getting the best of entertainment and the food is also top notch. Mr. Ounuma drives all the way to Canada and back within 24 hours without much of a break, just to pick up certain fish eggs and fish that fit his approval when it comes to sushi quality. His chief cook is no different. As a matter of fact, he is very hard to please.

One evening the restaurant ran out of meat for the hibachi, and Katie, the hostess and restaurant manager, went to the market up the highway to pick up a few rumps of meat. After returning, Katie had to run out of the kitchen with her hands covering her head so she wouldn't get hit when the Kobe chef threw the meat at her. He stated that the quality of meat she had brought to him was not acceptable in his kitchen.

Winter of 1990

We have a devoted group of theatre patrons, but it seems to me that people are not spending like they used to. Every once in awhile we don't have a full house at the theatre, and a few times we had the horrible experience of putting on a show for two people. But as they say in theatre, the show must go on.

Our music store is not doing the greatest either. Two stores in our mall have closed. I don't like to hear what people are saying, that we are going into a recession. The idea of opening another music store in Marlboro came to me as a possible salvation. Marlboro's population is at a higher level of finances than here in Howell where the average salary seems to be at the bottom of the totem pole. I wish I had thought about this a few years back. I have hopes that we might still be able to get our heads out of the water before the boat sinks. I am going to start looking for a place to rent in Marlboro.

If someone had told me that I could make a living out of selling chopsticks I would have laughed my head off.

I was doing my usual walking around New York City when I came across a huge Chinese store on the second floor of an old dilapidated building in Chinatown. The inside reminded me of a ten-cent store type of Chinese Salvation Army, except that everything was brand new and Asian of course.

I felt like I was in Chinese-wonderland when I found the most beautifully handmade lacquered chopsticks, with engraved mother of pearl intertwined with other colorful stones. I bought one dozen for a dollar a pair, figuring on saving them for presents during Christmas or something like that. But when I showed them to Mr. Ounuma, he offered to buy them from me for ten dollars each. I sold all twelve sets to him and he rapidly sold them to customers for twenty-five dollars each set.

When I returned to Chinatown to buy some more chopsticks, the owner was so overwhelmed that I wanted to buy three dozen more that he offered me a dozen chopsticks free if I bought a total of five dozen pairs. Mr. Ounuma was thrilled to buy all the chopsticks from me. I made out like a bandit and so did he. I am now in the chopstick business.

I love when people are honest enough to give me creative criticism. I thrive on that and believe that's one of the reasons I am successful in most everything I do. On the other hand, I've had people telling me that I'm too soft and easygoing. I have been encouraged several times to take a class on assertiveness. But I don't really want to be assertive and harsh like so many people I know. If that's assertiveness I would rather stay the way I am. When I say something I automatically consider what it would be like to be in that person's shoes. I thrive on making people happy and I go out of my way to do that. Maybe it is stupid like Tracey has told me several times, but I like myself better that way. I also believe that I have changed a lot in the last few years. I feel more secure in myself and I have become more open to showing my opinion even if not one hundred percent of the time. I also recognize that I can be very aggressive when I have to fight for what I believe is right. I just need a good cause to fire me up, that's all.

Francis says that there's nothing wrong with me being the way I am. Besides my friend Francis, Michael is the only one that understands me.

I've decided that it's not worth paying twenty dollars a month to store the stage props at the old chicken coop when I get seriously ill from the side effects of mildew. I decided to move everything into a clean professional storage space on Route 9. It's going to cost five times more, for less than a quarter of the space I have at the chicken coop, but my health is more important. I hate being sick.

I had a very touching experience when I was moving all the props from the chicken coop into storage. I was almost finished when I came across an old typewriter still inside its original case. Thank God that I opened the case carefully, because inside its center, between the keys, laying in a bed of soft pink insulation probably taken from the walls of the chicken coop, were two little baby mice. How the heck the mother mouse made the nest inside the typewriter I will never know. I laid the typewriter cover carefully back without putting any pressure to close it. Of all the props I had at the chicken coop, I left that one behind.

I look like a raccoon with huge dark circles around my eyes! I wanted a cute button nose and had nose surgery. But my nose is just as big as it used to be and I can't wear eyeglasses because the top of my nose is swollen and hurts really badly. What possessed me to do this? Vanity!

I should know better than to trust a doctor telling me that there was nothing to it. But he made it sound easy and never told me how he was going to fix my deviated septum, as he called it, or how painful it was going to be after the surgery. It was an outpatient procedure, but when I left the hospital I felt more like they had thrown me out into the street. They should have kept me overnight so that I could at least sleep it off. No, they needed the room, and I was to go home. Once I got into our van I immediately knew that I wasn't going to make the forty-five-minute drive back home with Al driving in a snow storm.

Stop and go, and slip sliding from one side of the road to the other side, after ten minutes of staring at the chunky snowflakes flying straight into the windshield, I yelled, "Stop! I have to lie down. My head is going to fall off. We need to find a hotel where I can lay down. Pleaaaaaase!!"

We found a hotel, thirty-five minutes away from home and it was the worst night of my life. I couldn't sleep because of the pain inside my brain, and even with my eyes open I was seeing ugly scary monsters and death-type roller coaster experiences and all I did was cry and sweat into episodes of pure panic and despair. I don't know what kind of drugs they had injected me with, but whatever they were it almost drove me insane.

Because it was the only hotel available we had to pay the incredible price of two hundred and fifty dollars for the night. The next morning I felt that I was entitled to keep all the towels and their Bible. Al agreed, and that's what we did.

Bill Daniels who is an actor and also has directed many plays for me, brought his wife Janet to the theatre to watch a rehearsal. Janet, who is a nurse, told me that the reason I had such a traumatic experience after the surgery is because the surgeon had put cocaine up my nose after the surgical procedure. No wonder I had horrible visions and I thought I was going mad. That must be what people call a "bad trip."

Michael said that if I had told him what I was going to do he would have discouraged me from it. He had the same surgery for a deviated septum a few years back, and now it's difficult for him to breathe through his nose because of extra cartilage growing as a result of the surgery. I am not looking forward to that happening to me.

It's been two months and my nose is still sensitive to the touch. The weight of eyeglasses hurts my nose. I'll have to look for eyeglasses that don't touch the bridge of my nose.

I have been using contact lenses, but I don't like wearing them because they are not comfortable.

Michael told me that he is concerned about me because I look like I am losing too much weight. He wanted to know if I was sick. I didn't have the courage to tell him that I am trying to shrink so that when we hug I can get into him like magic, and then I can always be with him. Even though he is the only one that understands me, I don't know if he would comprehend my intention.

It was a major task building the set for "Brighton Beach Memoirs," but I shouldn't complain since Barney was helping me. I couldn't ask for a better team of directors, I got both Sandi Van Dyke and Barbara Schiavonne, now that is what I call the very best.

We arrived at the Howell Music Center this morning to find the police and some people from the Health Department closing down the Chinese restaurant next to us! When we got there the police were taking away the restaurant's owners as they were crying while trying to explain to the cops that, in their country, cat meat is perfectly normal to eat.

A neighbor had called the cops after hearing some loud meows during the night coming from our building. The cops found cats in the cellar and vestiges of the dead ones.

I knew there was something weird about their food. Thank God I never got to eat the meat they were serving. But sometimes I did swallow their broccoli that had stewed for hours in the cat juice. I always thought the sauces were too gummy. I am never going to eat Chinese food again.

Michael brought his girlfriend to the Simy Dinner Theatre to see the show. She was not obese, just chunky and I didn't find her ugly either. Like Aunt Heydee once told me; "When you are young it doesn't matter what you look like. You can wear a toilet bowl for a hat and you are still a charming beauty."

His girlfriend didn't smile and I had a gut-feeling that she was aware of the love/friendship between Michael and me. Women have a sense for those things. After he introduced her I stayed away from them.

Do I care that Michael's girlfriend moved in with him? No, because I am not his girlfriend. We are friends that happen to love each other, nothing else; and Ronnie remembers that.

I have gone from a size eight to a size three. I have stopped eating, and I have no desire for food. Sleep is non-existent and if I fall asleep I wake up shaking.

I feel like I am dying. Since Barney used to be a veterinarian, I asked for his medical opinion. He said not eating and not sleeping means I have what's medically called depression.

That scared me. I don't want to be like my Aunt Ligia and be put in a mental hospital where they will give me electric shocks to put my brain back to normal. I just want to get as small as possible. I know it's a fantasy, but the idea is so very appealing to me.

Then it happened, I was taking a shower when Al walked into the bathroom. I guess he has not seen me naked for a long, long time because he was shocked as he screamed, "Oh my God, you look like a skeleton! Ronnie! You are skin and bones! What's happening to you?"

That did it. One thing about Al, when he says something, he says it exactly as he sees it.

I have started eating normally again, but sleep is still a problem. I have thought about leaving and going back to Portugal. In Eiriceira I would be far away from here and alone. The sun would keep me warm and the sea would provide me company.

But without money to pay for housing and food I have to stay where I am, amid the turmoil of my hopelessness.

I have asked Al several times to take on a hobby so that maybe we can have something to talk about besides listening to him telling me the news or watching television when he is home. I have started playing with the idea of asking for a divorce, but I am afraid of what Al would do to me, besides he doesn't even know that I am unhappy and I don't want to hurt his feelings.

Francis and her husband finally found a building in Newark where children and families with AIDS can have care until they die. Al was upset with me because I co-signed for the building in Newark and he doesn't want me involved with anyone that is personally in contact with other people with AIDS. He forbade me from going to Francis's house in case she is contagious. Of course, I still visit Francis, I just don't tell him about it.

The musical "Baby" brought laughter and music to the audience and also a family heartbreak to two actors that became involved in a love affair. If their marriages had been strong and healthy, that would have not happened. Maybe I am wrong about this assumption, but this is how I feel.

I got a letter from a company in New York wanting me to pay an exorbitant amount of money in royalties for all the songs we had used in the musical prior to "Baby." I didn't know that I had to pay royalties on songs we hear on the radio. I thought we only had to pay for professional musicals, like "Baby," which I paid a few thousand dollars in royalties for. They informed me that they keep track of every production around the country by having newspaper clippings mailed to them on a monthly basis. They found out about the show when the Asbury Park Press mentioned by title what great tunes we had presented on stage. Since it was my first offense, they let me off the hook, but from now on, any song that is out there in the music world is no longer available to be used, unless our theatre pays royalties.

I feel so sad all the time, but nobody knows it because I am always smiling — and I must do a pretty good job at it because everybody believes that I am the personification of happiness. I have thought about leaving a simple letter explaining to everyone that I am weird and need to be alone. Al is my husband and he is kind and supportive of everything I do, but we don't connect. Maybe I should visit my parents for a week and then take a train to France and back; anything to be alone would be good. After twenty-seven years of marriage I feel like I'm nowhere, as if traveling in a vacuum of emotion. I don't know what's going on with me. Maybe I am finally waking up from my deep sleep and I really want to live more than I realize. I dream of starting my life all over again, but in a different direction from where I am today.

I don't want to hurt my family. I hate to admit it, but maybe I am like my mother, looking for an answer to the meaning of life and longing for more than what I have. Her refuge has been writing passionate novels and poetry, an expression of her soul-seeking fulfillment. Maybe I am like my mother more than I want to admit.

I have Al's love and friendship, two sons that love me, Michael's love and friendship, good friends, a few businesses to keep me busy, like the Howell Music Center, Ronnie's Music Den and The Simy Dinner Theatre, and most of all we are all healthy! I should be satisfied but I am not. There's got to be more to life. Like the song says, "I'm gonna live forever, I'm gonna learn how to fly, high! Lalalalalala, I'm gonna make it to heaven, light up the sky like a flame, Fame!" I love the sound of this tune it makes me want to jump high and grab life in mid air.

When Michael and I kiss or hug I control my emotions to go blank of any thoughts except that my happiness is temporary and I should be content with just those moments that we are together. If I let myself fall under the influence of emotion I'll be lost forever. It's been two weeks now that I feel strong, like a rock, living free of silly feelings of love, thus maintaining my inner strength. I still see around me like "the fool on the hill" but I refuse to allow my heart to interfere and tarnish the truth.

I have noticed how people are always complaining. Poor souls that have succumbed to the human emotions of jealousy, desire, distorted ideas of what love is or is not. Not me. It all comes down to one simple answer, everything is transparent; everything is natural in its own way, and very beautiful if we accept our lives as is. The human existence is a joke; everyone puts more value into money and stuff, and there's never enough, more and more is needed. And when you actually believe that there's a human being that is pure and not for sale, you discover that for a couple of dollars his or her soul can be bought. It doesn't matter if it's one hundred dollars or a million. Everybody seems to have a price.

Al is not interested in possibly expanding our business. If that is going to happen I have to do it myself. It took me a few months exploring all the possibilities along Route 9 but I finally found a building for rent in Marlboro. Now all we have to do is move some of the merchandise from the Howell Music Center into it. Basically, we don't need to invest much except for the monthly rent. Everybody around us is going out of business. I am keeping my fingers crossed that our new Music Center in Marlboro will keep the store in Howell from going under. This will be my last effort to keep us afloat until the economy gets better.

I no longer go to New York City by myself because a young woman came into the Howell Music Center and, as we started talking, I learned that she had been hit over the head and robbed while walking in the city by herself. Her health has not been the same since that happened and she never really recovered from the trauma. It happened when she was twenty-three years old. She was in coma for two months after the beating. I figured it this way, if they had no pity and attacked a pretty young girl in the street, I would definitely be easy prey. I can't fight myself out of a paper bag.

Over the years, Al has been telling me over and over again not to go to New York City alone because of the crime there. I never believed him because I've never seen anything bad happen while I was there, but now that I met someone in person that almost died, that does it for me. From now on I will only go with company, like a friend or a family member. While one gets attacked the other can run for help.

Here I am at our store in Marlboro. Looks like business is bad everywhere, including here, but the sound of the music on the radio makes me happy, and since there haven't been any customers all morning I have been busy dancing between the pianos. The German side of me says, there are more important things to do, stop dancing and go dust the guitars! The Brazilian part says, don't worry! The dust is only temporary! Dance and be happy!

My Portuguese common sense came to my rescue; under the economic situation the country is in, you have done your best, take a well-deserved vacation!

I called Mama on the phone and told her that I am going to visit her and Papa this spring. Ralph heard about it and told me that he would like to go with me. So the plan is, instead of going alone to Portugal for a week, Ralph and I will be spending one week with my parents, and the other week traveling through Europe. You wish for miracles, and they will happen.

I have stopped collecting clippings from newspapers and magazines on personal interviews. It's a bunch of paper clippings that get yellow with time and I don't see any purpose to keep them. With about ten shows per year I have also run out of space in my closet to store VCR tapes. Besides, the tapes would be collecting dust in the closet since I have no intention of sitting down to watch the same show I have already seen performed for several weeks.

The problem is that there's always someone that films the opening night and then all the actors and directors want to buy a copy. I almost feel like a traitor when they offer me one as a present and I really don't want it. I get worried that everyone might think that I am not interested in the production, but I am: in the live productions. Once in a while I get embarrassed to say I don't need a copy of the VCR tape, and then I'll buy it anyway. I am such a nerd.

"Butterflies Are Free" was a brain twister because of the set. The low ceilings made it very difficult to fit a bunk bed on the stage. Barbara was adamant about having a "real" hippie bunk bed even if I had to knock out the ceiling and the roof of the building along with it.

I really had to improvise and wound up at a fence company buying metal pipes and cutting them to make a downsize bed frame, something that only a hippie would find practical. I enjoyed painting graffiti and a huge rainbow of colors across the stage walls.

Barbara was very happy with the "Hippie" set. The time period was well conveyed on stage. Once again the show was fantastic and we received great reviews.

"Educating Rita" promises to be one of those shows that I can take a break away from and relax, so I am going to use this opportunity to get away with Ralph. The only thing that has not been easy to find is someone to handle the stage lights and sound while I am away.

Michael and his mother are thinking about selling their home, and he is busy working and fixing their house. We still see each other, but I am not bothering him to come run the lights for us. He's got enough on his plate to contend with. Tracey will take care of collecting the money for the tickets and welcome the audience into the theatre. I called Bill Goods and asked for his help; after all he was the one that worked with Michael designing and setting the stage lights at the township stage a few years back, before The Simy Dinner Theatre even existed.

I am terribly disappointed. I found out that Bill may be great at designing and mounting stage lights, but when it comes to running the stage lights on cue, he can't handle it. It has turned into a nightmare for the cast and me. Two weeks into rehearsals and he still can't coordinate the light panel with simple things like turning the lights on or off when an actor touches a light switch on the wall. He is either too early or too late to be on cue.

I have spent a few nights awake, tossing and turning with the dilemma of hurting Bill's feelings. How am I going to tell him that I have to find someone else? Meanwhile, Ralph and I have already bought the plane tickets to Portugal.

When Bill called in sick with a cold, Jean, the stage manager's assistant, offered to learn how to run the stage lights. Amazingly enough, Jean was able to learn the whole lighting process that evening. The actors were beyond happy and asked me not to have Bill back to do the stage lights.

Bill came in Friday and I had to tell him that I was worried about his health, and felt better if I had someone else doing the lights.

What else could I say? I couldn't tell him the truth about how insecure everyone felt with him running the control panel with lights and sound. No matter how nice I was to him, he left very upset, and I know he will never return or be my friend again.

~ Chapter Three ~

Castaways in the Old World

Spring of 1990

I've been very sad over this whole mess with Bill and the stage lights, but business is business. The actors are a lot more relaxed now knowing that they can depend on having the lights and sound on cue. I have to accept the loss of Bill as a friend. After calling him on the phone, his wife told me that he wasn't going to talk to me ever again.

I am leaving on vacation without worries. The theatre is in good hands. Barney's wife asked me to bring her a couple of hand soaps. She swore that the Portuguese soap is the best she ever used. I am thinking that if they are that good I am bringing a soap bar for everybody I know. It won't be expensive, and it won't take that much space in my luggage.

While Ralph and I are in Europe, Al will take care of the Marlboro Music Center during the week and Ronnie's Music Den on weekends. Steve will handle the Howell Music Center. The Simy Theatre is also well taken care of by people I trust. When I get back, Al will be off from work for two weeks and I will cover for him.

I filled one big suitcase with presents for the whole family and a backpack for myself. With Al's blessing, Ralph and I got on the plane to Portugal.

We had a great flight. The plane was half full. I took two Benadryl capsules and taking advantage of the empty seats, I stretched myself across the three middle seats and Ralph did the same on the next aisle. We both slept through most of the trip. When I woke up I had some guy's foot close to my face. He had been sleeping on the seats next to mine.

Spring in Portugal is definitely the best time of the year to visit because the weather is perfect. I knew we would arrive at seven in the morning, and I had written ahead to my parents, telling them not to bother coming to the airport to pick us up that early.

No matter how many years go by, I will always remember how to get around Lisbon because this is the city I grew up exploring. From the airport we took the bus to the Plaza Praça do Chile, not too far from my parent's house. Each time I go to Portugal I notice how old and decaying the city of Lisbon is, falling apart at the seams. After twenty-eight years, my apartment building no longer resembled the way I had described it to Ralph. The pink marble was basically gray, and dirtier than the last time I had visited. The bright green exterior of the old times had faded drastically and the paint was peeling off like after a serious sunburn. But, thank God, Ralph is a lot like me, and everything he sees he appreciates. It also helps when there's nothing to compare it with, since this was his first trip to Portugal.

We rang the bell of my old apartment building, and when we got to the top of the steps, Papa was standing in the doorway waiting for us. He was crying as we hugged. This was the third time in my life I had seen my father cry, once in desperation, the other with remorse. That day he was expressing his longing for us. He was glad to see us.

Mama was waiting patiently in her bedroom. She was too weak to get up from her rocking chair. She was obviously drugged, (one of the benefits of having medical doctors in our family) because she cried calmly and softly without the usual drama.

By staying with my parents, Ralph got to watch them fight over the large fish head during dinner. They were willing to share the brain and the fish eyes, but Ralph refused to even try. He doesn't know what he is missing!

I was upset with the maid that was taking care of Mama. I should say employee, that's their new job title as per Papa correcting me. It has always bothered me when some people say they are very religious but they are the furthest away from God. Mama told me that Maria Fonseca, her employee, was helping Mama with bathing one morning and had said disdainfully, "As a devoted Catholic, I want you to know that since you are a Jew, every time I have to touch you to help you wash, it turns my stomach."

When the employee had to leave a few days later to have hand surgery I said to Mama, "I guess God gave her what she deserves."

Papa heard that and was very upset with me; "God doesn't give pain and misery to anyone. Each of us gets what we do to ourselves. God is good, and forgives everybody for their sins."

He was right. I had spoken out of anger, because Mama was crying when she told me what happened. I guess that living all these years in America I had forgotten the ignorance that comes with religion and prejudice. I asked Mama why she didn't fire Maria Fonseca for speaking to her in those terms, and Mama said that except for speaking out of turn, her employee was a good person. I believe that Mama and Papa, possibly because of their age, have become dependent on whomever they get as an employee. They no longer have enough fight in them to look for someone to replace a rude or ignorant worker. Papa told us that Lisbon is falling apart, and it reminds him of an old mouth with rotten teeth. Over the years Papa has lost his dry German outlook on life and has become dramatically Portuguese with his visual descriptions. But his observation is accurate. The buildings are decaying, the streets are dirty and smelly, and the cobblestones are full of holes. It's as if no one cares anymore. To Ralph everything was wonderful, but to me it was a great disappointment. Maybe what I remember being clean and beautiful is an illusion I created in my mind, because it relates to my childhood.

I had a lot of fun watching Ralph enjoy Portuguese food. As a matter of fact we both enjoyed it too much and were constantly bloated. My parents insisted we come home for all our meals, so we returned home for lunch and dinner because we didn't want to offend them. But when we went out exploring the sights, we would stop at local taverns and bakeries and try whatever seemed enticing by smell or looks. It was the palate experience of a lifetime.

My younger brother José barely spoke to us, probably because he was always heavily sedated. His medication gets added to the soup he eats, otherwise he won't take the drugs for schizophrenia. I remembered when he was a good-looking, bright youngster. I couldn't make myself look at him as he kept smiling and or talking to himself. He ate his food quietly and then he would go back into his bedroom where he sat at his desk resolving geometrical problems until he was called for the next meal.

Papa took me aside and said almost in a whisper, "Verónica, it was very nice of you to send your mother the trophy, you know, the so-called 'Academy Award.'"

I wasn't going to break down. I turned innocently to him and said, "Papa, it is a real Academy Award from the Simy Dinner Theatre Company. Mama deserved that award for her poem 'And the Black Panther Cried.'"

Papa said, smiling, "I am not stupid. I know exactly what you did. You are a good daughter and you made Mama very

happy when you sent her the trophy. And that's all that counts."
He gave me a long hug.

That night Ralph decided to explore the Lisbon nightlife
and I stayed home with my parents. They freaked me out over
the dangers facing anyone daring to go out alone into the big
ugly city full of sinners and killers roaming the streets at night.
Ralph doesn't speak Portuguese. If he were to yell for help,
nobody would understand him. I was very concerned when
he left to go out on his own exploring the nightlife of Lisbon.

The television was in my parent's bedroom and by ten they
wanted to go to sleep. Mama drank a glass of warm milk, to
which she attributes her youthful skin, and Papa ate a banana,
which he believes helps him to sleep like a baby.

I went into my bedroom and sat by the window from which
my brothers and I had done the silly stupid things that kids
do, like spitting and throwing dirt on the people walking in
the street below. I sat breathing in the cool night air and it
felt no different from twenty-eight years ago, as if time had
stood still. After a while I got chilly and went to bed though
I stayed awake waiting for Ralph to return, hopefully soon.
As I prayed for his safety, I kept pushing away the images of
gypsies robbing and killing him.

It was about two in the morning when I heard the front
door opening and heard him coming in. I thanked God for
his safe return and fell asleep in an instant. I was sure that in
the morning he would tell me everything that had happened.

This trip was quite different from the other times I had
visited my parents, when I had remained seated in their bed-
room/living room talking to them. This time I was showing
Ralph my country, and after two days in Lisbon with my
parents, Ralph and I decided to take the bus to Faro, in the
south of Portugal.

Ralph had a few goals in mind; besides seeing the family
and the country where I was born, he wanted to find the roots

of the Esagui family, and finish the family tree that he started years ago. We already have the complete Wartenberg family tree on my father's side, but when it comes to the Esagui family tree on my mother's side we don't know where his grandfather, also named Ralph, came from.

Mama told us that Ralph's grandfather was either second or third cousin to Nelly, her sister, but that was not good enough. Ralph needed better information than that to put the family tree together.

Mama informed us that the best place to investigate our ancestry would be at the Jewish cemetery in the south of Portugal. She also encouraged us to visit the cemetery in Tangier, Morocco. She gave us the address of an aunt who lives in Tangier, and most likely would be glad to let us stay with her for a few nights. In Tangier we would find her grandfather's tomb. He had been a rabbi and had started the first Jewish Temple in North Africa. He was considered a holy man.

"Where is the cemetery in Tangier? Do you have the address?" I asked Mama.

"It's easy to find," she said in a matter of fact way. "When the ship arrives at the dock you will see a large avenue in front of you. That is the road you want to take. It's called the Principal Avenue. After a few blocks you will see the cemetery on your right. You can't miss it."

Papa made us swear that we would not leave Tangier without trying couscous and said he wished he could come along with us, just to have some. We promised to find our aunt, have couscous, and definitely visit Mama's grandfather's tomb. Our intentions were then to travel through Spain and France before going back to Portugal.

Ralph and I left Lisbon very excited with the promise of an adventure about to unfold. This was going to be the trip of a lifetime since we would be following the footsteps of our ancestors, and putting together the many missing links of the Esagui family tree.

When I lived in Portugal I never had the opportunity or the reason to travel to the south of Portugal. I was finally going to see the cork and almond trees that had made the south famous.

Our bus traveled on straight roads through an endless flat terrain surrounded by arid, dusty land. I imagined Don Afonso Henriques, who became the first king of Portugal, riding his horse along with his men, in those dried fields. He would have worn the appropriate armor of those days, and carried the heavy tools of war to kill the moors and take over their castles. In that heat, they must have sweated their balls off! I couldn't imagine the weather being any hotter than on that so-called spring day. Growing up in Portugal had given me a chance to read many books about Portuguese history and their bloody battles. I had fun sharing the ones I still remembered with Ralph.

In Faro, we found a pensão, which was one notch above a hostel, for only ten dollars per night. The single beds had very thin mattresses and at night we both learned the meaning of sleeping on top of metal springs. The bathroom was down the hallway, but that was fine since the price fitted our next-to-zero budget. The front desk girl told us that the Jewish cemetery was up the hill about two or three blocks, on the right side of the road. Following her directions we found a cemetery up the street. It was a Catholic cemetery.

"Excuse me sir, but can you tell me where the Jewish cemetery is?" I asked the guard at the cemetery gate.

Visibly appalled by my question he yelled, "Why the hell would you want to know where the Jews are?"

I was very quick to answer, since my innate intelligence told me, that I'd better come up with a good answer or he was going to tie us up and burn us at the stake.

"We are news reporters from the United States of America and we need to see very old graves, you know... history!"

He got calmer, and tried to use some of his charm, "Why look at an old cemetery when you can look at this new one instead? Look over there," he said pointing to an impressive large mausoleum in the distance, "isn't it grand? Have you ever seen anything like it? This is the cemetery you should be writing about!"

I felt he was very passionate when it came to his cemetery, but Ralph and I were on a different assignment.

"You are absolutely right. I can see those tombs up there are a work of art, very nice indeed." I took a deep breath and went on, "but we need to write about the ugly as well as the beautiful. If you can direct me to the old junky Jewish cemetery we will start there, and then finish our American news investigation report here at this beautiful cemetery. How does that sound?"

He took a look up at the sky as if asking God to give him some form of endurance, and said irritated, "Americans! Okay, now I understand. But, you must come back, because here we have the best looking tombs." He added impatiently, "Go up that street, after passing the hospital make a right, and then cross the street. Just keep your eyes open, and you will see the darn place."

He turned his back on us knowing instinctively that we would not return.

That episode made me realize where we were, and I told Ralph that we needed to keep in mind three important key words: religious fanatics, ignorance, and the Inquisition. I am sure that not everybody is like that guy at the gate of the cemetery, but within the masses of the people, the curse of prejudice is still alive in Portugal as well as in many other countries throughout Europe.

Ralph became more aware of what I meant when we reached the hospital grounds and I asked two old ladies going by if they knew where the Jewish cemetery was.

They made the sign of the cross across their chest. One said, "Jesus!" and the other followed like an echo, "Jesus!"

Then one of them proceeded to spit on the floor, right in front of us as they kept walking and ignoring us.

We walked from one street to another, around and around the hospital we went, and a few people even tried to help us by admitting that they knew that the cemetery was across the street we were standing on, but they didn't know exactly where.

Finally, a man going by pointed across the street and said, "Right over there, can't you see it?"

The Walls of Flesh

Ralph and I stood motionless, staring across the street and we finally realized why nobody knew where the cemetery was. We had passed it at least three or four times and not seen it. Across the street was a wall, a thick, white-painted stone wall, so tall that it seemed to reach the sky, and it was surrounded by a huge parking lot with dozens of cars. The cemetery was invisible in a surrealistic manner, but once we became aware of its existence it became part of our senses. We ran across the street and looked up at the intensity of the mass facing us. Our ancestors were behind the white wall!

We ran around the wall eagerly looking for an entrance. We found a gigantic green metal door with a lock and thick metal chain around it, making it clear to us that no one was welcome. A feeling of desperation took over both of us. In America there are no walls or doors like that around cemeteries. It was as if the dead were hiding from the living! Ralph thought he might be able to climb the metal gate, but the sharp edges on the top discouraged him. The only way in was to use a very long ladder, he said. We stood at the gate admiring its grandeur. We were not going to give up that easily. I told Ralph, we probably could borrow a ladder and the best place to find one would be at a firehouse, which just happened to be a block away from us. Being newspaper reporters wasn't getting us anywhere. We needed a stronger, neutral title. We voted to be archeologists!

"Excuse me, we are archeologists from North America and need to borrow a ladder so that we can climb the wall into the Jewish cemetery."

But no matter how much I begged the fire chief and his assistant they would not lend us a ladder. Because we were Americans, they said that they were afraid we would fall and then turn around and sue them.

They did let me use their telephone to call the police station, but that didn't help either. The chief of police advised me to wait until Monday morning and to get the key to the cemetery directly from the city town hall. We finally agreed; it was probably the best and safest path to follow. That meant we were stuck in Faro until Monday morning.

When we got back to the pensão, the front desk girl recommended a restaurant she liked, but neglected to inform us that the restaurant didn't open for dinner until eleven at night. We soon found that out when we took a bus to the restaurant and found ourselves off city limits in nowhere land. It was cold, windy, and except for the restaurant building, which was still closed, there was nothing else around for us to take refuge. So we sat on the hard cobblestone steps of the building and waited patiently for an hour and a half with high expectations of a great dinner and entertainment.

The food turned out not to be typically Portuguese, it was made for foreigners, and very expensive. A young man with cerebral palsy played some boring organ music, and that was the entertainment. Ralph and I did a lot of talking. That was the best part of the evening. Afterwards, we took our time walking back to our pensão.

On Sunday morning we both slept late, and took a leisurely look around the historical town where not much of anything was happening. We just enjoyed being there and walking the same cobblestone streets that our ancestors had once walked on.

We were up early on Monday morning and ready for a great day as we went into the city hall's office where we were suppose to get the cemetery keys from an official person. When the well dressed man behind the desk asked me why I wanted the key to the Jewish cemetery, I thought that being in a government building where people are educated and supposedly are there to serve the people, that I would be safe to tell the truth.

"We would like to borrow the key to the Jewish cemetery so that we can visit the tombs of our ancestors."

His face went red with anger as he asked me, "You are Jewish?"

It was too late to back up, "Yes I am, and so is my son. We would like to see…"

I didn't have a chance to finish the sentence; he got up from his chair and threw us out of his office screaming, "I don't deal with Jews! Get out of my office right now."

Ralph didn't need me to translate what he heard and we both left the government building immediately. We walked for a few blocks silently, until we finally stopped to decide what to do next. At this point we both agreed that we were surrounded by a world of narrow-mindedness but nothing was going to stop us, if anything it was making us stronger. We decided to visit the local library.

Two young librarians went out of their way to help us, once they found out that we were archeologists from North America. They took us into a private room and put themselves at our disposal by bringing us the local churches' registers among many old documents of births and deaths in Faro from the last one hundred and fifty years.

Finally I took a deep breath and, crossing my fingers, I said timidly, "And…by any chance would you also have a list of who is buried in the Jewish cemetery?"

A miracle then happened! The two librarians were more than willing to help us, and within a few minutes they brought us three huge books, no less, to our table. In one of them I recognized the original Ezaguy name. In the books were the names of my great grandfather, his family, birth and death dates and even pictures of the tombs with their Hebrew names translated to Portuguese underneath the photographs. This was even better than having climbed the wall. We would have been at a loss looking at old tomb inscriptions since we do not read

Hebrew. We made copies of all the pages, and thanked the two good librarians. We were ready to continue our pilgrimage to Spain and then into North Africa.

We took a bus to Spain but it was nighttime when we got to Cadiz so we decided to spend the night there before continuing on to Algeceiras where we would board the ship to Morocco. While looking for a hostel for the night we came across a Catholic procession chanting in Latin. Each person was covered by a black hooded-cape, and held a lit candle, close to their faces. The only light in that narrow, gray cobblestone street was from the lit candles. The eeriness of the situation, and what we had experienced so far in Portugal, gave us an image of what an Inquisition procession must have been like in those days; after all, it had started in Spain. Ralph and I looked at each other and didn't need words to express our feelings.

The hostel we stayed in that night for five dollars was a bargain except for the bed bugs. In the morning I had their little bite marks everywhere on my body. Ralph was fine, which meant his bed was clean.

I wondered why sometimes we say, "Good night, and don't let the bed bugs bite."

Yeah, like we really have control over it.

When we boarded the ship to Morocco it seemed like a long trip ahead, and since I was tired, I laid down on one of the wooden benches and, using my backpack for a pillow, I slept for most of the trip. Ralph woke me up to tell me that we were approaching land. From the distance, North Africa didn't look much different than any other country. On the other hand, I had no idea as to what to expect; I just thought it would be different. The ship opened its bottom like a huge dinosaur's mouth and let out all the cars that had been carried in its inner guts. On the dock, waiting on the other side, were men dressed in the characteristic Moroccan robes, also known as thobes. We were definitely in Tangier, Morocco.

As we had finished going through the proper procedures of showing our passports and the inside of our backpacks, a man dressed in an impeccable gray suit and tie, like an official might wear, approached us and with a perfect British accent demanded our attention. He told us that he had been sent by the Moroccan government to stay with us and protect us from the riff raff waiting at the gate of the city ready to annoy and rob us.

Mama had been very explicit about us taking the main street ahead of us once we got off the dock. I told Ralph to ignore the man because we didn't need him. We could take care of ourselves. The man followed us like a fly on a horse's tail, and Ralph wasn't making it easy for him to leave us alone. Ralph kept asking questions concerning the city ahead of us. Nothing I said to Ralph could make him realize that I had a bad feeling about that man. One thing about Ralph, he never goes by feelings, only by concrete evidence or proof of what I am saying. But there are things that I can't explain. Then Ralph showed Mr. Marc Amed, as he had introduced himself to us, my Aunt's address that Mama had written in a piece of paper. Mr. Amed told us that he knew exactly where our aunt lived and he was glad to take us to her house. I still didn't want to hire Mr. Amed's services as our guide, if that was even his real name. But Ralph was totally sold on Mr. Amed's offer and said I had to stop being so skeptical.

"Mom, we are in a strange country. It makes sense that we hire him to guide us to your Aunt's house."

Once Ralph agreed to hire him, Amed asked for what I considered to be a small fortune, which he cut in half after I did my Portuguese bargaining.

It was agreed that he was going to take us to our Aunt's house. Ralph and I exchanged some of our money at the exchange kiosk for some Dirham currency and followed Mr. Amed.

Amed took us up a hill and into some very narrow streets saying, "It's still early in the morning, let me show you around the Kasbah, then I will personally take you to your Aunt's house."

Of course, Ralph said okay and against my intuition I went along with it. This is the part of me that still makes me angry. I don't have the assertiveness to argue my point. I just go along with whatever because I hate confrontation and arguments.

Amed took us to a carpet store where we were asked to sit down and they served us a very sweet tea with peppermint. We spent about an hour being pressured by Amed's "cousin," as he had introduced him to us, to buy one of the carpets.

If a car salesman ever wants to polish his expertise at selling cars, he should visit this guy's cousin. Talk about car salesmanship! Moroccan carpet salesmen have got to be the kings of forcefulness with all the annoying, pushy, selling techniques that are enough to make a saint become a murderer. It didn't matter that I told him we had no money, and we were on a tight budget. It didn't matter that all the rooms in our house were already carpeted wall to wall, because their carpets can go on the walls and over the wall-to-wall carpets. It didn't matter that we hated carpets. No one left his cousin's carpet store without a carpet! It's their policy, "legal" Moroccan, North African policy.

Finally I got up from the carpeted bench and announced impatiently, "We have to go."

Amed followed us, and was upset that we didn't buy a carpet. We had offended his "cousin" after he had spent so much time with us and had even given us tea. Once again Ralph and I went through the whole list of why we don't need a carpet and the only reason for us to be in Tangier was to find our Aunt.

"Okay, as you wish," Amed said with a smile as he bowed his head towards me. "I will take you both to your Aunt's house. But first, let me show you something that you will fully enjoy. It's still very early and you can't come to Tangier and miss the true flavor of the Kasbah."

He was very polite yet manipulative, and that kind of pressure is what I had become aware of from the first time he spoke to us.

Once again Ralph was open to his suggestion, and I went along like a good obedient girl. Amed took us through the open food market where the dead chickens hang from hooks in the open air and the flies were the only things moving. The narrow labyrinth streets finally took their toll upon my usual good sense of direction, and Ralph was no exception. We were now completely dependent on our guide, Mr. Amed, who told us about the "divine" blind men standing on the street corners begging. After seeing Mecca they no longer wanted to see anything else. They were blind because they had poked their eyes out to show their religious devotion. Now they were looked upon as godly men. He told us how lucky we were to be with him, since he was a good Muslim. The bad Muslims kill the foreigners without giving it a second thought.

It seemed to me that he was using a lot of psychology to scare us into trusting him. He also told us how the American shows on television were spoiling their women. They were being brain washed into having more freedom than they already had. According to him, women should only go out of their house to go to the market to buy food for their family, or to use the facilities in the bathhouses.

This would explain why we only saw men everywhere and no women around. The coffee houses, or I should say tea houses, were filled with men dressed in their Arab robes sitting outside in small groups and sipping on tall glasses of tea with peppermint. He told us that Muslims don't drink alcohol, it is against their religion, and they drink tea instead.

Ralph asked him, "Why do men have more than one wife? Are they that rich?"

"No," he told us, "quite the contrary. The poorer you are, the more reasons to have more than one wife. You can have up to four wives, and that way you have more sons to fight for the cause, but what you really want are girls. The more daughters you have, the more dowry money you get."

It was about three in the afternoon when Mr. Amed met another "cousin" in the street. After talking to him in Arabic, he said to us, "My cousin is a good man, you can trust him. I gave Mohamed the address you gave me and he is going to take you both to your Aunt's house. I have to go home to see my family. We will see each other again, don't worry." He was gone before we even had a chance to thank him. But it didn't matter, what was important was that we were on the way to see my Aunt.

The new guide took us around "looking for our Aunt's house." He would say, "I believe she lives here, let's see," and he would knock at different people's doors asking if our Aunt lived there. About two hours later we were still going from door to door and Ralph and I came to the conclusion that Amed's cousin was a jerk and was lost. Amed's cousin saw me with the camera in my hand and warned me not to take anybody's pictures, but when he was looking in a different direction I took a quick shot of a woman poorly dressed and without shoes. She was filling a plastic bucket with water from a broken-down water fountain. She had her back turned towards us.

The sun was going down when Amed suddenly appeared out of nowhere. He sent his "cousin" away, and then, looking at his wristwatch, commented, "Hum, it's getting late. How about if we start looking for your Aunt's address early tomorrow morning? I will leave you both at a very nice but inexpensive hotel, and in the morning, let's say about seven,

I will come by to get you both. I will personally take you to your Aunt's house."

We were too tired and hungry to argue back, and followed him like puppy dogs. We put our backpacks in the room we were going to share, and decided to leave the place on our own and find some couscous for dinner.

I was disappointed with the flat taste of couscous. I was also concerned with their sanitary conditions. Ralph thought it was great. After dinner, we walked into a small shop nearby to look at the out of the ordinary wares. The salesman inside was no different from the carpet seller and he wouldn't leave us alone, insisting that Ralph needed to buy one of the pipes for smoking hashish. It didn't matter if we smoked it or not, he was going to sell one to us anyway.

We decided not to look into shops anymore since it took a lot of work to get out of them without going through their annoying persuasive selling tactics. We decided to adventure further into other streets and see what was out there. Even though we had no idea where we were, we found ourselves out of the Kasbah. It was a relief for us to be out of those narrow labyrinth streets and in a larger more modern-like avenue. We could finally breathe, and felt more secure. Then we saw a cop directing traffic. I asked him if he knew of a Synagogue close by. Ralph and I were hoping to find the Temple that my great-grandfather had helped start in Tangier. The cop pointed to an old building not too far from where we were standing. We went in and waited patiently in the lobby for the men to finish praying.

When they came out of the room we were asked, "What is your family name?"

"Ezaguy."

Everyone surrounded us as if we were very special, talking about our heritage and my great-grandfather. Ralph and I are the descendents of Rabbi Ezaguy, the one that had gathered the community to build the Temple where we were standing on that day.

They were very excited to meet us, and one of them in particular introduced himself as the Portuguese Ambassador to Morocco. He was married to an Ezaguy, and that meant he was part of our family! He gave us his calling card, and was so thrilled to meet us that he offered his house in Marrakech where we were welcome to stay as long as we wanted. We thanked him, but had to decline since our plans were to meet my Aunt the next morning, see Mama's grandfather's tomb at the cemetery, and continue our travels through Spain and France.

Still remembering part of the way back to the Kasbah, we thought we could find our way back to the hotel, but it was completely dark now and the narrow, deserted streets became a lot more threatening than they'd been during the day. We seemed to be going around in circles and most of the stores were rapidly closing all around us as they were rolling down their metal gates. We walked into a very small spice store that was still open but the guy could only speak Arabic. Ralph told me to stay put while he was going to go around the corner to find someone to help us. I was standing in front of the spice shop when a young man dressed in a dark suit and looking like a typical gypsy asked me if I spoke French.

I shook my head and tried to ignore him.

He continued, "Are you an American?"

I shook my head.

Just then Ralph appeared, saying loudly, "I can't find anyone to give us directions."

The young man said, "Oh, so you are Americans! I can help. I speak English. What is the address you are looking for?" Ralph showed him the hotel's calling card with the address, and the guy said, "For a fee I will take you both there."

We had no choice. We were stuck in the middle of nowhere, and we agreed to pay him what he asked. Ralph and I held hands as we walked behind the dark shadow of the man who either was going to take us back to our hotel or to our death. Ralph and I were holding hands as if our lives depended on it. I could feel that Ralph was as fearful as I was because his hand was shaking as much as mine.

Our lives were in that stranger's hands and he knew it because he looked back at us and remarked with a snake's smile, "You are both frightened because you know that I could take advantage of you if I really wanted. But don't worry; I am only a poor student looking for a couple of bucks."

I don't recall how long we walked in the dark, twisted, and narrow deserted streets, but it felt like an eternity. Then, there we were in front of our hotel! We gladly paid what he asked for, and once we entered the hotel lobby we decided that this was it for us, we didn't belong in Morocco. Tangier wasn't a friendly city, and the people were too far-out in their culture. For us it was difficult to feel even remotely comfortable. We needed to get out of Morocco as soon as possible, and we would consider ourselves lucky if we got out without being harmed. We knew that Amed would be waiting for us early in the morning, and that thought was not a pleasant one for either one of us. We doubted that he was going to take us to my Aunt's house.

We then did the smart thing. We went to the hotel's lobby to find someone, anyone, who might speak English, and just our luck, the new person behind the counter could understand Portuguese. I gave him my Aunt's address and phone number and he called her on the phone. She was shocked that we were staying in the Kasbah, and said it wasn't a safe place to stay. She lived on the other side of the city, and our guide had to know that by the address we had given him. We had been taken. The decision to leave was not even a question, and

I told her we would be back some day in the future, but for now, we were ready to go back to Spain early in the morning.

Ralph agreed with me that we could not trust Amed who had lied to us by acting like he was helping us to find our Aunt's house, nor his partner in crime, "his cousin" who had taken us under false pretenses all over the Kasbah, like puppets on a string.

We felt safe inside our hotel room, but we decided to leave before the sun came up so that we would not have to contend with our dishonest guide, Mr. Amed. At that moment, the reality of the situation became even more clear to us; Amed was coming back to get us.

I didn't sleep much, and when I did there were images of Ralph and I being taken to the desert by our kidnapper. No matter how much I screamed and cried, they killed Ralph and I was kept as a sex slave and for the purpose of making bread for the tribe and giving birth to baby girls. The babies were put into boxes and kept until their ripe age of being sold as brides for dowry.

We were up and ready to leave by five in the morning. We gave the hotel manager an envelope with half the money our guide had asked us for, even though he had taken advantage of us, Ralph felt that we should pay him something since Amed had shown us the Kasbah and a way of life that we were not previously aware of.

We knew we were up on a hill; all we had to do was go down, no matter how many turns or twists. We walked at a fast pace. We were successful in our endeavor, and soon we saw the dock where the ships where waiting to take us back to Spain.

We were ready to purchase our tickets when a man looking like an official — very much like Amed — came up to us saying, "Passports, passports."

We had learned from our previous experience and were too smart now to fall for that again.

"We take care of our passports and tickets ourselves." Ralph said to him, quite annoyed.

He looked straight into Ralph's eyes and said, "I am not here to make money. I work here. Now… give me the passports so that I can expedite the tickets."

It sounded honest, and Ralph gave him our passports and the money for the tickets.

About ten minutes later, the man returned, "Here are the tickets and your passports. It's ten dollars for my services."

Ralph argued with the guy about him lying to us and refused to pay him. Of course the guy argued back, and would not leave us alone. He wanted the ten dollars. After a while I started getting concerned over the man's nasty attitude, since we were in a foreign country, and felt that it was wise to appease him so that he would go away. I opened my purse and took out one dollar in change and gave it to him, saying, "Sorry, but this is all I got." When he argued over the amount I told him, "It's better than nothing."

Ralph was mad at me for giving in, even if it was one dollar. He was right, once again we had been taken for a ride, but I just wanted to be free of all the hustling.

While waiting to board the ship, I saw near the dock a cart full of souvenirs, mostly stuffed camels. I told Ralph I would be right back and ran to the cart outside. I couldn't leave Tangier without a souvenir. I bargained and bargained for a ten-inch stuffed camel and finally the guy gave it to me in exchange for all my dirham change and my wristwatch.

Going through customs was a joke. One of the guards opened my backpack before Ralph's and when he saw my green silk pajamas he remarked scornfully, "Americans! Just go!" He waived us both to move forward and board the ship.

"If I had known that it was going to be this easy, I would have bought the pipe and the hashish." Ralph said, and he laughed.

Once in the ship we decided to return to Portugal. The idea of going to France and possibly Italy in the next few days was not appealing to us any longer. It made more sense to spend the time we had left seeing Portugal and enjoying our time there.

While traveling back from Spain to Portugal by bus, Ralph came down with a severe cold with no tissues available. I became aware of the most important item needed when traveling in foreign countries: toilet paper. There was no toilet paper or any type of tissue available at the pit stops. It was horrible to watch him dripping from his nose without stopping. We sat in separate seats in the back of the bus and away from each other, and took his dripping condition as a sign that returning to Portugal was definitely a great idea since we were both burned-out.

With the information we had gathered in the south of Portugal, Ralph figured out that Nelly, his grandmother had married Ralph, his grandfather, who was the son of the son of my great grandfather's younger brother. What a small world!

When we got to Lisbon I told Ralph, "Before we go to my parent's house, let's have lunch at a restaurant and have papasorda."

Papasorda is the Portuguese poor-man's regional dish. I had to eat a lot of Papasorda while growing up in Portugal when my parents couldn't afford to buy fish and potatoes. I hated it when I was a kid, but somehow it sounded very appealing to me after so many years. Memories, that's all I can say!

Papasorda is made from boiling old bread, fresh-minced garlic, cilantro, salt, and pepper. Then it gets mashed into a smooth paste. If you add extra water, the result is papasorda soup. If an egg is available you can add it raw to the boiling broth, and once the egg gets poached the soup is ready to eat.

The papasorda they served us at the restaurant was still as bad as I remembered if not worse. Ralph didn't like it either.

Mama and Papa were extremely happy when they saw us return early from our trip. When Mama found out that I had eaten papasorda at a restaurant, she was offended that I hadn't told her how much I had missed it. She was going to have her employee make some for dinner. I told her that I had hated that dish as a child, and even more now as a grown up, but if the employee was willing to make green soup, and white beans with cow's feet, I would be open to it.

The following days were some of the happier times of my life. I took Ralph to the top of the hill in Lisbon, to the São Jorge castle where we took lots of pictures and admired the city view. I bought a hand-made mandala with attractive purple stones from a young French craftsman. He said it would bring me luck.

We were walking back from the castle down the steep and narrow cobblestone streets when the smell of delicious food from a tavern nearby crawled up our nostrils. Ralph saw the barrels of beer, and asked for a glass of beer and a couple of Portuguese pastries filled with seafood. The place was packed, and everyone was standing while eating and drinking. Taverns are the best place to get real Portuguese food. When I heard what Ralph was being charged, I knew he was being taken advantage of.

I asked the bartender, "Hey, what are you doing overcharging my son?"

He was definitely surprised, "Oh, I thought he was an American. He didn't speak Portuguese to me."

I was pretty mad. "That's right!" I yelled at him. "He is an American, but he is my son, and you are not going to rob him."

The bartender was visibly embarrassed. "I am sorry." Then he added, "We always charge more to the tourists. They can afford it."

Ralph agreed that from that moment on if we bought anything, I did the talking.

The next day I took Ralph to the Jewish cemetery in Lisbon. I knew he would be interested in looking at the names of our family inscribed in the stones, and it was also my way of introducing him to his great grandparents and some other ancestors. Of course he would not meet them personally, but spiritually we were both paying them our respect. I told Ralph that we needed to pick a few cobblestones before we entered the cemetery since it is customary to leave a small stone on the tomb you visit. We picked up a few broken pieces of cobblestones and carried them in our pockets as we entered the cemetery. I took him to see where his great grandparents were buried, and some of our uncles and aunts, and then we started to look for Aunt Heydee's tomb among the newer area in the cemetery — which is where I expected her to be buried. We looked and looked, but she was nowhere to be found. I inquired with the cemetery maintenance man, who remembered Aunt Heydee when she was still alive, and he was glad to take us to her place of rest.

She had always wanted to be the first in everything, and she had made plans before she died to have her spot as close to the entrance as possible. Anyone entering the cemetery would see her stone first. We didn't expect her there. But at the same time we were not surprised. We were moved by her tenacity. She had managed to literally squeeze herself into the already overfilled old burial ground. I cried, and then laughed with joy because Aunt Heydee, even after dying, was still Napoleon Number One — as we fondly used to call her when she outdid herself.

Ralph and I felt that the best way to explore Portugal would be to rent a car for the five days we had left. The guy at the car rental office wanted to charge us extra insurance, swearing to us that we were going to seriously need it because driving in Portugal was an accomplishment that not many foreigners can boast about.

I told the rental person that Ralph and I were used to driving in New York City, and nothing can be more challenging or dangerous than that. We rented a car with a stick shift, and since I had not driven a stick shift for about twenty-five years, I felt it was safer if Ralph drove instead. At first Ralph thought the Portuguese were nuts when he saw them driving head on at us, but soon he realized that it was up to him to move slightly off to the side of the road and give the passing car space enough to go by. As he said, this would never happen in America. Once he caught up on the rules of the road, he felt a lot more secure.

We drove north to the town of Sintra and took our time looking inside the castles and palaces and the monasteries along the road.

In Eiriceira, Ralph fell in love with the typical fishing village. I was glad that he liked it too, since it is still one of my favorite places in Portugal. We spent the afternoon at the beach, and decided to stay the night at a hotel. We got a kick out of the owner not believing we were mother and son. This happens often because I don't look my age and Ralph insists on wearing a small goatee, which makes him automatically look older than me.

While in Eiriceira we found a seafood restaurant, a quaint little restaurant by the sea. It was Saturday night and we felt like celebrating with a banquet of all kinds of fresh seafood. Ralph ordered a bottle of white wine to which I said I would be better off not to drink; but he said, "Mom, don't worry if you get silly, just enjoy it."

So I did. After a glass, I found the menu to be the most hilarious thing I had ever read. I knew I was drunk, but I didn't care. I read the menu out loud as if I was reading a funny book and I laughed until my cheeks hurt. Ralph was cool about it, and wasn't even embarrassed by my silliness, and I was very happy that he and I were the best of friends. After the meal, which was fit for a king in size and price, the waiter took all the empty plates away from our table. Then he returned and proceeded to write, with a pencil, our total bill on the badly-stained white paper covering our table. Ralph gave the waiter his American Express card. The restaurant didn't take American Express, only Visa. My card was also American Express, and we didn't have any money except for some small change. We had run out of cash because the term "banking hours" is part of the Portuguese way of life, and on weekends the banks are closed. We had a dilemma on our hands. I went looking for the owner who was busy cooking in the kitchen.

"I am very sorry, but we can't pay for our dinner because we only have American Express and no cash. But my son and I are more than willing to help you tonight in the kitchen, and also tomorrow, and Monday morning we will go to the bank and get whatever we owe you to pay for our meal." I said in Portuguese.

He looked at me and started to laugh, "Are you kidding? Take a good look at the people eating. They are all tourists! I will be making more than enough money on them. You and your son just go on home, you don't owe me anything." Ralph was shocked when he heard about it and said this would never happen in America. Funny, but Al said the same thing when he first came to Portugal to marry me. He was just as surprised as Ralph by the cultural differences between the United States and Portugal.

Sunday morning Ralph and I got back on the road, and while driving north to the town of Coimbra we became aware of the eucalyptus trees surrounding us mile after mile. I can only say what an incredible experience it was to travel with Ralph. We stopped the car and I lay on the ground breathing in the aroma. Some people like to make angels in the snow by moving their arms and legs; I enjoyed making angels amid the ground covered with eucalyptus leaves.

The eucalyptus forest had taken on a complete new meaning to me, perhaps because I had someone to share it with. If I had laid myself down on the ground like that when I was with Al a few years ago while visiting Portugal, he would have called me a nut case.

I watched Ralph going up to the trees to touch them, picking up the leaves and smelling them and I was happy. We decided to take a few tree branches and put them in the back seat of our car. They were going home with us, back to America!

I didn't worry about asking Ralph to stop the car whenever I saw something I liked to investigate, because I knew he felt the same way as I did. There was only one thing that I didn't care for, the way he drove and the speed at which he drove. I am nicknamed the Roadrunner of New Jersey, yet by my standards on safety I was scared that we were both going to wind up at the bottom of a ravine. By the time we got to Coimbra I knew that I had to quickly brush up on my stick-shift driving technique or we were both going to die on one of the steep curves. When I complained about his speed around the curves he remarked, "Mom, when you drive in Europe, you have to drive like a European in order to get the full experience."

The more he drove like a European the more I disagreed with his philosophy. So, after we got to Coimbra and took the car to a garage because it had a flat tire, I decided it was only fair that since he drove going north I would be driving south.

I thank God for that insight, because when we were driving back, the road suddenly stopped at an abyss. This is so typical of Portugal. No signs to tell you what to expect ahead, you are supposed to know that there's no road ahead. Now it's my turn to say that would never happen in America. If Ralph had been driving I don't believe he would have been able to stop in time. Of course, I will never know the answer because I was driving. We did stop in time, but it wasn't easy to turn the car around. He had to get out of the car and instruct me until the u-turn was completed in the narrow path. Afterwards, we were lost and couldn't find the main highway. So when I was going through a little village, I drove up the sidewalk to get directions from a policeman standing by a store talking to some people.

Ralph cringed, and yelled out, "No, you can't drive on the sidewalk! Are you out of your mind?"

To which I was proud to say, "This is the norm in Portugal. You don't yell at a cop from your car and bother him asking for directions. You drive up to him and show him respect."

The cop gave us directions and we went on our merry way. I felt I had impressed Ralph with my driving skills, and once again he remarked, "This would never happen in America." Of course not, each country has a different approach concerning legalities. A good example was when Ralph and I were walking around Lisbon and we both noticed a huge hole in the middle of the street.

Ralph said, "This is incredible, right in the middle of the street! Someone could fall into it. Aren't they worried about that? Ask them, what would they do if that happens?"

I asked one of the workers at the bottom of the hole, "Excuse me, but aren't you worried someone might fall in the hole you are working in?

One of the workers below, asked, "Who wants to know?"

I pointed to Ralph saying, "My son, he is an American and he is curious as to what happens if somebody falls in there. There are no warning signs up here."

"American, hum. Well, tell your son that if he falls inside this hole, tomorrow he can read the headline in the newspaper, 'Stupid American fell into a large hole in the street.'"

When we returned the car to the rental place they wanted to charge us $150 for a missing hubcap. After almost an hour of arguing that we were not at fault, I finally convinced them to call the garage affiliated with their company in Coimbra. They agreed that they had forgotten to put the hubcap back on after they had changed the left front tire. I learned from this experience that anytime I have to rent a car in a foreign country, I would always remove the hubcaps and then put them back when returning the car. It was a miracle that we didn't lose all the hubcaps after hitting so many potholes on the road.

Did I have any serious thoughts about Michael or Al during this trip? No. While in Portugal I was Veronica, not Ronnie. I was happy showing Ralph my country and seeing my parents and family. Soon I would be back in New Jersey and in Ronnie's world across the Atlantic Ocean with Al. I was not in any hurry.

What a fantastic trip! I believe that every mother should take a vacation with her son or daughter, and one at a time so that the bonding becomes a powerful experience of love and understanding between the two of them. My intentions are to do the same with Steve next year. The only downer was that all the soap bars I bought to give as gifts must have been confiscated out of my luggage, because when I got home, out of the two dozen that I had enclosed in the luggage, there were only three soap bars.

I am so happy to be home! This is where I belong, with my family, friends, and businesses. Michael's mom called me at work to tell me that she and Michael had been trying to get hold of me. They have officially put their house up for sale. Her husband is never coming back, her daughter Robin has gotten married and moved out with her husband, and Michael had broken up with his girlfriend who is moving out of their home at the end of this month. It's going to be just Michael and her alone in that huge house. They can't afford it, and they are planning to move to South Carolina as soon as they sell the house.

I drove over to their house and found Michael working hard at repairing the wall in one of their bedrooms. After that he plans to start pulling the steps off the front of his house and putting on a new entrance. I offered to come by and help him whenever I have free time. We kissed and hugged and then said goodbye once again.

Someone called me at the Howell Music Center this morning telling me that they laminate and frame news articles, and that they had done mine from the March /April issue of Monmouth County Business Today. I had forgotten about that interview. They are going to drop it off for me to take a look, and if I like it, I can have it for twenty-five dollars.

I told my friend Joe, the owner of Crazy Joe furniture store across from Howell Music Center, what happened to Ralph and me in Morocco, and how we had been basically kidnapped and taken into the Kasbah. He told me that he was not surprised, and that if he had known that I was going to Morocco, he would have told me not to go. He had been there a year ago with a tour group, and some of the people in the group got robbed, including a young girl with extremely tight jeans. Until today he can't figure out how someone was able to put his hand into her pocket and take the money out without her even feeling it.

Joe's wife is funny. She always says to me as I leave their store, "We have to do lunch one of these days."

We have known each other for years and we've never had lunch together.

I've been busy putting the set up for "Bell, Book, and Candle," and Monday I have to send out press releases to all the newspapers that we will be having auditions for our next production, "Bedrooms."

I had to agree with Al and Steve; the laminated presentation of my interview with the Monmouth County Business Today looks very nice even though I look like a nerd. They put under entrepreneurs, "Ronnie Esagui, Energy in Action." I put the plaque up on one of the back walls of the Howell Music Center.

"Bell, Book, and Candle," is doing very well. Sandi Van Dyke, the director, picked a great cast, and this production makes theatre a very enjoyable experience. Michael is busy with his house, and I try not to bother him with the theatre unless it is absolutely necessary. Through the years I have gathered a good crew, and lately I have been busy just being the producer and set designer.

One of our customers at the Howell Music Center told me that he did janitorial work. Our store is humongous, and with what he charged by the hour I would have been a fool not to hire him. He cleaned the place twice, but then he called me on the phone saying that he took the job not for the money but because he wanted to see me. I responded by telling him not to come back, and that I am a happily married woman. I am definitely developing a strong inner self. If this had happened a few years ago I would have given the phone to Al because I would have gotten all flustered, but now that I am like a rock I can take care of myself. I feel invincible.

I can't believe I got food poisoning again. This time I thought it was going to be my last day on earth. God must have some incredible future plans for me or he made my stomach out of iron. I tried something new at the Kobe; rolled eel. To describe how I felt when I got food poisoning before is to say I fell off a bike and broke all the bones in my body. To depict how I felt this time I would have to add that after falling off the bike and breaking all my bones I got dumped into an active volcano. I hope and pray to God that I will never have this happen to me again. It is beyond my physical endurance.

The next day I told Katie, the hostess at the Kobe, what had happened. She said she was very sorry and was going to let Mr. Ounuma know. He then told me that it couldn't be from what I ate and it had to be from something else I had ingested earlier that day.

That evening, Mandy, one of the Japanese waitresses, came upstairs to the theatre and told me as a friend that she would, never eat eel at the Kobe, because they get it frozen from Japan. If the eel was spoiled before being frozen, the poison comes alive after cooking it.

I will never eat eel again, not at the Kobe or anyplace else.

Michael and his mom have started moving things to South Carolina. Soon he will be gone and far away, but I choose not to think about it. I have been helping them as much as I can, and his cellar is just about empty, like my empty heart.

Tracey gave me a two months' notice to find someone else to do the props for the theatre. She is too busy being a grandma, and besides that, she confided that she is scared about dying soon, since her mother died about the same age she is now. Being fifty-eight years old and with high blood pressure, she feels the odds are against her. Personally, I don't believe she is going to die any time soon. This is just a psychological thing with her. Either way, we will remain friends forever.

Selfishly, I keep thinking it is a blessing that Tracey left. Since the theatre has not been doing so well lately with attendance;

a dollar saved is a dollar earned. I gave it some consideration and decided that I will not get another partner. I will do the props myself.

Through the years that Tracey and I worked together I always shared the money we made from each show, just like I have done with Michael. Even if he is not at the theatre for every production, I can always rely on his help and I feel his help is well worth it. Once he leaves for South Carolina, then I'll classify him as no longer being part of the theatre.

I no longer can count on Tracey because she quit, but I felt that it would only be right that she receive the five hundred dollars she originally put into the Simy Dinner Theatre, as a thank you token for all those years of working together. She said she would still be around and come to sit with me whenever possible while waiting for the theatre patrons to arrive. We have too much fun talking to each other, and we want to keep our friendship going whenever possible.

Summer of 1990

I hate to admit it, but it looks like Mama is partially right; there's no such thing as a platonic relationship between a man and a woman. "Bedrooms" was the perfect example of what happens between two actors that are not happily married. I'm afraid that their marriages will not survive.

Michael and I said goodbye and he said he would be back to New Jersey every chance he gets to work on his house — which is still on the market. He promised that he would call me when he is back in New Jersey. I am not thinking about him; I'm too busy. My feelings have not changed, but I am more mature now, and I realize that life is what it is.

Al decided to have the screws removed from his leg. It was a personal decision since his doctor said his leg has healed perfectly and it was up to Al whether to leave the screws in or take them out. Al told his doctor that he wanted the screws back and he gave them to me thinking I could use them in the theatre. I showed them to Barney who said they are special screws, and very expensive. If he were still in practice he would probably buy them from me. I am so impressed with their value, that I have kept the screws in a plastic bag and have been showing them to everyone I know.

How many times do I have to do something that I know is not good for me before I learn my lesson? I really don't know.

It was hot, very, very hot and I was outside hanging on to the Kobe's outside sign, pulling out the letters and putting in the new ones announcing the next show. When it's hot like that my maximum capability of standing in the heat is about fifteen minutes. After that I start getting dizzy with a pounding headache, and the weird sensation that I am going to pass out anytime. I believe this happens to me because I don't sweat. I don't think I have sweat glands. Without sweat I am unable to cool down. I am so jealous of people that sweat! Finally I put the last letters up on the marquee sign and dragged myself into the Kobe Restaurant where Mrs. Ounuma saw my flushed face and went to get Mr. Ounuma. He became concerned with my overheated look and handed me a tall glass of cold plum wine, which he said would help me cool off.

Did I tell Mr. Ounuma that I couldn't drink wine because it makes me sick and act weird? No. I wasn't going to offend him. Besides, I'd never had plum wine, it sounded to me more like fruit juice and I was very thirsty. I drank the wine as if it were water. Rapidly. Yummy, yummy, cold, sweet and…Oh my God! Help! My heart was beating very fast, and I was even dizzier than before. My head felt too heavy to hold up. Since I was seated at the sushi bar I bent forward and laid my head on it. Suddenly I became a lot more aware that the Kobe was in dying need of something more than that constant Japanese music, over and over again, ding a ling ding, ding ding ding…I knew exactly what I was doing, but had no control as I started singing "This land is your land. This land is my land, from California to the New York Island…"

With Mr. Ounuma on my right and Mrs. Ounuma on my left, they carried me upstairs to the theatre and laid me down backstage on the couch where I remained paralyzed for who knows how long. When I was finally able to get up and make it down to the restaurant, Mr. Ounuma said with a smile, "You should not work outside when it's too hot," and he pointed his right index finger towards me while moving it side to side. And he said to his wife, "We don't give any more plum wine to Ronnie."

I love Mr. and Mrs. Ounuma! I wish I were a Japanese child so that I could adopt them as my parents.

Al says everything is fine economically, but I don't agree and neither does Steve. In the last year and a half we have been barely paying our bills. We are struggling financially. We have become very aware of our declining economy. Steve and I recognize this fact because someone will sell us a used Fender electric guitar for $10, which is basically giving it away, but when we try selling it for $50 no one can afford it, even though the instrument may be worth $800.

Businesses are closing left and right. This is not a Recession like the news wants us to think. I believe that we are in the midst of a Depression. In our mall there are only three stores still open besides ours, everybody else has closed for good. How long we can hold on, I don't know. I called the mall's landlord and asked him to reconsider not hitting us with the extra-added cost for the problems he is having with the sewage in back of the Howell Music Center. If anything, he should think about giving us a break until we all get back on our feet. He said that was not his problem.

I showed Ralph our bills and the store's records. He was very direct; we need to go bankrupt like he had done a year ago. We are deep in debt.

I gave it a lot of thought in the last few days and brought up the idea of consolidation, which is another way of pulling all our resources together.

We closed the Marlboro Music Center, and moved all the instruments and equipment back into the Howell Music Center.

It's been a month now since we closed the Marlboro Music Center and Al feels that we should do the same with Ronnie's Music Den, the music shop we still have going on weekends at Collingswood market. In his opinion it's not worth keeping it since it's doing poorly.

I decided to take a chance and put an ad in the Asbury Park Press and sell Ronnie's Music Den for $10,000 instead of closing the place down. Al told me that I was wasting my time and that only a jerk would buy a tiny shop of 5x10 feet with barely anything in it except a couple of cheap acoustic guitars and some picks.

Two people called the next day.

I sold Ronnie's Music Den to the first buyer that showed up with a $10,000 check. Too bad I didn't think of doing the same with the Marlboro Music Center. Now it's too late, and it doesn't do me any good to cry over spilled milk.

I have a serious problem on my hands with one of my actors in the present production. Larry has an obnoxious attitude and no regard for anybody's feelings. Even though his wife is always with him and does a pretty good job at keeping him calm, she can only do so much. He is actually very nice to me, but this will be his last production with us because there is too much tension when he is around. It's too bad because he is a great actor. Larry made the mistake of using his nasty attitude on Ben, the bartender hired to work upstairs during the shows. Ben took upon himself to get even with Larry by replacing the cup of tea he was supposed to drink on stage, with whiskey. That night Larry was on stage performing and thank God that he only took a sip, because according to his wife, he is highly allergic to alcohol. Larry managed to recover his voice on stage, but his wife wants to sue the bartender for almost killing her husband.

After that incident, Mr. Ounuma fired Ben.

Two months ago, a member from the Cultural Arts Committee in Howell called to ask me if I would consider becoming a member again. She said she had heard about all the work that I had done when I was a member and they would like me to return.

I told her, "I don't know if you guys really want me back. I have no problem attending the meetings, but I will be delegating the work to every member, and that means everybody will be very busy working."

I was smiling as I accented the very busy on purpose. She said she would pass the message to the group and then call me back. She never did.

I called a bunch of hospitals trying to find a straight jacket we could borrow to use in our next production. I found out they no longer use them, but when I called a mental hospital in North Jersey a doctor answered the phone and told me she could get me a used one. Dr. Seine gave me directions to the hospital where she worked, and the building number where she was the head of the department. I made an appointment to meet with her next Thursday morning at ten.

If Tracey were still with us she would make us a straight jacket in a jiffy. But I have no idea how to make one that will look even close to real.

The mental hospital was a conglomeration of heavy massive brick buildings with jail-like narrow windows covered by black metal bars. The humongous property had one entrance, a large double black metal door, which gave the buildings in front of us the seemingly austere look of a top-security prison. I have never been to a mental hospital, but it matched exactly the way I imagined it to be. It gave me the creeps.

"This place must have been something else in its old days," said Al, also impressed.

We parked the car and went into the building looking for Dr. Seine. They told us to wait in the lobby. To make matters worse Al kept repeating over and over again that he wanted to get the heck out of there. We decided to sit outside on the steps of the building. Dr. Seine was one hour late and couldn't find the office key in her coat pocket. She started looking for the key in her deep, obviously overfilled handbag. Then she lost her patience, mumbled something under her breath, and got on her knees to hastily empty all the contents of her large handbag on the floor. Her eyelids kept flickering and her hands were shaking as she searched among a bunch of make-up items, a hair brush, two eyeglass cases, a bunch of papers, and what looked like bills including a couple of small note books, a few pens and pencils. She is on the edge of a nervous breakdown, I thought.

Upon finding her key to her private office, we were asked to follow her in and to have a seat. I waited until she was seated and breathing normal. Once again I introduced us as being from the Simy Dinner Theatre in Howell.

When she looked at me with a blank look on her face I reminded her, "Dr. Seine, I spoke with you on the phone three days ago and I am here to borrow the straightjacket for the show I told you about."

She had no recollection of talking to me. But since I was there she would call someone in building number four and most-likely they could accommodate my request. We were to drive over there and someone would be waiting for us.

I was proud of Al that he didn't say anything while in her office. But as soon as we left the building, he remarked, laughing with gusto, "That's a psychiatrist? I'd hate to see her patients!"

I had to agree with him.

When we got to building number four Al told me not to take too long as he was going to wait in the car, right at the front door.

I ran into the building. There was nobody in the large waiting room. There was nobody behind the large reception counter either. I rang the counter bell and called out, "Is anybody home?"

I waited a few minutes and then started to see if there was a door I could use to get inside the building. There was one door behind the counter. I was happy to find it unlocked. The hallway was empty with not a sound around except for my voice, "Hello, is anybody home?"

A woman dressed in a nurse's outfit showed up at the end of the hallway and walked hurriedly towards me.

I was sure glad to see her. "Hi, I'm here to pick up the straightjacket."

The woman was strange in her behavior as she questioned me, "What are you doing here? How did you get into this hallway?"

"I used that door over there." I said pointing to the door I had entered from.

She became very serious. "That's impossible! That door is always locked!"

I got a weird feeling that I was in a bit of trouble, and if anything I should respond calmly.

"Look, that door was open; otherwise I would not be walking in this hallway." Then I decided to be a bit more assertive and stick to the reason I was there in the first place and asked her, "So, do you have the straightjacket? Dr. Seine called here not even ten minutes ago."

She grabbed my hands and said sternly, "Show me your wrists!"

At this point I started to get really worried, as I could sense that she must be thinking that I was a mental patient trying to escape. I showed her my wrists and she seemed to feel more comfortable, but she made me walk in front of her as she took me into a room and locked the door behind her.

She pointed to a chair saying, "You sit there, while I check with Dr. Seine. It's strange that she didn't call me."

Of course Dr. Seine was not in her office, and to make things worse, nurse Watters wouldn't believe the reason I was there, no matter how many times I told her that I had a dinner theatre and needed a white straightjacket as a prop for our next show.

"Straightjackets are no longer being used!" She argued back as she got up and grabbed my arm forcefully, adding, "Follow me and don't make a fuss."

Holding hard to my arm she took me back to the hallway and I walked along with her wondering where she was taking me.

I was getting scared and tried to reason with her, "My husband is waiting for me in our car by the front door. You can take a look if you don't believe me. If I don't come out of this building very soon he is going to come in looking for me, now let me out!"

She took me to the front door, saw Al in the car, and said with a hand gesture, "Okay, you can go!"

I got into the car and Al wanted to know what had taken me so long, where was the straightjacket, and not to count on him anymore to go looking for props for the theatre. I didn't dare tell him that I had almost become a hospital inmate. Thank God that I had asked Al to come with me.

The Howell Music Center is not making enough to pay the rent. I called the landlord once again to see if he would charge us less just for a couple of months so that we can get back on our feet.

He laughed. It looks like we will have to go bankrupt after all.

We will need to start selling everything as fast as we can. We are going to need some money to get started someplace else, definitely out of New Jersey. I went to visit Crazy Joe at his furniture store. He said he is not worried about the recession. His business has dropped considerably, but he has enough money that he can wait a few years for things to go back to normal. He must be richer than I thought.

Autumn of 1990

Al and I went to visit a bankruptcy lawyer. We have no choice in the matter, since New Jersey is a goner and the whole state is going berserk. The latest in bumper stickers says it all, "The last person leaving New Jersey, turn off the lights."

I have racked my brain trying to think of ideas on how to save our music store but nothing is feasible. According to Ralph, when he went over the books, we are $250,000 in debt.

Al and I turned in our Life Insurance and put the money aside along with the $10,000 we made from selling Ronnie's Music Den at Collingswood Flea Market. We are going to need every penny we can get together to get started with another business again. I am thinking that perhaps we should check out the possibilities in Florida since we had so much fun when we were there with Ralph and Steve when they were kids.

Most of my directors at The Simy Dinner Theatre have a certain group of actors that they are used to working with because they are extremely talented, easy to work with and reliable. But we still hold auditions for just about every production. This is our way of finding new talent to add to our already awesome group of performers. I have to be on vacation or pretty sick to miss a show or rehearsal. The theatre is my escape, but it's no longer a pleasure for me.

Michael is now living in South Carolina. A day doesn't go by that I don't think about him. I wonder how he is doing out there in the "boondocks," as he described the place where he and his mother are living.

Setting up a stage with Al's help is pure torture, as we don't work well together and I run several times to the bathroom and cry in desperation. I count my lucky stars when Barney helps me out.

I am very disappointed with Joel, one of my stagehands. He was one of the three high school students helping me to build the set last month. I gave each kid a $50 check for a day's work, which I believed to be very fair. Today I got in the mail a copy of the checks for the month, and to my surprise one was made out to Joel for $500 with my falsified signature.

I called him to ask him what that was about, and he said that he didn't know anything about it. Before I dared to accuse him, I went to the bank and they showed me on video Joel, wearing a hooded jacket, cashing the check. I called Joel back on the phone and told him that he had until the end of this week to bring the $500 to the Howell Music Center; and if I didn't get the money by 9AM Friday, I was calling the police. He came by on Friday morning and handed me the money. He didn't even say he was sorry; instead he blamed me for giving him a blank check because it had been too much of a temptation not to take advantage of the situation.

Now I understand what Papa once told me, the majority of crooks and criminals in jail tend to blame their victims. Joel is no different; he must have thought that what he did was not a big deal, because he asked me not to fire him since he loved working with me. I bet! I didn't say anything, but I don't rehire robbers.

I got a letter from Mama, telling me that Alice, her new employee, was trying to convince her and Papa to allow her two young daughters, who are prostitutes, to come live with them. Mama and Papa talked about it and came to the conclusion that they would not be comfortable having the girls living in their home because this is a way of life that they don't find respectable. Mama was also upset because Alice is engaged to a guy who is in jail for selling drugs, and when he gets out in about a year from now, Alice is engaged to marry him. That means that most likely Alice will be leaving my parents. Mama says she don't know how she is going to manage without Alice who is a caring and loving employee to her.

When the teachers at the Howell Music Center heard about our financial predicament, all nine teachers got together and unanimously offered to work for free until we could get out of debt. I thanked them from the bottom of my heart, but that would be a drop in the bucket, and it's not going to help much.

Now I stay awake at night thinking about their future, and what they are going to do to make a living when we close down the Howell Music Center.

After going from one beauty shop to another trying to borrow some beauty equipment, I was starting to give up when; miracle of miracles, Barbara came to my rescue. She made a deal with the owner of the beauty shop she frequents. In exchange for advertisement in the playbill, they offered her all the beauty shop props we need for "Steel Magnolias," including four old, beat up professional beauty chairs with the hairdryers included. They are perfect props for an old town beauty shop.

I get a warm fuzzy feeling just thinking about the end result of "Steel Magnolias" with Barbara as the director. Her shows are masterpieces.

For the last four or five years, Joe, the owner of Crazy Joe Furniture has been our theatre patron-saint. I give him a full-page advertisement in the playbill, and two theatre tickets with dinner included. Any furniture we need can be borrowed from him for the duration of each production. Now that I moved all the props out of the chicken coup and into a real storage unit, we have very limited space to store large pieces of furniture. The beauty about borrowing furniture from Crazy Joe is that I can pick the furniture style we need, and I don't have to worry about storage. At the end of the run I just take everything back to his store. I couldn't ask for more. Some of the odd larger props, like fireplaces, bars and stools, and other large items that don't fit into the small rental unit, I keep at home as part of our home decoration. Al complains a lot, saying that our apartment looks like a consignment shop. I kind of like it though, our place always has a new flair. Now I understand why Mama was always moving the furniture in our house from one room to another; it gave the rooms a fresh new look every few months.

At present we have in our apartment two beautiful fake fireplaces and a dark African wood bar with three matching stools covered with leopard skin, that are the envy and desire of everyone that sees them on stage. The front of the bar has three carved African-like masks and the front of the stools have the same matching carved masks. More than once I have been approached by someone who either wants to buy the bar and stools, or wants to know where I got them. I got them as a donation a few years back, and I don't even remember who gave them to me. I only remember Michael being impressed when he saw them. "Ronnie, as always, you have outdone yourself."

It's funny how I remember all of his compliments.

Ralph got into a car accident. He went to see another chiropractor, and now his back is killing him. The chiropractor was a real jerk and popped his back really hard and hurt him. I would have to be dying to allow myself to be treated by a chiropractor. Just the thought of it gives me the willies.

I got a very disturbing letter from Laurie, who used to be my stage manager. She moved to Georgia a few months ago with her family. Her high school teacher told her that she was not allowed to talk to black male students or something unpleasant was going to happen to her. In the south, white girls are not allowed to speak to black boys unless they want to jeopardize their own lives. I was shocked to learn about this as if we were still living in the middle of the '50's or '60's.

I always felt that people from different religions had it bad when it came to prejudice, but having your skin a different color has got to be the worst curse one can have when it comes to having a normal life among a bunch of ignorant white people. I would never be able to live in the south; I don't know how Michael can stand to be living in South Carolina. He can't be happy there.

For the last two weeks I have been looking for a bug pin. "The bug pin for 'Steel Magnolias' has to be three inches in diameter no more and no less" said Barbara firmly.

Every bug pin I bought didn't fit Barbara's standards.

I found a golden spider with fake diamond toes and green eyes for $50 at the Freehold mall. The mall gave me the heebie-jeebies. Half the stores were closed, and there was nobody shopping. It looked like a ghost town. Obviously businesses are doing badly everywhere.

I presented the spider pin to Barbara during rehearsals that night. She must have liked it because she said, "It will have to do."

I'm keeping the pin after the show.

Our future has been written. We are definitely losing our music store. We have been selling everything below our cost for the last two months, and with Christmas at our doorstep, it has helped us a lot since there are still people that buy for the holidays even if they can't afford it. With the low prices we are offering, they would be fools not to take advantage of our downfall. We are basically giving everything away.

Once again Barbara Shiavonne's production was flawless. The critics raved about the show, and many of the patrons commented that "Steel Magnolias" was better than the movie. I never saw the movie, and now I have no reason to see it.

The New Year's Eve show "Adults Only" was sold out by the end of November. I called it "Adults Only" because I now have enough experience to know what titles attract audiences. Mr. Ounuma said that I am a real businesswoman and I am the best thing that has happened to his restaurant. He said that if he goes out of business, he will move back to Japan with his family, but he is keeping his fingers crossed, hoping that things will get better. He finally listened to me and agreed to advertise with coupons in the newspapers, but at the same time he gets upset when the customers bring the coupons in and calls those customers "cheapskates."

Tracey and her husband Sam joined us for the New Year's show at the theatre, and we had a chance to reminisce during intermission over the "old days" and how much fun we had doing theatre together. She reminded me of the very over-weight couple with an attitude who came to see every show. One day the woman came out of the bathroom and the toilet paper was still stuck to the back of her glittering red pants. It took us a while to stop laughing before I had the courage to tell the patron about the toilet paper sticking out of her pants and dragging on the floor. That was, indeed, a very embar-rassing moment.

Winter of 1991

Moving to Florida still seems to be the most practical idea, since we had a great time many years ago when we went there on vacation. I don't know yet what I am going to do with the dinner theatre if we leave New Jersey. Without Michael, I no longer have any desire to continue with it; it's lonely and empty, and I feel constantly sad when I am there. Yet it is still my own personal hideaway. Interestingly enough, I am not concerned about losing our music store. That simply means that we have to do something else to make a living. When one door closes another will open; that's my philosophy.

I got my friend Rosanna excited about starting her own tele-vision talk show after she told me that was her dream, but she didn't know how to go about it. I told her the way to do anything in life is by doing it, that's how we learn. We talked about it on the bus all the way to New York City and back. She treated me to what she calls, Dim Sum Hopping, in some of the best Chinese restaurants in Chinatown.

I had never had dim sum and I enjoyed it a lot, even though I refused to eat chicken feet and other oddities like duck tongue that she wanted me to try. I feel like I am quite adventurous when it comes to food, but there are some parts of animals that I refuse to eat.

On the way back to New Jersey, Rosanna said she would do it, but she would need a cameraperson and someone to edit the show at the television station. I volunteered to do it as long as someone shows me the process. It was agreed that her first production on television will be a talk show for singles. She also wants to do a community talk show about local events and interesting people. I told her whatever she wants to do, I will be there for her.

Two stagehands bringing the couch downstairs to my van bumped into Mrs. Ounuma's favorite glass vase arrangement and broke it into a million pieces. We rapidly cleaned up the mess. Thank God there was no one else in the restaurant except the three of us. We put the broken glass in a container to take with us on the way out. One of the guys said, "What are we going to do with those ugly maroon flowers? They sure are huge!"

Knowing how much Mrs. Ounuma loves her maroon flowers, I couldn't possibly throw them away. It would be a criminal act. But if I left them on the counter, Mrs. Ounuma would know that I was guilty of not paying attention while guiding the guys with the couch down the staircase. My only option was to put the flowers into a garbage bag and take it home.

Al said they were the ugliest fake flowers that he had ever seen, so I hid them under our bed. I don't know how I am going to live with myself, knowing that I have Mrs. Ounuma's flowers. I can't just throw them out, and I don't know what to do with them. I feel like I'm hiding a dead body under my bed.

I have asked myself this question many times. Why do I let Al come to the Kobe? He always makes some kind of comment that is either derogatory or dumb. Either way it's trouble for me. It took me months to convince Mr. Ounuma to finally do some advertisement in the newspapers, and then Al came in and in two minutes destroyed everything I worked so hard for. Mr. Ounuma was making small talk when he told Al that he was hoping the newspaper advertisement this month would bring new customers to the restaurant. Al said, "What a waste of money! Nobody is going to even look at the ads."

By the time Al was finished telling Mr. Ounuma all the reasons for not advertising, Mr. Ounuma was convinced that advertisement was a waste of his time and money and he told me that he would no longer be advertising in the newspapers.

Katie called me at the Music Center asking me if I could get to Kobe two hours before "Move Over, Mrs. Markam" was to go on. Katie, Mrs. Ounuma, and Hiroko, my favorite Japanese waitress, had a mischievous look on their faces when they insisted that I follow them upstairs to the theatre's dressing room. I trust them enough that when they asked me to undress down to my underwear I did it while giggling along with them. They dressed me in a complete kimono outfit with every detail being carefully addressed from my head to my toes. Mrs. Ounuma apologized for using a cotton summer kimono, to which Katie said that she had an extra winter kimono and next week she would give it to me as a present. First they had me put on an embroidered white chemise that had to be used in a very specific way so that it could fit just right under the beautiful green cotton kimono with flying white geese pattern. They spent some time making sure that the back of my neck was properly displayed since in Japan that is the sexiest part of a woman's body. A black silk sachet went around my waist where they hooked up a black silk pocket they called the hump. They inserted a white doughnut shaped plastic piece wrapped in a green scarf into the hump and tied it in along with another black scarf. Then they used dark and light green cords around my waist. By the time they were finished, I was so tightly bound that I couldn't take a deep breath. They fitted me into a pair of odd white socks where the big toe was separated from the other toes and gave me a pair of black sandals. Then they proceeded to comb my long hair up and stuck some fancy ornamental hairpins into it.

Mrs. Ounuma smiled along with the others. They were content with the results achieved. Katie said to me, "You are like a sister to us. We all appreciate you. This is our way of saying thank you. Everything you have on is a present from us." They bowed and I bowed back to them.

Except for my face I looked quite Japanese, and I got a lot of compliments from everyone at the theatre and the Kobe staff.

After the show everybody left in a hurry, which is what happens after a Sunday matinee, and besides it was starting to snow. Everyone was anxious to get home before it would get any worse. My van thrives on slippery icy roads, and I have never had to worry about a snowstorm except for the one time when my windshield wipers were not working. Since I didn't want to go home, I hung out at the bar downstairs talking to Jerry, the bartender, and another couple who was not worried about the snowstorm either. I was telling Debbie and her husband Dan, the couple at the bar, that I was looking for a double-sided desk for the next show and they had no idea what I was talking about.

They kept asking Jerry and me, "What is a desk?"

Finally Jerry said to them, "You know, a desk, where you put the typewriter, and do your typing!"

I found out that the word desk is not pronounced with an X but an S sound. Everybody thinks it's cute the way I talk and nobody ever corrects my words, but after being in the United States for twenty-seven years I say it's about time I get with it. I begged the couple not to give up on me, and to keep repeating the word until I had it to their satisfaction. I repeated it over and over again until I felt it was impregnated into my memory bank. I finished my club soda with lemon and decided that I'd better get going. Wrapped up the way I was in my kimono, I could only take rapid little steps through the snow-covered parking lot. I got into my van smiling happily while I kept repeating "desk, desk," over and over again. My van went as far as one block. I had a flat tire. Thank God the gas station was not too far, but I still had to walk quite a distance in snow up to my knees. I was shivering and feeling absolutely out of place in my sandals and kimono, when I opened the glass door to the room where two gas station attendants were sitting down talking and drinking hot chocolate by the lit stove. They both looked me up and down and remained quiet.

"I work in a Japanese restaurant." I tried explaining, and smiled at them.

They smiled back. So I went on, "My van is just a block away from here and it has a flat tire."

"Mam, this is a gas station, not a garage!

"I know, but can you help me to change the tire, anyway? I have a spare!"

Nope, they were not getting out of their warm environment. I called Al and he came to pick me up.

Veronica's Room" will be starting February fifteen. Did I agree to produce "Veronica's Room" because it has my name on the title? Honestly, it helped my decision. Besides, Barbara will

Miso Cold

be playing the psychotic main character, and the actors will be in the same caliber of professionalism as she is. It's going to knock everybody's socks off as a thriller.

When Al and I got to the top steps of the Court House, we wondered where to go from there.

A guard came up to us and announced, "The bankruptcy room is on the third floor."

We admired his extra sensory perception, and I had to ask him, "How did you know that's what we were looking for?"

"Lately, that's what everyone is coming here for."

He was right; the courtroom was packed with people overflowing into the hallway waiting to be called in.

Our bankruptcy lawyer told us that the landlord had to give us one-week notice, but he never did. January 15th, the Howell Music Center, our Alamo last stand, was closed down and taken over by the landlord who grinned at Steve saying to him, "This black baby grand is going to look great in my living room."

Poor Steve was by himself when they came in with the court papers and asked him to leave. Of course, we knew this was going to happen very soon, we just didn't know exactly which day. Thank God that a week before this happened, I took home the "Toolbox" where I had been keeping all the cash we made, as I had a feeling that it would be safer there. Except for the baby grand and a few guitars, our Music Center was basically empty.

Between our Life Insurance, what we sold in the last few months, and the money earned from selling Ronnie's Music Den, I had saved enough money in the "Toolbox" to keep us afloat. I divided the monies equally between Al, Steve, and myself.

I made it clear to Al that no matter what happens, this money doesn't exist, at least not for me; it belongs to the future. What future I don't know. But if all our cash is gone, we will have absolutely nothing to fall back on. He agreed but I don't know how long he'll go before he spends his share of the money.

I heard from our neighbor upstairs that a restaurant in Freehold gives away fresh chicken gizzards to farmers to feed their animals. I went to the restaurant and asked the manager if I could have some to feed my family. She asked me how many buckets of gizzards I needed.

One full bucket was definitely enough for a month of cooking!

Rosanna is live on Monmouth Cablevision Public Access with her fun and exciting talk shows, and I am the director. At first it was challenging to learn to enter the data in the computer, but they were very patient at the television station and I finally learned the procedure including running the two cameras in the studio. I enjoy seeing Rosanna happy.

"Et tu, Brutus?" Yep, that's how it feels to be knifed in the back by someone you trust and believe is your friend.

The Spring Lake Theatre went ahead of us and put on "Veronica's Room." How did this happen? Hum, let's see. It just happens that one of the actors in our present production is also a member of the Spring Lake Theatre. He was present at one of their board meetings and overheard our supposed friend and director, telling their theatre group, "Let's beat the Simy Dinner Theatre by producing 'Veronica's Room' before they do it."

When I found out I was devastated, and so were the actors that were already two weeks into practice. To rub salt in the wound, the critic for the Asbury Park Press buried the Spring Lake Theatre group alive to say the least. After the general public reads that review they will have no desire to see our production.

I called in a meeting with the actors and director and decided that if we didn't do this show the other theatre would certainly have us under their thumb. Our traitor, as I call her now, knew that we were planning on putting "Veronica's Room" in February, because I had shared my plans with her.

Why did she do that? I will never know! Malice or jealousy; it doesn't even matter anymore. One thing is for sure, it will stay in her conscience, and God has already paid the other theatre group back by turning the critics against them. Oops, my father would not agree with what I just wrote, so

I'm fixing it right now. God had nothing to do with their show being terrible. The only ones to blame are they themselves for putting on a lousy production. Now we have to prove what we are really made of. I feel so secure with my cast and crew that I have decided not to cancel the show.

I sent an invitation to Yolanda the critic for the Asbury Park Press. She called me to inform me that she couldn't come; it would be pure torture for her to see that show once again.

I told Yolanda about my first experience with "The Pirates of Penzance," at the Lakewood Theatre, and what happened when I saw the same production directed and performed by another theatre in Massachusetts. It had been like night and day. I begged her to give us a chance to prove ourselves, and promised her that she would not be disappointed. I added that with the cast I had, if she didn't come, she was going to miss the best show she could possibly imagine. Finally, out of desperation, I offered to pay for her dinner if she didn't like the show, because in that case I didn't expect her to do a review of the play.

"Okay, I'll come to see the show and do the review," she agreed. "But if the show is as good as you say, I will pay for my own dinner."

After the opening night of "Veronica's Room," Yolanda told me that she still didn't like the subject of the play, but the quality of the production was, without a doubt, way above what she had been exposed to at the other theatre. She kept her promise and paid for her dinner, but she also said that she would have to be true to her readers.

Yolanda's review raved about the quality of the production, but went on further to speak against its subject of incest and murder. Such review demonstrated how people love dirty laundry, just like the song says. People are attracted to violence and sex. Our shows were sold out every night and I had to extend the production an extra weekend.

I knew it in my heart that the production was extraordinary when one of our patrons had to be held back as he tried to climb on stage to save Katie Grau from being murdered. That's how real the acting was. When Barbara Shiavonne cried in the end of the last act, she brought cold chills down every patron's spine, and I had to hold my own tears back because I knew that her crying was not an act. I felt so bad about it that after the first performance I offered to replace her with another actress, but she swore that she was fine and if anything it helped her come to terms with her own emotions and what she had gone through as a child, being physically abused by her mother.

I got a really good deal on plane tickets, and all of us, including Ralph, went to Florida to see what might be available for a new life down there.

The trip was disastrous, and proved to me that when you go somewhere on vacation with plenty of money in your pocket it can give you the impression of an idyllic situation. But it's a completely different story when on a budget. The car we rented to drive around from town to town was small and had enough ants living inside to fill a stadium. For five days we stayed at the cheapest motels and ate our meals at McDonalds. We didn't go to Disney, and there was no leisure time cooling off at the pool. Where we stayed there were no pools. We drove through a couple of towns and cities, and I still don't know what we were really looking for, but nothing was appealing. It was hot, and humid, and worst of all we had no idea in what direction to go. There were already music stores in all the towns we traveled through, and we came to the conclusion that moving to Florida was going to be a big mistake.

It's not that easy to just move to another state and put down your roots in a strange territory. We were all quick to realize that we were better off looking at different options in New Jersey.

Following Rosanna with the video camera takes me to places that I would otherwise never have the opportunity to see, like when she was covering a party on a golf course in Rumson and the featured guest was Geraldo Rivera. I was to do the video with Rosanna interviewing him. While we were waiting for him to show up, Rosanna started getting sick to her stomach and we had to leave before he arrived. I began taking the equipment back to her car, and on the way out I couldn't help grabbing a puffy cream-cake from one of the dessert trays in the lounge. When I got to the middle of the parking lot a chauffeured black limousine was pulling in, and to my surprise Geraldo himself—and what looked like his family—came out of the vehicle and were walking towards me.

Like a robot I walked up to him and, trying to remain calm, I said, "You are one of my favorite television stars. Can I shake your hand?"

I was holding the camera with my left hand and the cake with my right hand. In order to shake his hand I quickly stuffed my mouth with the cake. To my surprise he smiled at me, said thank you for the compliment, shook my hand laden with whipped cream, and then kept walking towards the building. I just stayed there frozen on the spot. It was my first one-on-one encounter with a famous person.

Rosanna came walking in my direction and asked me if I had seen a ghost. I told her, "My God, Geraldo Rivera just shook my dirty hand and he didn't even complain."

It made my day to find out that he was a really nice person.

I have become very creative cooking rice with chicken livers, sandwiches with liver pâté spread, stewing rice and chicken hearts and, our favorite old-timer, chicken soup. There is meat everyday at our table, and plenty of rice to keep us full.

Steve wanted to see what a television studio looked like, so I took him to see Rosanna's live show. I did the computer entry and then went into the studio to run the cameras. Rosanna is doing well between both talk shows.

After the singles show was over, her guest remarked to me, "Did you see that young man in the hallway? He looked at me and I almost dropped to my knees! Do you know his name? Can you get me his phone number?"

Rosanna tried to control her laughter as she introduced the woman to me and then added, "By the way, Ronnie is his mother."

Rosanna's guest didn't even blink as she said, "Forgive me. But if he is not married, please give him my home phone number."

Of course I didn't give Steve her phone number. He already has a girlfriend.

My van is gone. But Al's car won't be taken away for another week. I told Mr. Ounuma about our predicament, and that Al and I were planning to move out of New Jersey as soon as we figure out where to go. Of course, I didn't want to close the theatre, so I promised him that I would start looking for someone to take over. Mr. Ounuma was very sad and asked me to sit down at one of the dining tables. His wife brought me dinner and he asked me to eat and wait until the customers were gone.

When everybody was gone, Mrs. Ounuma started to cry softly as she hugged me for the first time.

Mr. and Mrs. Ounuma spoke to each other in Japanese, and then Mr. Ounuma asked me, "How much money do you need per month, to pay your bills? We don't want you to leave us. Our restaurant depends on the theatre crowd to survive."

I told him that what I make with the theatre is very unpredictable, and some months are better than others. If I were to stick to an indispensable amount, we would need about $250 per week to help pay our basic monthly bills.

He asked me if Al would mind doing some work around the restaurant in exchange for the weekly pay, and I told Mr. Ounuma that we would both be glad to do that.

When I got home, Al agreed to work at the Kobe helping with painting and any other building maintenance.

Al and I left the Welfare department very disappointed. We decided never to return to their office. Besides, Al was worried someone we knew might see us there.

A woman without any sense of humor told us to come back when we no longer have a car, and then she'll talk about us getting food stamps. As long as we have a car we are not entitled to any financial help.

"And how do we get here, if we don't have transportation? We are already here, so why can't you process the food stamps?" I asked, surprised.

The woman answered annoyed, "Take a taxi!"

"We can't afford to pay for a taxi!"

"Bring the bill and the Welfare Department will pay for it." And she asked us to leave since she couldn't help us until our car was gone.

No wonder the government is losing money; they have no common sense. We were there already, why didn't she give us the food stamps? It made no sense.

We didn't tell her that we have a condo and are paying a mortgage, since we didn't put that into the bankruptcy statement. Without the apartment we would have no place to live.

With what Mr. Ounuma gives us weekly, and what I collect from the theatre, we have barely enough to live on. Al and I need to start looking for regular jobs, but we will need a car to look for work and then to get back and forth. Living out of the city limits puts people in the predicament of not being able to get anywhere without some form of transportation.

I heard that the maintenance man in our complex got fired and the main office is looking for another custodian. It took me a while to convince Al that he could do the job. If necessary I volunteered to be his assistant. Of course, when I came up with the idea he said I was nuts and no one in their right mind was going to hire us. I wrote a letter anyway, with both our names, to the main office.

My letter did well. They liked the idea that Al has a wife as his assistant. We were hired. The good news is that Al is not only well paid, but as soon as the old maintenance man leaves his apartment in two weeks, we can move into it. Meanwhile we will look for someone to rent our condo, and the rent money we get we will use to pay the mortgage there. Thank you God, for everything!

~ *Chapter Four* ~

The Chiropractic Miracle

Spring of 1991

Buddy, Ralph's friend, who is a car salesman, sold me a used car for $200. I have to use a stick shift, and the car is very small, but its green color is striking and highly visible on the road. Everybody that sees this car comments that it is the most charming car they have ever seen. Nobody can imagine the problems that I have had with it since I bought it.

It drives fine as long as I don't stop at a light or at a stop sign. If I stop the car for any reason, I have to keep turning the key over and over again until it catches and starts to run again. On the first day I took it from Buddy's used car lot, the side mirror fell off. The next day my driver's side door stopped opening as the handle came off in my hand, so I have to get into the car from the passenger side. But it is a pretty cute car.

Ralph and I have been dreaming about going into business together, though he is still doing very well at Bell Core. He has a good salary and he even has edited some books for a couple of physicists that work there, but he says he is ready to start doing something else that's more challenging and fulfilling. First we talked about opening a Portuguese Restaurant. I even wrote a detailed menu and did the art work for it. But it takes more than a menu to get a restaurant started. Once we started looking around for a place to open a restaurant, we came to the conclusion that even if he matches the $20,000 that Al and I have saved, it won't even cover a down payment on a broken down shack in the middle of nowhere.

I was not surprised when Al used his ten thousand dollars to buy himself a new vehicle. Steve also spent his money quickly so Ralph and I can't count on either one of them for any financial help. We came up with a better idea, a fish farm! I still have my ten thousand dollars. We can rent space in an empty lot and dig a couple of pools, fill them up with water, add some fish eggs and just wait for the fish to hatch.

We've moved into the apartment where the maintenance man and his wife used to live and I like it there because it has an extra bedroom — which we use for all kinds of storage including some of the props for the theatre. Luckily, Al and I found a tenant to rent our condo. We are paying the mortgage there with what the renter pays us monthly.

I did meet the maintenance man that used to live here once when he was still working in our complex. He came over to our apartment to check a water leak in our bathroom. He told Al and me that his wife had gained a lot of weight since they had gotten married a year before, and to him that meant she was satisfied with her new life. Of course, I didn't say anything but I thought, maybe food has become her only source of happiness.

Ralph did a lot of research on fish farming and came to the conclusion that it's not an easy business. There's a lot more to raising fish than we thought. The water has to be constantly treated and there are all kinds of diseases that can kill them all in one shot if we don't really know what we are doing — and we don't know what we are doing. Fish farming is too much of a gamble for us to get into. He is going to continue working at Bell Core and in the meanwhile we will both keep our eyes open for other business opportunities that may come along.

Mr. Raster, the owner from Westwood Greens, an independent senior facility where I applied for a job a week ago, called me on my birthday! I got hired as their Activity Director! This is what I call a birthday present, but I am a nervous wreck. I have to learn to play cards! The old folks love to play cards, and they want me to deal. I don't like to play cards because I don't know how, and I can't shuffle them either.

What makes it even more amazing is that the retirement home is only a ten-minute drive from our apartment — which is very handy since I have a very unreliable car.

I gave the good news to Mr. Ounuma, he no longer needs to help us financially. We are doing fine on our own now. I told him that he could still count on me to help at the Kobe when they need me to answer the phones on weekend mornings. I will be working at Westwood Greens from Monday through Fridays only. Mr. Ounuma accepted the offer gladly. This is the least I can do for him after he helped us financially through some tough times.

Now that Al and I have real jobs, I started sending money to my parents again. It's only $50 per week, but when I make more money I will send them more. The pension check Papa gets from the German government doesn't seem to be enough to live on. But our cousins from England are helping my parents financially every month to compensate for the small income he gets from Germany. According to Papa, if it weren't for his family in England, he and Mama would be destitute.

My job at Westwood Greens is giving me anxiety attacks. I know they are anxiety attacks because my heart beats faster when the old people fight over their mid day fruit snacks! They fight over the bananas or if an apple is too small they want two apples without regard for the other folks. They run after the fruit cart and try to steal a piece of fruit as if they were children. Then I got into trouble with Mr. Raster, the director of the place, because I didn't have control over the seniors and I ran out of fruit. Like, what can I do? Scream at them? Push them out of the way? Run them over with the fruit cart? Smack them on the hands if they grab the fruit? I truly love my job but only until three in the afternoon, then the fruit

The Fruit Zombies

zombies go nuts. I stay behind the kitchen doors, hoping they don't see me until the very last moment, but at three o'clock sharp they sit anxiously waiting in the lobby, their eyes fixed on the kitchen doors, waiting for me to show up. As soon as I enter the lounge with the fruit cart, the ones that can get up on their own — and that means about half of them — stand up and come my way, surrounding me like a swarm of bees.

Now that I let off steam I can talk about the good things at Westwood Greens. I get to pick what activities I want to do with the senior residents, and I also get to drive the facility's van and take them out on trips twice a week.

I got turned in by one of the seniors for speeding at fifty-five in a fifty zone. That's because when I take them out shopping there's always one or two that disappear on me, and by the time I find them I am running late. If I don't get them back on time for the fruit madness at three in the afternoon, the poor starving seniors waiting at the home get upset. This is not an easy job!

Theresa, one of my favorite residents at Westwood Greens, really fooled me today. She was all excited as she took me to the side and whispered, "My high school sweetheart is coming to take me away this week. We are getting married this Friday, here at the home. Will you come to our wedding?"

I hugged her, of course, as I was very happy for her, and said, "Wow! That is so exciting. I will definitely be here. At what time is the wedding?"

She had a beaming smile as she announced, "11:30 in the morning, right here in the lobby."

I made sure I announced the good news to a few other seniors seated in the lounge, "Did you hear the good news? Theresa is getting married Friday, to her high school sweetheart."

They started laughing, and Sofia who can be malicious said with a smirk, "Theresa is crazy. She is wacko in the head. Who would marry her, just look at her. She is ugly."

I felt bad, really bad. When Theresa went by, she reminded me, "Don't forget, this Friday. It's my wedding."

I answered, "Don't worry Theresa. I wouldn't miss it."

All week long I hoped for a miracle of love, and that Theresa's wedding would come true, but it didn't. Now I understand. Theresa is living a dream, but it is a good dream, it brings her joy and hope. On Friday when Theresa came up to me and told me her wedding was next Friday; I promised her that I would be there.

Some of the people that work at the home explained to me that Theresa has been in foster homes since she was born and now she spends her adult life in places like this. Theresa's life has been spent in institutions. She was an abandoned child. I was very sad when I heard that. I believe that people, much like animals, are either lucky or not. Some animals are tied to a post outside in the cold or in the heat and barely fed. Others are loved and cherished dearly by their owners, like in Portugal where there's even a pet cemetery where pet owners pay a small fortune just to have their little pooch happily buried on the Lisbon zoo grounds.

The theatre is very unpredictable at present because of the ups and down of the economy; sometimes we have good attendance and occasionally the numbers are low, but it's still going. Every now and then I sit upstairs, staring at the darkness, and dream about the good old times when Michael used to be part of the theatre and my life. I miss working with him, our talks, the hugs and kisses. I miss him a lot. I keep busy, and I'm always surrounded by people, but I feel very lonely. One can be in a crowd and still be alone.

I can't just sit and watch other people work while I sit around. I get help building the sets and running the theatre, but I still do a lot of heavy work which makes my lower back horribly sore. Barney is no longer with us; he simply stopped coming in with his wife Patricia. All of that coincided with what happened with "Veronica's Room." I must have said something to offend them, but no matter how much I go over it in my mind, I don't have the foggiest idea of what I could have done to make them angry with me. Like the song says, nothing lasts forever only the earth and sky.

While putting the last set up, the door resting against the wall fell on my head, when I let go to pick up some screws off the floor. Now I understand the full meaning of seeing stars.

Once a week I drive my seniors somewhere special for lunch, besides going out shopping. I also enjoy taking them out on adventure trips. I took eight of them to see a baseball game at the New York Stadium. The owner of the home and another staff member came with us. Between the three of us we didn't lose anybody. I still have no idea what baseball is all about, but I was too embarrassed to ask anyone to explain it to me. I like football a lot better. It makes more sense to me.

This morning I woke up with my right eye red and gooey. I had to go see an eye doctor that told me that I have "pink eye," and that it's highly contagious. I have to use special eye drops, but it felt more like burning acid than medicine. I called their office just to make sure they had not given me the wrong prescription. With my luck with doctors and medicine I was convinced that they had given me sulfuric acid by accident. But they said that's the way it's supposed to feel.

There's one couple at the home I call the Windsors, because they are always properly dressed, and they don't mingle with the other residents. Robert wears a black suit and a white silk scarf around his neck and his wife Jocelyn wears a tailored outfit with matching pocketbook, hat and gloves. They act like royalty and are always dressed as if the Queen of England is coming over for tea.

All the seniors know that they have to give me five dollars each, and that the money is to cover the cost of their lunch and tip. The Windsors came along for the first time two weeks ago and right after they finished their meal they left the table and went outside by the van waiting to be taken back to the home. I had to go outside to get the money from them, and that was not an easy task since they didn't want to pay for their food.

I told Mr. Raster, my boss, what happened and suggested that the home collect for the lunches before I take the seniors out. It's working a lot better this way.

I can't believe who I met today after so many years. I was getting stamps at the post office in Lakewood when the man behind the counter looked at me for a few seconds and then asked, "You are Mrs. Esagui, aren't you? You don't remember me, but I was the one that drove the ambulance when you and your husband took your little boy out of Fitkins Hospital and to the hospital in New York. He had Meningitis if I remember correctly. Did he live? I always wanted to know what happened to your son."

He was extremely happy when I told him that Ralph was not only well and healthy, but he was 28 years old! He said he had never seen two parents so devoted to their child and with all we went through to save our little boy he was glad to hear that Ralph was alive and doing well.

I have to be careful with Mr. Mafioso, as everybody calls Frank, one of the old seniors at the home. Supposedly he was involved in organized crime in his younger days, but when he got too old and hard to reason with, he was put away into this retirement home.

I didn't believe it when they told me that, so when he was going by in the hallway yesterday I asked him, "They say that you used to be in the Mafia, is that true?"

Right after I said that I knew I had made a mistake.

He looked at me with his knife-like dark beady eyes and harsh face and retorted, "I killed many people with my own hands." Then he pointed one of his fingers at my face and said, "For one dollar, I would even kill you."

That did it for me; he had been a Mafia member. or he was crazy, probably both. I particularly don't like when Frank hangs around the poker table while I am dealing the cards. Frank never plays. He mumbles nasty words towards everyone seated including me, and when I try shuffling the cards and fail miserably he looks at me with his usual killer look and tells the folks, "You should get rid of her. She can't play cards for shit."

I told Mr. Raster, that I would do anything at the home except being a card dealer. It is not going to work with these people, they all get hot tempered and smoke and yell and the atmosphere is very nasty all around the game room. I don't feel comfortable.

Mr. Raster said he was already aware of my problem because he had so many complaints. He agreed to find someone else to play cards with the seniors since I can't shuffle cards even if my life depended on it. He was very delicate about it.

Tracey and I enjoy going to New York City several times a year. We like to walk around and visit art museums and look at the art shops. This weekend we got to see how far artists can get away with their creativity. We went to check out a prestigious gallery and they had a piece of cardboard hanging on one of their walls, with a price tag of twelve hundred dollars. What a joke! Being that Tracey is an artist, she knows a lot about art and I get a good education from her concerning the paintings we see, and how the time period had a lot to do with the technique used. Once in awhile her son Kirk, who lives in New York City, meets us at the Port Authority and takes us around the city.

Kirk is an actor, singer and definitely an entertainer. During Christmas he was invited to sing at the White House for the president of the United States. Tracey told me that pictures of Kirk's body have been used several times for billboard advertisements, but they always attach somebody else's head to it. I have not told Tracey this, but I believe that the reason they don't use Kirk's face is because he looks too much like Robin Williams.

We were walking on 42nd Street when Tracey said, "Wouldn't it be fun to go to one of those sex shops and see what goes on inside?"

I have always wondered that myself. How can women show their naked bodies for only twenty-five-cents a peep? The peep shows are advertised all over the dark-painted glass windows and when the front door opens, there's a black curtain in the doorway so that no one walking on the street can see anything inside. I agreed with her, and Kirk said, "Okay, girls, just follow me across the street. We are going inside that shop and upstairs where the girls wait for their customers."

I must say that I was a bit nervous as we followed him across the street. The three of us walked through an adult sex store with all kind of sex magazines and pornographic material including plastic penises of all sizes, and blow-up plastic dolls with vaginas. This was my first time inside a sex shop, and I wanted to stop and look but Kirk told us to keep walking and follow him closely. He walked briskly through the shop, and we climbed a narrow flight of steps into a badly-lit hallway on the first floor where three girls in skimpy clothes were standing by what looked like the doors to their private rooms. The girls were very polite and each said hello to us and we answered hello back but we didn't stop to talk. We followed Kirk out to the other side of the hallway and down the steps we went, and once again hurriedly crossed the sex shop. On our way out, we were all laughing and giggling like juveniles. I was laughing along with Tracey and Kirk, but in my head I could hear the lamenting sound of the song, "The House of the Rising Sun."

It took me a while to fall asleep that night. I felt sorry for the living dead above the sex shop in New York City, but I didn't say anything to Al, because he would not approve of my outing with Tracey and her son.

I guess I am bonding more than I realized with my old folks at the home. We were having our usual Wednesday lunch at a restaurant when Marcy, one of the residents, pulled her underarm deodorant out from her pocketbook, unbuttoned her shirt, and proceeded to apply the deodorant stick under her armpits. Some people at the table next to us were whispering to each other and shaking their heads in disapproval while looking in our direction.

I turned to them and said, "What're you looking at?"

I couldn't believe I had said that, but how dare they look down at Marcy! She used to be an artist, a very talented and successful artist, but since the car accident her brain had gotten damaged including her overall health, to a point that she became a burden on her family so they put her in the home. Marcy is the youngest senior at the home; she is only 51 years old. She also has a bad bladder and can't go more than half an hour before she has to rush to the bathroom. Even though she wears diapers, she'd rather go to the bathroom like everybody else. If I am taking the seniors on a trip that takes longer than half an hour drive, Marcy can't come with us.

Yesterday, Rose, who is seventy-two years old and has been diagnosed with dementia, left the food market walking arm in arm with an old lady from another retirement home. When I asked Rose to come with me, she said, "I want to go with my new friend."

The other senior said, "Yes, I am taking her with me, we are friends."

Of course the other senior also suffered from dementia just like Rose, and she couldn't understand why Rose couldn't go with her. It was very sad to see both women hugging each other, crying as the other woman's caretaker helped me to separate them. We took them away, each to their own home.

Rosanna took me out to lunch on Saturday, and I told her what was going on at the Westwood Greens. She made me swear that if she ever goes senile I am to tell her as soon as she starts to show signs of mental instability. I didn't know what to say except that I asked her to do the same for me.

Used cars are a pain because you are inheriting someone else's problems. Al was right to buy himself a new car. I was driving on a busy intersection in Manhattan, New York when my little green car broke down. Tracey and I stood by the car hoping not to get killed by the oncoming traffic, and waited patiently for someone to help us get the car started. A street person was walking by and after taking a look under the hood he said that for five dollars he could fix the problem, but he needed a paper clip.

I stayed with the car while Tracey went looking for a paper clip at one of the stores close by. She brought us a couple of paper clips and the man stuck one of the paper clips somewhere in the engine and when I turned the key the engine started. He told us not to stop the car until we got home. I gave him the well deserved five dollars, and he gave us a letter he had written about the world blowing up at the end of this month. Then, to make us feel better, he reassured us that the paper clip would keep the car running until then.

John Fraraccio is one of my very best actors. He played in our productions of "Don't Drink the Water" in 1988, "The Nerd" in 1989, and "Bell, Book, and Candle" in 1990. When he mentioned a few months ago how much he would love to direct "The Playboy of the Western World," a very old Irish play written in 1907 by Synge, I told him the month of August was open. This will be his first directing job, but after producing theatre for so many years, I know when someone has the potential to be exceptional. I am looking forward to John's production. John is having the actors learn the Irish accent.

John introduced me to a good friend of his that just happens to know a lot about Irish culture and the wardrobe style of the early 1900s. Her name is Katherine, and she has volunteered her time to design the wardrobe for "The Playboy of the Western World." With the help of Susan — the stage-manager, who just happens to have a sewing machine — both of them will be putting together a truly all-Irish wardrobe.

Summer of 1991

"Talk Radio" was another very successful theatre production at the Kobe. It was directed and performed by Carlo Durland, who was the personification of a radio talk-show host-with-the most. He kept the audience in the palm of his hands, and we had pretty large crowds. But without Michael, the theatre doesn't seem the same anymore. I need to do something else besides theatre, but I don't know what.

I sewed a long black cape made of glitter material for Steve to use while performing solo last Friday during one of my weekend musicals. The production was called "Friday Night Live at the Kobe."

I got a smoke machine, and the effect was very theatrical when he appeared on stage. He sang and played one of his original tunes on my red electric Yamaha guitar. I gave him the guitar a couple of years ago when he played with his band at the Freehold High School Battle of the bands and won second place. Personally, I think he should have won first place. I am not just saying this because I am his mother, but when I say that Steve is like a lightning bolt of energy and talent when he is on stage, and his band members are glued together in perfect harmony, I really mean that.

"Playboy of the Western World" is under rehearsals, and Katherine, the costume designer, told me that she couldn't be at the Kobe next Monday because she has an appointment to see her chiropractic doctor that afternoon.

I asked her what was wrong with her and she said, "Nothing, that's why I get adjusted by my chiropractor once a month, to maintain my health."

I had to control myself from laughing. There's nothing wrong with her and she is seeing a doctor? That's weird! She is a bit strange.

Since the first day that I started working at Westwood Greens I've taken notice of the three sweet old ladies that always sit together on the lounge's larger couch. When I get to work at eight in the morning, they are already comfortably sitting on their couch. They always smile at me, and I hug them and they always say how young and pretty I am, which is probably why I liked them from the very start — and also because they never run after my fruit cart. They sit there all day like frogs on a pond. They get up to go to the dining room for lunch, and then return to the couch where they sit talking to each other until the next meal. That's the extent of their physical activity.

This morning I squeezed myself between two of them and told them that I had a secret to share with only the three of them. "Can you keep a secret?" I asked them.

"Of course we can!" was Joan's answer. She is the speaker for the group.

With a very convincing look on my face, I lowered my voice as I said to them, "What I am going to tell you will shock you. As a matter of fact, you may never believe me. Okay, here it goes. I am not as young as I look. I am older than you are. I am more than 100 years old."

I expected them to start laughing, and they did.

I waited for them to stop and went on, "About fifty years ago, my actual age was exactly 100 years old, and that's when I decided to become very active, and guess what, my age started to reverse itself."

At that point they started listening with a look of tell us more. I had their attention so I kept going, "I am forty-seven years old (the only thing I said that was true), and I am still reversing my aging process because of the way I live."

Once again Joan spoke for the other two ladies, "I am ninety-two years old, and both Martha and Susanne are eighty-nine years old. Tell us what to do, because we are getting closer to 100."

I had them where I wanted them to be and I continued to talk in the same secretive manner, "In order to reverse the aging process, you need to do things you never did before, and they must be exciting and adventurous. Now, this is a very important question, if there were no barriers and nothing was impossible, what would you all like to do, and remember it has to be something special that you never did before."

I waited, keeping my fingers crossed as they talked among themselves. Joan said with a twinkle in her eyes, "We have never been to a race track. Will you take us there?"

I immediately got up from the couch saying to them, "I'll be right back."

I ran to Mr. Raster's office to clear my plans for next Wednesday and he said, "If you want to take them to the racetrack, that's fine with me, but I would like to have the wooden massage roller I have seen you use on the backs of our residents. My wife is pregnant and I know that she would love that."

I took the roller out of my carry-on bag and gave it to him. It's set for next Wednesday. I will be taking Joan and her two girlfriends Martha and Susanne, plus anyone else, up to eight people total that want to sign up, to the racetrack with me next week.

When Al found out about the massage roller being gone he was upset, "He had no right to ask you for it. Why didn't he go buy his own? Now we are without a massage roller."

And so are the old folks.

Ten people signed up for the Wednesday trip, which was more than I would like to handle by myself. I drove them to the Monmouth Park Racetrack, with everyone singing, "99 bottles of beer on the wall…"

Before I took everyone out of the van I explained that we needed to stay close together, and it would even be a good idea to hold on to each other's arms because the Monmouth Park Racetrack is not the place to lose one of them. It would be as difficult as finding a needle in a haystack.

Everything was going well, as I got them all seated in the lower bleachers. The racing was about to start, and the seniors wanted me to get them some refreshments. I wrote down their orders and once again I asked them to stay seated and wait for my return. When I came back I counted heads and there was one missing. Joan was gone. I waited what felt like an eternity, hoping that she might have gone to the bathroom and would soon be back. Finally I gathered everyone together and asked them to follow me as we looked together for Joan. We could hear the crowd screaming, as the horses raced around the track. After walking for a while back and forth looking for Joan, I had to call security as it was almost time to go home and I couldn't go back with one resident missing. The cops went looking for Joan. I was going to lose my job. Who could have kidnapped a ninety-two year old woman, and why?

Then we saw Joan in the distance. She was boasting a beaming smile as she walked towards us, holding on to the arms of two "good-looking cops," as she referred to them.

"These two good-looking young men were kind enough to escort me down to the promenade. What more can I ask for?"

Somehow she had gotten to the bleachers way on the top, and from there she had watched the race. Now she could proudly brag about her mischievous adventure to her family as well as to the old folks at the home, she said proudly. She'd had the time of her life and was ready for more new adventures.

The racetrack story grew to delicious disproportions and Joan found herself surrounded daily by the other residents who wanted to know exactly what happened to her. Everybody wants to go on my weekly trips. The word around the home is, if you hang out with Ronnie you get younger as the days go by.

I did a lot of research before designing the set for "The Playboy of the Western World," and if I ever go to Ireland, I know exactly what to expect to see in an old Irish tavern. I am proud to say that this is one of my best designs in creating a sense of realism. Katherine did an amazingly good job designing the time period costumes and coordinating the colors, they are absolutely perfect. John Fraraccio, the director, went out and bought real antique pottery and an antique table to decorate the set. The table lasted until the very last show when the actors became more than rambunctious. During the fistfight, one of the actors took it upon himself to go flying over the old table. As he fell on it, the legs on the old table gave way, collapsing under his weight. It was a dramatic scene. The interesting thing about the play is that it brought out a large crowd, and also some additional people that were under the impression we had something to do with the "Playboy" magazine. Still, no one left unimpressed with our production.

James Gardner from the Asbury Park Press wrote "… The Simy Dinner Theatre Company does poetic justice to this great play, which ages like the finest wines in the Western world…this production is vintage Synge, and very much worth tasting."

This was one of our proudest moments in the history of our dinner theatre company. "The Playboy of the Western World," fooled everyone into believing that the cast had been imported directly from Ireland.

They were short-handed at the home, and I was asked to help in the kitchen. I will never, ever again eat in a restaurant. It is gross, absolutely gross what goes on behind the scenes. One of the cooks had a cold, and he would wipe his nose on his sleeves and hands and go on mixing the greens for the salad. Also because it was very hot in the kitchen, another cook was sweating droplets into the food.

I no longer have lunch there, now that I have seen what goes on in the kitchen; what an eye opener. Except for the Kobe Restaurant — where everybody is very particular with the food preparation, at least from what I have personally observed — I will never eat out again.

Katherine the costume designer and I have become good friends during the production of "The Playboy of the Western World," and when she asked me if I could give her a hand with moving, I was more than happy to help out. Katherine and her husband are selling their house and moving to Florida.

Katherine's house turned out to be a beautiful old mansion by the sea. First she gave me a tour of the place, which knocked my socks off and then she said, "Let me know if you see anything you like, I have to get rid of a lot of stuff."

No way in heaven was I going to ask for anything, those were her belongings. After two days of helping her packing, she took me to her attic where — a sight to behold — presented before my eyes were rolls and rolls of cloth, and a world of crowded antiques and treasures that I never thought possible to exist. I was in Aladdin's cave. She confessed that among many other passions she also loved cloth, and when she travels she buys whatever is pleasant to her eyes.

As we were leaving the attic she asked, "Anything you want?"

I was going to say no, but I didn't want to offend her when she and I both knew that everything in her attic was beautiful.

I pointed to an extremely elegant umbrella and said, "That is so exquisite!"

She was impressed with my choice. "Good taste. It's an antique British umbrella. It's yours, and here, let me give you this long skirt of gold and browns. I never used it. I bought it because I was attracted to the material, and the way it drapes." She mentioned to follow her and then added, "Let's not worry about the attic. I am going to have someone come in and just pack everything into boxes."

Wow, if I were a kid I would have loved staying a little longer looking through so many attic treasures.

I went to put the umbrella and the skirt in my little green car so I wouldn't leave them behind, and when I got back Katherine was in the kitchen preparing lunch for both of us. I offered to help, but she said she had everything under control.

She sliced a fresh tomato and proceeded to scoop out the seeds and the juicy pulp, my favorite part of a tomato. Then she used the same technique with a cucumber and cut it into small chunks adding them to the tomato pieces. After seeing how it's done, I figured that I had never learned how to properly slice tomatoes or cucumbers for a salad, but at the same time I was glad I had never learned it since I love veggies guts.

We had a nice relaxed lunch in her backyard, and afterwards she took me to one of her kitchen pantries and asked me if I wanted some tea boxes. She had collected tea boxes from all over the world, particularly England. I thanked her for the offer but I didn't really drink tea.

I mentioned how much I liked the salt and pepper set on her kitchen windowsill and she responded by giving them to me as she explained that they were antique and very valuable. Then she handed me two serving trays with duck designs and two beautiful Japanese serving trays as she declared that there were never enough trays in a household. I have never used a tray in my life, but I figured that I could always use them for display since they were all very striking to look at. She also gave me a set of four English dishes that dated back to 1657. She observed that if I ever have a tea party, those dishes would make a unique statement since they have an indentation just big enough to put the matching small saucer on therefore keeping the saucer from slipping off the dish.

"I have three bathrooms each decorated in its own style. Which bathroom do you like the most?" she asked me as we were walking on the second floor.

I looked at the bathroom with the white bear rug, and then the other bathroom down the hall with antique decorations, and the third bathroom, which was mostly duck décor. I thought that she was just asking for my opinion as to which bathroom I liked the most in the sense of decoration. But I have to confess that I have a weakness for ducks, and for a brief moment I wished I could have all the bathroom duck décor, including the duck towels.

Having a gut feeling that she was about to do just that, I said shyly, "Of all three bathrooms I love the bathroom with the ducks."

She responded, "I want you to have everything from that bathroom. It's all yours."

Mama mia! Lush, quality towel sets with duck designs, a see-through shower curtain except for the colorful ducks, duck soap dishes, duck planters, duck tissue holder. She brought up a couple of boxes and I promptly filled them up with all the duck stuff. I was never so excited in my life as when I put all my loot into my car.

On the way down the hall, I became greedy as I noticed a pretty colorful lamp in one of the bedrooms. I mentioned how pretty the lamp was, but she said, "It's a real Tiffany lamp, and it's very rare. I can't part with it." She said as she kept walking.

I returned Sunday morning to Katherine's house to help pack, and she encouraged me to take whatever was in the closet downstairs. I took the wooden, green, mini-alligator box with big teeth, and a children's puzzle box. I had enough stuff.

I went by one more weekend in the morning to help out, but every time Katherine offered me something I said that I already had one of those at home. Sunday it was agreed that everything had been basically packed. Katherine and her husband took me to the park by their house and, to my surprise they gave me a sealed envelope that I thought to be a thank-you card. We sat there talking, and they told me how much they appreciated my help, and wished they could pay me more than they were giving me. I opened the envelope; they had put three hundred dollars inside with a thank-you card. I told them I didn't want the money, and I tried to give them the money back but they would not take it. My feelings were hurt, because friends are not supposed to pay for help. I smiled and made believe that I was happy when I left them, but I was sad.

I felt that the stuff Katherine had given me had been more than generous on her part. Today I realize that I am not good at receiving, only at giving, and that was the reason I was uncomfortable when they paid me for my help.

Sometimes I can't sleep until I come up with an idea for doing fun things with the old folks. They never know what I'm up to. This week I took them to a lake after lunch. I took my tape recorder with me and played a waltz and told them that they were free to dance with each other, take in the fresh air, and breathe in their beautiful surroundings, as life is to be felt with each breath. I felt like Aunt Heydee was guiding me in what to say to them. After the race track event they were all eager to do anything I ask them to do.

When I cook, I like to make large batches of food. I find it very practical to prepare more than enough food so that I can separate it into individual containers for when I don't have time to cook. If I am not home, Al can just go into the freezer and pick what he likes. With that in mind I made a huge lasagna dish this morning, big enough to freeze for eight individual meals. Saturdays and Sundays are my best days for cooking, because I don't work at Westwood Greens, and I don't have to be at Kobe until later in the day, unless I'm covering the phones for them in the morning.

Because our kitchen is very small and narrow, when I open the oven door to put anything in I have to bend sideways, which is a bit difficult when I have something large like the lasagna dish I had prepared. When I twisted sideways to put the heavy tray into the oven I felt a pop in my lower back and couldn't stand up. The pain was very sharp. I made it to the living room by taking little tiny steps, and then I curled up on the floor waiting for the pain to go away or someone to come home to help me up.

Steve is living with us again after he broke up with his last girlfriend. Lucky for me, Al and Steve got home at the same time and I asked them both to stretch me out. It made sense to me that if Al pulled at my arms and Steve pulled at my legs my back would get straightened out again. But it made it worse. They helped me to get up, but I couldn't sit down.

I called Sarah my stage manager and Connie who is running the stage lights and asked them to run the show without me. I would be there Sunday I was sure.

I spent the night trying to sleep by standing against the bedroom wall, because I couldn't sit or lie down. I spent the next morning standing against the walls, and then, when it was time to go to Kobe, I actually got myself into my car. I believe that being half German makes me the kind of person who will not allow futilities like pain to stop me from going about the things I must do, no matter what. I was convinced that if I didn't pay attention to the throbbing pain I would recover soon enough. I didn't count on the car giving up on me before it even left our parking lot, and I wasn't going to waste precious time walking around our apartment complex looking for Al to drive me to Kobe. I decided that I would use each valuable step to walk to the Kobe. After walking one block, the freaking pain was going down my right leg, crippling me. I knew it in my guts that, just like the car, I was breaking down. I took one small step and stopped. Took another step and stopped again. One step at a time I made it back to our apartment. I called Sarah and asked her to tell Connie that once again they were on their own. I wasn't going to make it to the theatre. Sarah told me not to worry. Everything had run fine the night before, and they didn't expect anything different this afternoon.

Al came home, had dinner, and sat to watch television. I got myself in the shower. I figured that a hot shower might help my back muscles relax. It didn't. I stood up against the living room wall and watched television with Al. When he went to bed I also went into our bedroom to stand against the bedroom wall. The next morning I asked Al to drive me to work at the home. I would just have to do things with the old folks while standing up. I got into his car, and for a while it wasn't so bad, but when it came time to get out of the car I couldn't.

I was scared when I told Al, "I don't know what in the world is wrong with me, but I don't feel my legs."

He said he was driving me directly to Dr. Lehman's office. He is the doctor that did the surgery on Steve's clavicle when he was a child and he also had helped me a lot when I hurt my back working at the bakery a few years ago.

Going up the steps to Dr. Lehman's office was like climbing Mount Everest. Dr. Lehman tried to make me move in different directions but I couldn't without crying. He told me I needed to go to the hospital immediately.

"No way! I have to go to work or I will lose my job." I was feeling desperate. "Why do I have to go to the hospital? Why can't you fix my back here in your office?"

"You are a very hard-headed person. I'm your doctor and you need to listen to me. You have to go to the hospital, right now."

He had to be kidding. I couldn't believe what was happening, what kind of a doctor was he that he couldn't fix my back. If I went to the hospital I already knew they would keep me there for God knows how long, just like the last time.

I asked Al to drive me back to work instead, but when we got to Westwood Greens, once again I couldn't get out of the car no matter how hard I tried. It was plain ridiculous; one day I was fine, and the next I was paralyzed. One thing was for sure, one never knows what can happen from one day to another, and that is the reason one should always give thanks to God for each blissful minute of the day. Man, do we complain about so much junk! Having legs that work, should be part of our daily thanks.

The idea of getting fired from my job was too much for me to bear; but I couldn't move, so I agreed to be taken to the hospital. I just didn't understand why Dr. Lehman didn't give me some medicine for my back. What else could they do in the hospital?

When I got to the hospital I couldn't lie down, so I was given a shot in the rear-end that knocked me out instantly into the land of darkness. I woke up when I heard them telling me to stay awake. I was inside some kind of a white plastic tube, which I learned later on is called an MRI machine.

It's been two days and I am still in a hospital bed, flat on my back. I have a herniated disc in my lower back, between L4 and L5 and I am not allowed to turn or move in any direction. Even if I want to change positions I can't since I have weights on my feet. The apparatus is called traction and I believe that it's supposed to pull my back into place. I am in a lot of pain, but they can't give me drugs for it because Dr. Lehman still remembers how I reacted when he gave me medicine for back pain a few years ago.

A neurologist came to see me this morning and asked me to wiggle my toes. I thought I was moving them until he said I wasn't, and that I was faking it.

What an idiot! Yeah! Like I love not to feel my toes, and I want to be stuck in a bed day after day like a prisoner while missing days from work and the theatre. When the rude doctor left I was feeling sad. Then an older lady came by my bed and told me that she was a volunteer and wanted to paint my fingernails. She said she liked making people happy. It was a nice feeling to get pampered and to have someone hold my hands.

Mr. and Mrs. Ounuma sent me a huge flower arrangement of exotic, colorful plants. It's been placed across from my bed on a table. When I wake up in the morning that is the first thing I look forward to seeing. I never thought I could enjoy having fresh cut flowers just for my pleasure. I look at them, and it makes my day bright. I always believed it was a cruel thing to cut flowers and put them in a jar with water just for our own decorative purposes, but now I don't feel that way anymore. I have changed a lot in that aspect. I love looking at the flowers across from me; they remind me that there is a beautiful colorful world out there that I am missing, and that I must get the heck out of here if I am going to live. Staying in a hospital is contradictory to that happening.

Dr. Lehman came to see me, and I noticed that he limped when he walked towards my bed while holding on to a cane. He told me he has a bad hip. He looked at my weights and yelled at the nurses for putting the weights on my feet incorrectly. The side where I needed more pulling was not being pulled like he had given them instructions to do. Then he sat next to my bed, and I asked him why he didn't have hip surgery since it was hard for him to walk.

He confided, "My colleagues have offered to do the surgery at no cost, but I am no fool. At my age, it's too much of a chance. I am afraid the surgery might kill me."

I thought that he was very nice to tell me that much about his personal life and also his fear of surgery — or, as they say in Portugal, going under the knife.

Four days after being in the hospital bed, a physical therapist came to see me. His name was John Johnson, or Jay for short, and he wanted me to start exercising my muscles.

I got worried about that, and I told him, "I don't want to have muscles like a man. I am happy with the way I am."

He laughed saying, "You have a good sense of humor. The exercises I'll be showing you are to help you tone your muscles so that your back can get strong again."

I didn't understand what that had to do with my back hurting. I didn't say anything more because I didn't want to hurt his feelings. The exercises he showed me made my back hurt even more. That afternoon I was taken to the hospital basement and put into a large metal hot tub. Because I couldn't move my legs, Jay and a nurse put me into what looked like a leather harness and they lowered me slowly into the hot water.

The hospital gown came up in the water like a balloon, and I felt so silly that I asked Jay, "Will you help me to take this ridiculous gown off? It's a nuisance."

He consulted with the nurse and she said to me, "I agree. The gown is annoying the way it goes up like that. But most of our patients are too embarrassed to be naked."

"I really don't care. I'm in too much pain to worry about that."

She took my gown off. The hot water felt fantastic and I let myself relax. When the nurse left the room, Jay came from behind me, above my head, and massaged my neck, saying, "You are very beautiful."

I didn't answer; instead I closed my eyes and imagined I was by myself. Like, who cares what I looked like? I was nothing but a cripple, an invalid. If looking at me naked made him happy, then I was glad for him. Suddenly I understood Aunt Heydee's philosophy about bringing happiness to those less fortunate, like the time we both went to a movie theatre in Lisbon, and the man sitting behind us slipped one of his hands between the seats and finally rested it gently over one of her breasts. She felt so sorry for his obvious loneliness that she didn't do anything about it.

Jay came by my room last night. He put me in a wheelchair and said he wanted to take me out for a little ride down the hallway. Then he set me up in front of one of the windows as he said, "It's raining outside, isn't it romantic?"

I said, "How can rain be romantic? It's cold and wet outside!"

I got annoyed about his attention. Why I don't know, maybe it's because my life is over, and I am in a situation where I have to be dependent on others. I can tell that he is lonely, but romance is the furthest thing from my mind. Also, the thought that I will never be able to walk and will have to be stuck in our apartment for the rest of my life with Al is driving me crazy. I am better off dead.

I have a chest cold, which I believe I caught from the moist heat pads left on my back last night. I called and called on the push button for one of the nurses to take them off my back, but no one came, and when I woke up in the morning I was feeling chilly from the dripping wet pads and towels.

Dr. Lehman came to visit me and he said he wants to give me an injection into the spine, and if that doesn't help then surgery is to be considered; after all, I have been in the hospital for two weeks and I am not getting any better.

I didn't say anything. I waited for him to leave, and then I called home. I wanted to get out of the hospital as soon as possible. Al couldn't come because of his job and Steve was nowhere to be found. Ralph offered to pick me up. I can't stand the idea of shots or surgery on my back. My instincts tell me that drugs or surgery will be a mistake; besides, I am scared.

Ralph wheeled me out of the hospital, and on the way home we stopped at a Chinese restaurant for lunch. He helped me out of the car and I walked in, taking painful little steps like a broken down old lady, while grabbing on to Ralph's arm. I kept complaining during lunch about my situation.

"Mom, this is the way it is, and nothing more can be done to make you better again. You have to get used to the reality of the situation and accept it."

Accept it my foot!

I've become aware that I have a high degree of pain tolerance. It's partially my fault for being this way. I worry about being called a crybaby. I have an invincible type of attitude. This is really pathetic when I think about it, because when I finally cry out that I no longer can take the hurt and I am at the end of the rope, nobody believes me. I have to start paying more attention to when I don't feel good and take care of it as soon as it starts. No more being a superwoman from now on.

I have been home now for two days, lying in bed and sleeping as much as I can so that I don't have to face my destiny as a worthless invalid. Dr. Lehman has called me twice already telling me that back surgery is really the only thing that might put me back on my feet. Surgery sounds like a death sentence to me.

Ralph is not giving me any positive reinforcement, he keeps telling me that I have to accept that this is what it is, and crying about it isn't going to help me.

I refuse to accept that I am going to be this way for the rest of my life. I wish there was something else that could help me return to normal. There has to be another solution.

I got a call this morning from Mr. Raster. He wanted to know how much longer I needed to be off work. I told him I had been in the hospital with back pain that was so bad that I couldn't even walk.

"You must be kidding." He said. "I thought you had the flu or something like that. Call my chiropractor, Dr. Peruzzi, right now. Go see him today and then come back to work Monday. Everybody misses you, and we need you here."

Mr. Raster had to be joking. When Ralph heard about my boss's advice, he reminded me that after he had gone to see another chiropractor the second time he got hurt in a car accident, his back had been hurting since, and Al stated that only a fool would go to a chiropractor and have their neck twisted and broken. They both agreed that some people had either died or become paralyzed for life after getting "cracked" by a chiropractor.

I decided to call Mr. Raster's chiropractor. I am already paralyzed from living my life, the worse that can happen is that Dr. Peruzzi will kill me, but that is a chance I have to take. I also must keep in mind that Ralph got a lot of pain relief after seeing a chiropractor the first time. True, the second chiropractor that treated him had hurt him, but that is just a reminder to me that the same can happen with medical doctors. I am the living proof of all the medical screw-ups that have been done throughout my life. I only know that I can't stay this way, and I am desperate enough to try anything, even if it kills me.

I was quite scared when I entered Dr. Peruzzi's office, and it wasn't helping that Al came along because, upon entering the chiropractor's office, he remarked, "I hope you are not going to be sorry for allowing some quack doctor to treat you."

Dr. Peruzzi is quite old, probably in his mid seventies but he looks like he works out. Even though his face has a lot of wrinkles, and he has gray hair, he also has a great physique. He wore a white doctor's jacket, which struck me as funny since he is a chiropractor and not a medical doctor. His handshake was very strong, and that made me even more scared. He sat behind a large desk, and he showed me a plastic spine and told me all kinds of nonsense about the nerves from the spine going through the body and that once I got my spine adjusted I would be back to normal. I didn't believe one word he said. He asked me to follow him to the adjusting room where I assumed the torture would soon begin.

I decided to beg for mercy the best way I could, "Dr. Peruzzi, whatever you do, please, don't touch me, my back hurts too much already."

He looked patiently at me and, making a loud sigh, he said, "I have to use my hands to touch you. But don't worry; I am not going to hurt you."

I asked myself what the heck was I doing in a chiropractor's office, but it was too late to turn around and leave. His exam consisted of gently touching my back everywhere except where it was hurting, and that made me relax a little. He asked me to lie down sideways on a low table, to breathe deeply and relax. Then he "punched" me on the left side of my neck, very close to my ear. I felt my brain leaving my skull, like in one of those cartoons I used to see with my children on television, a long time ago. My brain hit the wall and went back into my head. It was that painful, but when he asked me to get up and walk, I had no back pain and I could feel both my feet.

I got hysterical and jumped on top of him, hugging him, "This is a miracle! I am your slave forever, anything you want, just ask." I said with tears of joy running down my face.

Of course, Al was standing there when all of this happened, and he thought that maybe I had been hypnotized to not feel pain, nothing else made sense to him. After suffering for a week in the hospital, I felt I had experienced a personal miracle.

Dr. Peruzzi was also very emotional about it and his eyes seemed to have gotten teary as he said, "Witnessing my patients getting better like this is what I live for."

Wow! That's all I can say. I walked to the car and got in without a problem. I was high on happiness. When I got home

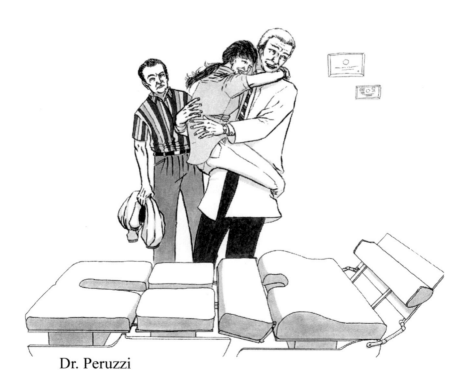

Dr. Peruzzi

I immediately called Dr. Lehman to share the good news with him. I told him I had gone to see a chiropractor and I was walking painlessly.

His reaction was weird. "You were very lucky that the chiropractor didn't kill you. Please, listen to me, whatever you do, don't go back to see him."

I immediately felt that there was some kind of jealousy between the two professions since the chiropractor had helped me more in one single visit than Dr. Lehman had in two weeks.

I hung up, saying, "Oh, okay, Dr. Lehman. I won't go back to the chiropractor, and I'll see you soon."

I lied. I have no intentions of returning to his office.

Later in the evening my lower back started to hurt again, but not as bad, and I could still feel both my feet. To me that was a real good recovery.

I slept like a baby, and when I woke up the next morning I started thinking, what would take to be like Dr. Peruzzi. It can't be that difficult, if all I have to do is learn to punch people in the neck to get them out of pain. Right after that thought I woke up Al to tell him that I want to be a chiropractor. He laughed and called me nuts.

I called Dr. Peruzzi and made an appointment to see him that afternoon after work.

Dr. Peruzzi was surprised when I told him that I wanted to be a chiropractor like him. I also wanted to know how long would it take.

He seemed to be annoyed, "I don't mean to discourage you, but it is a long process. Pre-meds and then Chiropractic College, it will be about five or six years in school." He made one of his long deep sighs and then continued, "I have to tell you this…what a waste of time studying anatomy, pathology and chemistry and whatever more they are coming up with these days, when all you need is to learn to adjust the spine."

He went back to talking nonsense about the nervous system, and how through spinal adjustments we can all be healthy, and there is no illness in the world that can't be treated by getting the spine adjusted.

At that point I got scared again about his lack of medical knowledge, and decided that I was better off getting out of there as soon as possible before he killed me. Even though I wasn't completely recovered I was not going to let him know that, he might want to twist my neck and my back and I may not be as lucky as the first time.

So I got up from my seat across from his desk saying, "Well, thank you for your time, Dr. Peruzzi." I stretched my arm out to shake his hand, as I continued; "Now I have to go, and by the way my back doesn't hurt any more..."

He pulled his hand abruptly away from mine and yelled at me, "What do you mean you have to go? You are here, and you are not leaving without getting your spine adjusted! Have you not learned anything from what I have been telling you all along?"

Shit, I thought, he has no medical education, he only believes in cracking bones. I was lucky to have survived the first "adjustment," but one cannot push their luck twice in a row. My God, what am I going to do? Now he is upset and he is going to break my neck for sure! But I couldn't say anything even though I felt I was going to pass out with fear. I followed him, feeling as if I was going to be sitting on an electric chair, but still being the non-assertive person that I am I followed him without a word. I didn't want to hurt his feelings by telling him that I had lost my confidence in him as a doctor. He took me into the adjusting room and once again he did the "punch" on my neck. He calls this adjusting technique, Toggle. I was surprised, because this time the adjustment didn't hurt at all like the first time. Then he said, "You told me you wanted to be my slave, have you changed your mind?"

I was tongue-tied for a few seconds. "Yes, of course I still want to be your slave, but first I want to be like you and help people. Where do I go from here, is there a school for chiropractors?"

He told me his favorite school was Life College in Georgia, but he had heard about another college in Pennsylvania that had a strong chiropractic philosophy and should be getting accredited soon. I found out that there are no chiropractic schools in New Jersey.

I thought about my options on my way home. This is the opportunity of a lifetime, the miracle I have been wishing for, to go away from home as far as possible for six years and at the same time learn how to help people to get out of pain without drugs or surgery. What more can I wish for?

I told Al, once again, that I wanted to be a chiropractor.

He knew that he couldn't make me change my mind and said, "Once you put your mind to doing something, there is no stopping you. If what you really want to do is to become a chiropractor, go ahead, it's fine with me even though I think that, at your age, you are wasting your time going to school all those years."

Al is a very kind and supportive husband.

I am not intimidated by Dr. Peruzzi anymore, and because I want to learn as much as possible from him about chiropractic, I have been going to his office three times a week like he told me I should, to get my spine adjusted. He said that since I will be his colleague in the near future, he no longer would be charging me for my adjustments. He is my chiropractor, but he is also my friend now, and he showed me a secret door, which is covered with an ugly brown curtain in one of the treatment rooms. That door is the direct entrance from his meager looking office to his luxurious house attached to the office. From the street outside, looking at his office building no one would even imagine that his house was attached to his office. His huge living room is covered with windows that go all round to the back, like a huge glass boat. The furniture is like that of a movie star's house, very modern. In the corner of the room there is a glass atrium with exotic plants where he works out. It is his personal gym. His house is absolutely gorgeous, and I even took Al with me one afternoon so that he could also see it. Al was impressed too. Dr. Peruzzi showed us both his karaoke machine attached to his television in the living room and he sang to us a boring tune from Frank Sinatra's repertoire. Dr. Peruzzi is very old fashioned. I am surprised that he has such a modern house with modern furniture.

I took my seniors on a shopping spree to the Ocean County Mall, but they were only interested in K-Mart. This was good because by the time I got them there, let them browse through the store, and put them back into the van, it was just about time to get them back to the home for their fruit treats. Laura, one of the seniors, never lets go of my arm when we go out, and she is always depressed and overwhelmed by negative thoughts. I've tried saying silly stuff to make her laugh, but it's a lost cause so I decided to use psychology on her today. She was complaining about her age and how being eighty-one years old sucked, when a miracle happened. A young man dribbling at the mouth and seated in a wheelchair was just being pushed into K-Mart, by what seemed to be his mother. I used that situation as my encouragement to make a point to her.

"Laura, how old do you think that young boy in the wheel chair is?"

"I guess about twenty years old."

"How would you like to change places with him and be young again?"

"Oh no, that is a terrible way to live."

"That's right Laura, you are indeed very, very lucky to have had a good, long, healthy life. You told me that you traveled to many countries in your youth, and had five wonderful healthy children, and now look at you at eighty-one. Here we are both using our feet to walk anywhere we want to go. Let's thank God for everything we have, including our age."

I had spoken to her from the heart, from personal experience, as I believe there's nothing like being able to walk. She hugged me and said she understood my point.

Just to make sure she did I added, "Laura, keep the image of that young man in the wheelchair in your mind every time you feel depressed, it will help you give thanks for what you have."

Thank God that Aunt Heydee taught me to think this way.

"Sleuth" was basically a gift from the Gods. The director took it upon himself to build the set and to get all the props. I didn't have much to do with this production. Even the lights are being taken care of by the stage manager. During the week I'm at the theatre to oversee the evening rehearsals for the next show "What the Butler Saw," otherwise I'm free to roam. I hang out a lot with Rosanna.

Dr. Peruzzi has a very depressing personality; he is always talking about his mother, and he gets all teary. Poor man, he regrets every day of his life that he wasn't a chiropractor because he could have saved his mother from dying of cancer. He truly believes that adjusting the spine cures every disease known to mankind. I only believe that it takes away the pain as it does for me. Maybe I am too medical.

Katherine is a tall, slim senior who likes to sit quietly on the closest chair to the entrance of the home. Every time I go by, she says "hello" and smiles kindly and then goes back to staring at the front door. I imagine that if she could be a bird she would quickly flap her wings and leave the place. There are four other chairs along the wall always taken by other seniors that sit along with her, but they stare at the wall in front of them. Katherine is the only one with a sparkle of life left in her eyes. I was going by this morning and, noticing a vacant chair next to her, I sat on it and asked her why she always sits there by the front door.

"Because I wish I could go outside. But I don't have anyone to walk with me."

I immediately took her arm saying, "Let's go then, just you and me."

"You, you will do that for me?" She said surprised.

"Yeah. Let's go now, before somebody stops us."

She got up as if seated on a spring-chair and, holding my arm, we walked out into the parking lot. She would take a few steps and stop, take a deep breath, smile with contentment and then walk again a few more steps.

"Would you mind if I take these silly bedroom slippers off? I would love to feel the ground on my feet."

"That's a great idea Katherine. Kick them off like I'm doing with my sandals." I said to her.

I held her arm on my left and carried her slippers and my sandals in my right hand. It was only a ten-minute walk, and we were laughing as we entered the home. We hugged each other and she thanked me for paying attention to her needs, nobody had ever done that for her. I promised to take her out every day from now on.

Katherine was born in New York City and she is eighty-nine years old. She was one of the very first women allowed to work in the Fire department. She showed me a picture of her in uniform, next to other firemen. She had been happily married twice. She loved to be physically active and walking is now one of the things she most misses these days. I understand that feeling completely.

I got called to the main office. Someone snitched on Katherine and me for going out for a walk. I am not to take her out anymore during my working hours. Mr. Raster said I could do whatever I want when I am not working for him. So now I take Katherine out for a walk after I'm done for the day at 3:30.

Sofia, one of the residents at the home, likes to sit at the corner of the lounge downstairs and complain about everything and everybody. Katherine and I believe she is the one that turned us in. Everybody agrees that Sofia is a spy for Mr. Raster. I'd make a bet that Sofia was this way even before she became old.

Inspired by the lady who had done my nails at the hospital, I bought myself a little star-shaped basket with a handle and filled it with different colored nail polish bottles, nail polish remover, some cotton balls, and a nail file. I brought the basket with me to the home and decided to start with Sofia.

The reason I picked Sofia to be the first one to be pampered is that I am hoping she will break down and become a kind person, by realizing that not everybody is out to "screw her," as she constantly says. I sat next to her and offered to do her nails.

She looked at me for a moment like what do you want? Then remarked, "You must be kidding if you think I am going to fall for it. You are not getting a dime from me."

"Good because I am not charging you anything. It's free."

"Nobody does anything for free. I'll give you a dollar."

I maintained my smile, as I was not going to give up that easily.

"Sofia, I can't accept your dollar. I will do your nails only if you don't pay me."

"Well, if you are that dumb, go ahead and work for nothing."

Sofia was happy with her ruby-red nails because she smiled condescendingly and then said, "Thank you, it looks nice, but if you are smart, you will charge the others for the work."

Tomorrow I will be going to Brookdale College to find out what classes I need to take so that I can be eligible to enter Chiropractic College.

Once in awhile my back feels weak and I get scared that I won't be able to walk again. I try my best not to lift anything heavy at the theatre, but once in awhile I forget, or take a chance on moving something heavy that I know perfectly well I shouldn't be lifting. It's very hard to stop old habits.

Ralph is doing well financially and he is a successful engineer at Bell Core, but he still feels like he has reached the top and there are no more challenges in that field. He is ready for a career change. He is a lot like me.

I think that after being a witness to what happened with my back, and how much I have recovered, it has given him inspiration to look into the health profession, either as a chiropractor or a medical doctor. He is not one hundred-percent sure about which direction to go.

I found out that I have already accumulated a few science credits and a bunch of art credits from all the classes I took in the past at Brookdale and Ocean College. In order to get accepted at Chiropractic College I will need a lot more science courses like chemistry, anatomy, biology, and physics and so on. I am not afraid of what's ahead of me, because when it comes to taking subjects that have an aura of difficulty, I simply recall people I know who I don't think of as even being that smart, but have done it.

Classes are starting next month, and I will have to stop working at Westwood Greens so that I can concentrate on studying instead. The courses that I will be taking are brain-busters, and I will need all the free time I can get to study. When my low back starts to hurt, I go see Dr. Peruzzi and that gets me back on my feet. But sometimes I lose my patience with my slow recovery, and this week I went to see another chiropractor in the hopes that he can do better than Dr. Peruzzi and cure me.

Dr. Holdman explained that I will need chiropractic care for the rest of my life, because my back is trashed and, if I'm not careful and insist on lifting stuff that's more than ten pounds, I can have a relapse of the herniated disc. I don't know why I feel like he knows more than Dr. Peruzzi, but on my third visit I asked him what kind of advice he could give me so that I will be a good chiropractor.

He whispered in my ear as if he was giving me the secret of life and death, "Your intention is the key."

I thought I heard him wrong and repeated, "My intention? What does that mean?"

He pointed a finger to his chest and said with emotion, "Your intention comes from here, your heart. That's all you need in order to be a good chiropractor."

I didn't have the courage to tell him that I still don't understand what he means by intention and what does that have to do with the technique of adjusting the spine?

Between running the theatre at the Kobe and going to school fulltime, I will be very busy. I don't mind that at all, I'm looking forward to it. I honestly don't want to be married any longer. I don't know how to ask Al for a divorce without hurting his feelings. We hardly talk to each other. We sleep together, but that is it. I love him as a friend and the father of my children, but there's nothing physical or intellectual connecting us anymore. When we talk we argue. I wish I could come up with a solution.

Right now I have to concentrate on getting financial aid since we have no funds for my tuition. I refuse to use the money I saved for a rainy day. The College wants me to bring records of how much money Al and I earned last year and now. If it's below what they consider a normal amount to live on, I will be eligible for financial aid.

I gave Mr. Raster one month's notice to find someone else to take my place at the home. It's ironic that he is the one that encouraged me to see a chiropractor, and now I will be making a career change in part because of him.

There's no doubt in my mind that we are all connected to each other in one way or another, even a stranger walking across the street from us can make a change in our lives, very much like a ripple in the ocean. I am a Twilight Zone believer. Things happen that make no sense now, but they do later. Even something simple like getting somewhere on time or getting there too early, perhaps that's what saved our lives. Everything in life has its own fate, like the fuzzy warm blanket I kept in back of my van for years in case I should get stuck somewhere in the bitter cold.

This is because about two winters ago I was driving my Howell Music Center van in Lakewood on Route 9, when an accident happened ahead of me. It was snowing heavily, and a young bicyclist had been run over by a car. He was lying on the cold, snow-covered road, bleeding from his head and shivering. I took my blanket from the van and laid it on top of his body, trying to keep him warm. When the ambulance came, they put him on a stretcher and I told them that he could keep my blanket.

The blanket had been bought and kept in my van all those years just to keep that man warm, not me.

Mrs. Thompson and Sofia could each win a personal award for being plain mean.

Mrs. Thompson, a senior resident at the home, has re-inforced my belief that all those awards of appreciation I received from the Mayors in Howell and Jackson, and all the newspaper interviews and so on are merely pieces of paper that, as time goes by, will turn yellow and finally turn into dust if one likes it or not. My philosophy through life has always been that, when helping others, one should never expect any-thing in return, otherwise there's no value in what we've done. But some people, like Mrs. Thompson, believe that awards of any kind are like medals and should remain pinned on her chest for the remainder of her life and she should constantly pat herself on the back, and the world should consider her above the rest. Give me a break! That's not reality; awards are just thank you notes, nothing more.

Mrs. Thompson's Medal of Honor box is under her bed as a reminiscence of her past good deeds. I was walking in the hallway and she came out of her bedroom and grabbed my arm, asking me to follow her. She closed the bedroom door behind us and proceeded to show me the contents in the plastic blue container under her bed. She wanted me to see how vital she had been in her community, and how much she had done for those "ungrateful bastards," as she called them. Now that she was old, nobody called her or came to pay her respects for all the work she had done. Instead, she had been put away, discarded by her family and phony friends. This was the reason she was so full of anger at everyone and she wanted to apologize for coming across that way to me. She asked me not to leave her and not go away to school. She promised to behave from now on.

I told her I was not leaving because of her behavior. I was leaving because I had new wonderful plans in my life, and in order for me to follow my dream I had no choice but to go away for a little while.

She held my hands on her lap and cried as we sat on her bed. Then, while still weeping, she told me about Robert, one of the residents, who had been her constant companion for the prior six months. She had broken up with Robert two weeks before. They had been a couple until sleazy Pamela, as she called the newcomer, had arrived at the home. She had found Robert and Pamela talking to each other very closely-seated, and it was obvious to her that they were more than just friends. I was in the middle of a teenage love triangle but I was not surprised; just because you are old doesn't mean you no longer have feelings. At the home there are plenty of love affairs, and emotions run strong among the residents. Mrs. Thompson always has a frown along with her despondent attitude, two bad attributes I believe no man can be attracted to, especially when one considers the calm softness that Pamela radiates.

Ralph has been busy researching the medical profession versus chiropractic. He wants to see which profession will be the most gratifying in the sense that he can actually help people get better and still have time to spend with his own family — which he hopes to have someday. He is investigating, and has already talked to several medical doctors who shared with him that they are not happy with their demanding profession because it has a negative impact in their families.

Knowing Ralph, when he is finished researching he will know exactly which way to follow. I am hoping he chooses chiropractic and goes to college with me.

I bought an anatomical bone chart last week, and every day I memorize two bones. My idea is that by the time I take the anatomy class I will recognize and name all the bones in the body.

It was very, very difficult to say goodbye to all my senior friends at the home. I made Katherine promise me that she would never walk outside by herself. Marilyn, who always dresses in pink and used to be a ballerina, started to cry and asked me not to leave, but when I told her I was leaving to become a chiropractor, she said, "Will you come back and fix my back so that I can be a ballerina again?"

I told her I would return, and we hugged each other and she was as happy as anyone can be.

"You just hurry back," she said smiling.

I thought I had hugged everybody, but when I was getting into my car I heard Mr. Phillips, one of the residents at the home, yelling out at the front door, "Wait Ronnie, wait, don't go yet."

I waited as he shuffled his feet all the way across the parking lot, and as he got closer to me he said, "Please, let me hug you before you leave. I am going to miss you a lot."

We hugged and we waved goodbye to each other as I drove off.

Autumn of 1991

I've been granted financial help at Brookdale College, and I have a full-time schedule. I got myself a small pull-cart to carry the books back and forth between classes and to the car. Dr. Lehman gave me a handicapped sticker so that I don't have to walk too far to get to my classes. Walking can be difficult sometimes; I have good days and bad days. I do all my studying at home while lying flat on my back with a pillow under my knees. With the chiropractic adjustments and taking care of myself, I am definitely getting better each day. I have become a master at putting up stage sets with the least amount of lifting when I'm by myself. But most of the time,

I have help. Little by little, I am learning to delegate the work that I really shouldn't be doing. My main weakness, which I call my Achilles, is lifting.

The anatomy teacher is a super cool person. She insists that everybody must smile at each other before starting to take the tests. She said that smiles cause a release of good chemicals from the brain; that in turn helps us to relax and think more clearly. The first time she told us to smile at each other it was a forced smile, and then it slowly melted down into a more natural expression as it turned into contagious laughter. Smiling is now the solution to engaging my memory bank into gear just prior to taking a written exam.

I am really focused on doing well in school, but it is hard for my brain to suddenly switch gears from arts to science. It hurts inside my head from thinking so deeply.

It's amazing how many future doctors and nurses are attending Biology class with me. I find Biology very interesting but also very difficult. I tried a few times joining a study group, but they are either too fast or too slow. I have to study at my own pace.

I bought a dissection book with very graphic pictures of body parts. I don't have the courage to look at more than one page a day. I believe that this kind of book will get me mentally prepared for when I start doing human dissection at Chiropractic College. At Brookdale College I was told that dissection labs use cats and rats, but when I start Chiropractic College I will have to cut up human bodies — or, as they officially call them, cadavers. As if the name changes anything for me, they are still dead people. The idea terrifies me. I have only seen two dead embalmed people in my life. When Joe's father-in-law died, Al tried to hold me back from going into the wake room to look at the corpse. I am glad that I was curious enough at that time to insist on viewing the body. I didn't know what to expect, but it wasn't scary because he didn't look alive or dead. He looked more like a mannequin covered with make-up and dressed in a white suit. Also, when my friend Maryanne's teenage son died in a car accident she had him dressed in his jeans and favorite leather jacket, trying to make her son look alive I guess. But the boy looked unreal, and I felt that this kind of thing called a "wake ceremony" should be made illegal. I don't understand how they can put the dead through that kind of display and say they are paying them respect.

I imagine that the corpses we will be working with won't be wearing make-up, and they will definitely be undressed. I can't even imagine having to open a chest to look at the heart by cutting and pulling away the bones and muscles. This is the only thing I am concerned about not being able to do in Chiropractic College, and that's the reason I got this sickening dissection book to look at once a day.

My first dissection specimen at Brookdale was a rat. I could tell he had been gassed because he had the expression of "Oh, no!" His eyes were closed tight as if he was protecting them from the burning fumes. His arms were extended out, and his little paws were clenched tight. We followed the teacher's instructions on how to open the rat's chest. There they were, the lungs, and the little heart, not much different from a human being, just smaller. I didn't cry, I just stood there staring at the rat, and a light of knowledge came to me. It felt like I was staring at the beginning of life and this is what I envisioned:

Once upon a long time ago, on another planet too far away from us to even conceive the idea of distance is where God lives. Yes, it is a planet of good beings, called man and everybody lives forever and everybody is happy. There is no war or even greed, only love and understanding. Then, for a reason that no one knows, including God who pondered on what could have gone awry (possibly a gene that went wild, or something like a virus that entered the planet after crossing the universe and decided to stay), an epidemic of nasty symptoms came upon a few of the man. Just to name a few of the symptoms: greed and jealousy started taking over these once godly beings. God had to intervene immediately because they were enjoying killing each other just for the pleasure of it. In its infinite wisdom, God gathered those that had become infected with the virus, which he called Hu, along with many of the animal species from their world, so that man would not feel lonely without all the creatures they had grown up with, and transported them all to a planet called Earth, which was on the other side of the Universe. God would not punish, kill, or try to make man change their minds. Instead, he gave them the power of choice, and God called them Hu-man as he hoped that someday the good would take over their Hu and they could return home to their real world, as man again.

It's not that I love rats, but by cutting up the innocent rat — a victim of science and men's quest for more knowledge — I felt like I had found the explanation to why there is so much cruelty and also so much kindness on earth. We are the descendants of man! This is the reason why some of us believe in changing the world for the better and living in harmony, and others are capable of murder. It is a constant inner battle between Hu and man in all human beings. Until we can overcome the Hu, in all of us, I am afraid that we will never have peace on earth and we will never be able to return to God's planet where our ancestors came from.

When I tell someone about this idea, which came to me clear-as-a-bell during a rat dissection, they get very quiet and don't know what to say afterwards. They are probably starting to wonder themselves.

My next specimen in dissection was a cat. I had a housecat and it was very difficult to identify each muscle. I found out that housecats have blubbery muscles, and they are far from being toned, probably due to their lack of physical activity. I felt a bit jealous of the student next to me who was working on a street cat, or as everyone calls them, alley-cats. These cats are well-defined which explains why people that are inactive disintegrate, and people that are physically active stay in form and are healthy. This is what I have learned from my own observation in the anatomy lab. I wonder, if the seniors at the home were to become more physically active, instead of sitting all day, would they be healthier, not only physically, but also mentally? It's back to the Old Portuguese proverb, "If you don't use it, you lose it."

Pietro, one of the students in the Anatomy class and I have become close friends. We both can identify with having problems with the English language. Pietro, whom everyone calls Peter, was born in Italy and moved over here with his family when he was only twelve years old. He is twenty-two now, and his dream is to become a medical doctor. We were standing by one of the lab tables with human bones of all sizes and shapes, and we were talking about our plans in the future. I was telling him how much I was looking forward to becoming a chiropractor and helping people to get rid of pain without drugs or surgery.

Pietro said passionately, "I want to be a medical doctor so that I can help people too. I intend to charge very little for my services, that way everybody will be able to afford medical care."

"Me too, I'm going to treat everybody even those that can't afford it." I said.

There was another student next to us who, upon hearing our conversation, remarked, "Well, I am going to be a medical doctor too, but at least I am honest enough to tell you both that I am doing that for one main reason, to make money. Being rich is my goal."

Pietro tried to reason with Josh by telling him that a doctor's duties should be to help and care for the sick.

But Josh left the lab, laughing as he said, "You are both either naïve, or freaking liars."

This event is what brought Pietro and me to be good friends. We study together twice a week.

Poor Pietro, he is in love with one of the girls in the class who is forty-five years old, married, and has a child. Supposedly she confided in him that she is not happily married and wants a divorce. He keeps hoping that maybe she will see him as a man and not as a kid, since he would like to marry her. He keeps asking me for advice, but I don't have much to say in the love department.

I am definitely allergic to formaldehyde. But of course I already knew that from breathing the formaldehyde fumes in our motor home and then in the modular house in Freehold. But this is worse; the specimens in the dissection lab are impregnated with formaldehyde.

Even though my body is not exposed and my arms are covered with long sleeves, the formaldehyde fumes have penetrated through my clothes, and my skin is the color of a boiled lobster with bubbling sores, like second degree burns.

I showed my skin to the Anatomy teacher, she became concerned and said I would no longer be allowed into the dissection lab. She arranged for me to continue dissection studies along with two pregnant women in a different room where there are no fumes. The cats are inside a glass wall box, and we use thick rubber gloves to reach inside and cut their muscles and ligaments and pull their organs out. I don't like dissection!

My little green car has expired for good. The paper clip must have fallen off the engine, but the world is still turning on its axis, thank God!

Every car I get from Ralph's friend falls apart soon after I get it. Sometimes it runs all the way from Buddy's parking lot to Route 9, and then it dies just like that. Buddy told me that he has no idea what's wrong with his used cars, he buys them as is, in bulk. The good news is that, since I am Ralph's mom, I can keep exchanging the cars as they break down. Buddy only charged me for the first car he sold me, the green car. The others are now free for the exchange. Still, I never know when they are going to break down, and I'll find myself in a bad predicament, stuck on the highway with my thumb up.

"Driving Miss Daisy" was cancelled due to the illness of the main character. With live theatre, one has to deal with what life brings along, and I have learned that when one show can't go on, another one will pop up from the woodwork. I have noticed that from a chaotic situation, a masterpiece can take its place. It happens that way every time, it's really amazing.

I feel slightly like a traitor, leaving Brookdale College to continue taking my pre-requisites in January at the Ocean County College because it's closer to home. Not that I can walk to Ocean County College, but it seems to make more sense that in the winter I will be closer to it. I already have to contend with English being my second language, and my hearing loss, which sometimes makes it hard for me to hear in class. But I'm not under pressure when I talk because everybody can tell that I have an accent, and they are willing to understand that I'm doing the best I can. Reading and writing become real challenges when taking tests. I don't need to be extra stressed wondering if my car will get me as far as school early in the morning.

Winter of 1992

I have started offering the latest form of entertainment, at the Simy Dinner Theatre. The audience is encouraged to participate in the show and guess who the criminal is. I call it "Murder for Lunch" and "Murder for Dinner." I rent out the theatre for groups, like corporate companies, clubs, and so on. Mr. Ounuma is very happy with the idea of bringing large groups into his restaurant. Truthfully, it feels kind of weird to me; like it's not really theatre, because it's not structured like a play. But this is a new trend that is catching on in the entertainment world, and I have to move with the times. The audience loves being part of the plot.

Last weekend I was accused of being the killer because I looked too innocent in my pink silk outfit — which had some ruffles around the hips making it perfect to conceal a handgun. That didn't make much sense since I was not involved with any lines or stage appearances. I spent most of the evening behind the bar, running the stage lights and sound effects. Some people shouldn't even try being detectives.

I won't mention the actor's name, because what he said was absolutely ridiculous, but he remarked that the reason I am so successful with my dinner theatre is because it is in a Japanese restaurant!

Controlling my laughter, I said, "Yes, that has to be the reason." Poor man, he doesn't even realize how wrong he is. If the Simy Dinner Theatre was located in an American greasy restaurant, we would be a lot more successful. It's because the theatre is in a Japanese Restaurant that we miss out on people like the senior crowd. Our audience's average age is between 35 and 50 years old. Since the very beginning I have had to struggle with the prejudice of the older folks around here who refuse to go to a Japanese restaurant even if it's to see an American play.

Public Speaking class has opened an avenue of creativity that helps me to mellow out between science courses. Once I got over the first speech, where I was sure that I was going to die in front of the class, I was okay after that. But nonetheless, it was an odd feeling, having my heart ready to jump out of my mouth. I couldn't breathe and I felt dizzy. I couldn't control my hands and legs from shaking as I held myself against the podium and took a good look at the staring students. Obviously they were as scared as I was, and soon they would be in my place trying to utter a word, and trying not to faint while attempting to project a sense of confidence. In order to survive the ordeal and feel confident, I reasoned with myself by feeling sorry for them.

The teacher's advice to everyone at the beginning of the term was, "You need to start your speech with something exciting to draw the audience's attention, and keep them in the palm of your hands until the very end, where you must finish with a good punch line. The topic should be original if possible, and being controversial helps a lot, too."

I took a deep breath and did my first speech following the teacher's recommendations to the letter. I showed the class a few handmade birthday cards I had made. I explained that I had started making them a few years ago when my father told me that he hated birthday cards unless they were handmade, only then did they mean something to him. Then I told the class about what I felt made sense to write in a card if it was addressed to a family member or a friend, and how you should always be honest when wishing your best to the ones you love.

A good example of what to write for a birthday card would be something like, "Happy Birthday, dear friend or relative! I hope you have a long healthy life, and when it's time to die, may you drop dead."

That was my final punch line.

The students were taken aback, including the teacher who asked, "What kind of good wish is that?"

I was ready for the answer, "Given a choice, do you want to drop dead at the end of a long, healthy life, or do you want to die slowly and agonizingly while hooked up to wires?"

Everyone agreed it made sense, but it didn't sound good for a birthday wish. Of course, nobody wants to face their own mortality. People like to believe that if we don't talk about it, it won't happen. Death is part of living, like the seasons; spring, summer, fall, and winter, each is an example of Nature. Each season is a demonstration of what happens to each of us.

There's so much I need to talk about, but when I get home I have no one to talk to. I tried a few times talking to Al about the meaning of life and death, but he thinks everything I say is a joke, and I wind up feeling like a fool.

I miss Michael so much! I miss how we used to talk while working at the theatre, and I miss our drives to the countryside. Thank God for school where I can spread my wings and express myself. I wish I were single. I want a divorce so badly!

"Bathroom Humor," by Billy Van Zandt, was another fun show. All his plays are crowd pleasers. But the props were a real challenge until I found a store in Howell that sells bathroom fixtures, and was willing to work with me. In exchange for a full-page advertisement in the playbill, they lent me the three most imperative props: the tub, the toilet and a matching sink. They not only delivered them to the theatre, but they also put everything onto the stage for me. When things like this happen, I feel like the luckiest theatre producer in the world.

I take my schoolbooks everywhere I go. While the shows are going on at the Simy Dinner Theatre, I am busy studying behind the bar. Every minute counts. There's a lot to memorize, and I am finding out that in order for me to remember something important I have to scribble the information on a paper. Then, when I am having a test, I'll recall my scribbles, and that is how I find the answers to the questions on the tests. I call this technique the doodle association method. I have tried word association and riddles, but all that does is mess me up because I'll be trying to remember what the associated word is instead. Besides smiling to help me relax and to give me a certain feeling of confidence, graphics are the one sure thing that sparks my memory bank. I am a visual person.

I used to get A's with high honors in all my classes prior to taking my pre-meds to enter Chiropractic College, but now I am worried that with all these science classes I'm taking, my grade point average is going to slide down. The reason I did so well until now is because creativity is fun, but when it comes to something abstract like numbers, atoms, and protons, my brain can't deal with it. Still, it is a miracle that I am surviving. I believe that it's because I am an adult and have a mission to accomplish. I am going to become a chiropractor no matter how hard the road ahead is.

The second speech in school was about smoking and how bad it is for your health. I had to come up with something strong and visual since everybody already knows that smoking is not good.

I kept it short and sweet, and finished by saying, "Do you want to see what happens to your insides when you smoke?"

Then I turned my back on the class and inserted into the right side of my mouth a brownish plastic roach and a black spider on the left side. They both looked very realistic, which is the reason why I bought them.

Keeping my mouth closed, I carefully smiled at the class, lit a cigarette and put it up to my lips and slowly pushed the black spider out the corner of my mouth, with my tongue. The look on most of their faces was that of unbelief. Encouraged by the effect upon the class, I continued and slowly pushed the black roach out from the other corner of my mouth. It was unanimous; everyone was at least partially grossed out.

They were impressed, principally one older female student who told me, "Your talk was very illustrative. I am going

Smokin' Butts

to skip my next smoke break. Who knows, maybe I'll quit smoking? Thanks."

After the second speech for Public Speaking class, the teacher said I sure knew how to throw everyone for a loop with my speeches. I am proud of them too. It helps that I am Portuguese, which means I have a natural streak for the dramatic just like my mother, who is Brazilian.

Steve is quite busy doing massages. He never learned how, he just has a natural ability, and his clientele are mostly women. He gets paid $100 an hour plus tip. When he massages my back or my neck, I instantly feel better. Maybe this is what Dr. Holdman meant by using intention when I treat a patient. When Steve gives a massage, his intent is to take away the muscle ache. It works.

I am almost done with General Chemistry I. Next quarter I will be taking General Chemistry II and Physics I. Physics scares me, so I keep telling myself that I am going to have fun, fun, fun. It's not easy to put my brain into science gear. Ralph has assured me that if I make it through the pre-meds, then Chiropractic College would be a lot easier. He is impressed that I can walk again, and for the most part I am almost without pain. I use very tight jeans, which work as a girdle to support my back, and I am also very careful not to lift anything heavy.

Mr. Johnson, our neighbor above our apartment, hurt his back at work and is talking about having back surgery. He is going through the same suffering I went through. I have spent a lot of time with him and his wife, trying to convince him to go see Dr. Peruzzi, but he says he doesn't believe in chiropractic. He acts as if chiropractic is some kind of religion. He doesn't believe in it? What kind of dumb statement is that anyway? I used to think like him, but at least I had the guts to try it. Men can be such babies.

For my third, and last speech it took me a few days to come up with a good idea, and I had to do quite a bit of research before I put it together. It was a lot of work, but I believe that's what awarded me an A with high honors. Gosh, how I miss my A's with high honors, B's are what I have been getting in science; it is so depressing.

I called the company where my friend Rosanna's daughter-in-law had her second insemination — by the same donor, because she wanted the two children to be related. So, I got to thinking about that. If she uses a specific donor, and then her neighbor happens to get the sperm donation from the same donor, does that mean that her children are half-brother or sister to the kid's neighbor? Of course they are. What if by any chance they were to grow up and fall in love and get married, then what? I called the company and asked that question, they said they had no comment and hung up on me.

Rosanna showed some concern when I explained my thought process to her, and she said it made a lot of sense. Brothers and sisters could be getting married without even knowing it. Rosanna showed her apprehension by observing that a semen donor might even marry his offspring without knowing it, since a lot of men nowadays marry girls that are young enough to be their daughters. I used her point in my speech.

The insemination subject was very effective with the class, with some of the students getting upset that nobody was investigating this concerning subject any further.

Mama wrote me a very macabre, strange letter. She was very, very upset and had been crying inconsolably for days. All the money she had been saving for years in a little box locked inside her closet has disappeared. She had found the box empty except for some ashes in place of the money. That money had been to cover the funeral costs for her, Papa, and

José when the time came. Mama wore the key to the box in a chain around her neck and never took it off unless she was being taken to the hospital, in which case she gave the key to Alice, her employee. The only two people that knew about her savings were Papa and Alice, whom Mama says is like a loving daughter to her. I don't know what to say; obviously someone took the money from the box and played a cruel hoax on her by putting the ashes inside. I told Mama to be aware of Alice, the woman that is taking care of her. The robbery had to be from someone inside the house that knows her habits and where she keeps her valuables. Who keeps the key every time she goes to the hospital? Alice!

Mama wrote back saying that she trusts Alice with her own life.

The whole thing sounds peculiar to me, since Mama keeps telling me that she gets my letters but there's no money inside of them. Who goes downstairs to pick up the letters? Alice! I have stopped sending cash inside my letters. In my heart I believe it has to be Alice, even though I've never met the woman, it makes the most sense.

I heard from Mama that Papa fell down while putting on his trousers. He was standing, lost his balance and hit his head against the bedroom armoire. He got a severe head concussion, and was taken to the hospital where they had to make a hole in his skull to remove a blood clot.

Being that Papa is eighty-nine years old, the doctors said it was remarkable that he had survived the surgery.

Papa is home now and Mama has been taking care of him. Ironically, she had been the one constantly in and out of the hospital, but since Papa came home she stays busy caring for him and won't allow herself to be sick. She also mentioned in her letter that she couldn't even imagine living without Papa

~ *Chapter Five*~

Freedom has been Granted

Spring of 1992

I have decided to stay focused on saving my marriage. I think that it's only fair that I should at least try. I told Al that I would like to re-do our marriage vows in Portugal.

"What for? We are already married!" he said, surprised.

"Because it would be romantic. Pleaaaaaaase!"

"If it makes you happy, okay then."

I wrote to Mama, letting her know my plans. I will be going to Portugal during my next school break and dedicating the first four days to be with my parents, and then Al will come and meet me in Lisbon. I will be waiting for him at the airport like the first time we met, and we will re-do our wedding vows at my parents' house with a little party. I'll buy a small cake, and we will have fresh flowers around the house. Afterwards, Al and I will take off in a rental car and travel for the next four days into the countryside up to the Serra da Estrela, which I've heard is very beautiful. We will be starting our life again like newlyweds.

Of course, I didn't tell Mama that I am trying to save my marriage. She would flip out if I told her that I am not happy. I simply told her that thirty years of marriage deserves some kind of celebration. I'll be leaving for Portugal once "Room

Service" our next production is on, which coincides with my spring break from school.

Al will not do any kind of handyman work whatsoever on weekends. He says he was not hired to be a slave, which I agree. But this weekend he went beyond limits when it came to having an attitude problem. Arlene, the neighbor on the third floor of the building across from ours called us on the phone screaming, "Get Al here right away, there is a tire on the roof!" She has a heavy Swedish accent and sometimes it's difficult to understand her.

"Al, our neighbor Arlene says there's a tire on the roof, and she wants you to take a look right away."

"Yeah, yeah, just tell her that I'll take care of it on Monday."

I told Arlene what Al said and she yelled back at me, "You stupit! There a tire on the roof! How man times I am going to tell to you?"

"Okay, compose yourself," I tried to calm her down the best I could. "I'll talk to Al and get him to take a look at it right away."

She kept on screaming at me and calling me names.

"Arlene is really hysterical, and she called me stupid. Even with her heavy accent I can tell that something is wrong. Why don't you at least go talk to her and see what it is all about."

He wasn't going to budge. "You go talk to her." Then he continued to watch television.

I went outside and started to walk towards Arlene's apartment, and there she was at her window pointing to the apartment across from her, "Look, look, the tire on the roof!"

The smoke from the fire was not only coming out of the roof, but also the windows of the third floor. I ran inside our apartment to call the fire department as Al went out to see what was going on. He had everybody evacuate from that apartment section. Thank God the firemen got there in time

"Tire" on the Roof!

to prevent the fire from spreading throughout the whole complex and they were able to stop the flames from burning the building to the ground.

Nobody got hurt except the tenant from the apartment where the fire got started. He couldn't get out through the front door and had to jump from the small, narrow bathroom window, falling on the hard concrete ground below. He was taken to the hospital for burns and both legs were broken. They say he is in fair condition. Supposedly the fire had started in his kitchen where he was baking a turkey. He had fallen asleep on the couch (some said he was drunk), and didn't wake up until the flames engulfed his apartment. All the apartments in that building section suffered serious damage. All of the contents were destroyed either by fire or smoke.

Al and I have been waiting for the insurance to do an appraisal of the burned building before we are allowed to start cleaning up the two apartments below, which were damaged by smoke more than anything else. The two apartments on the second and third floor will have to be rebuilt from scratch, and that is not a job for us to do.

I was emptying the drawers in one of the bedrooms into the trashcan when I found a large pin with a Picasso style silly face. Instead of throwing away the broken pin, I kept it to sew onto my pin jacket. I also found a diary that curiously enough had not burned completely in the fire. I took a quick look at some of the pages that were still intact. It was from a woman writing about her indiscretions with other men. She loved her husband but she needed more than one man in her life to be satisfied. I threw it into the garbage can that Al was using to dispose of small items. After almost an hour of picking up stuff and having to listen to Al complaining about everything under the sun, I excused myself with homework and left. We can't work together without butting heads.

I was on the plane to Portugal the day after my last exam. Once again I found Papa with hair almost down to his shoulders, except for a few strands at the top of his head and sides that stuck out as if he had put his head into an electric socket. He asked me if he looked like Albert Einstein.

I made him happy by saying, "Yeah! But you are a lot more handsome."

Papa told me that he had stopped going to the barber once he knew that I was coming to visit them. He preferred to have his loving daughter cut his hair. He already had the scissor and comb waiting next to his chair when I entered their bedroom. I felt very special and honored that less than an hour after I was at my parent's house, I was already giving Papa a haircut and pulling the little hairs off his ear lobes with tweezers. He proudly showed me, not one, but two holes in his skull, the result of the head surgery he had to have just a few months ago. The indentations were deep as he put one of my fingers into each of the spaces in his skull. He was like a soldier proudly showing his scars. Mama didn't speak much; she just sat in her rocking chair looking at me with pride in her eyes and said we had plenty of time to talk to each other later.

Papa confided that he felt humiliated having to sleep in a separate bed from his wife and, to add salt to the wound, he had to sleep in a crib type of bed. The doctors insisted that he needed protection from falling out of bed during the night, and the side rails were to be pulled up on both sides once he lay down. He told me that not sleeping with Mama was devastating to his male ego and he felt like a nincompoop.

"I may be eighty-nine years old, but I'm still a proud man and I like having my woman next to me, if you know what I mean," he said very seriously.

On the other hand, Mama confided that she was finally sleeping a lot better without Papa kicking her during the night. According to her she had suffered for many years with Papa's nightmares. She would get hit several times during the night by his flying arms and kicking legs as he dreamed that he was running away from the Nazis. The other problem, she said, was something that couldn't be helped; her new twin-size bed had a mattress that was hard as a rock, and in the morning her whole body was sore.

With my mind set on finding something that would make Mama's bed more comfortable, I went looking in downtown Lisbon for some kind of sponge or foam to put over her mattress. It took me the whole morning, but I finally found an old warehouse that sold me a three inch thick foam piece to go over Mama's mattress.

Papa made me laugh, when a very attractive physical therapist came to their apartment to help him with some exercises.

Papa winked an eye at me, stating, "If I had known a physical therapist looked this nice, I would have requested one sooner."

The therapist asked Papa to lie down in bed, on his back. She told him to raise his feet up and move both his legs as if he was biking. He was definitely enjoying the attention, and decided to show off by doing the exercise as fast as he could. I could see in her face that she was not expecting to see an eighty-nine-year-old invalid in such good shape. She had come in expecting the worst since he was supposed to be in bed suffering from a head injury.

Mama and I were laughing as Papa peddled away as if on a racetrack. With both his hands behind his neck as if he was having fun, he was a sight to behold.

The therapist was shocked, "Mr. Wartenberg, you are in very good shape!"

To which Papa answered, without stopping his leg exercises and without losing his breath, "This is child's play. I can do it all morning and I can also do a dozen push-ups. Would you like to see?"

She took his blood pressure and pulse and left.

Papa can't help being a show-off but at the same time what he did was actually easy for him. He keeps in shape by walking at a fast pace, up and down the hills in Lisbon and doing all kind of errands on a daily basis. He goes to the supermarket and carries the groceries home. He goes out to buy Mama's medicine and to the German Embassy to get his retirement check. Once he came home from the hospital he didn't stay inactive. He went right back into his normal routine. He walks all over the city and keeps mentally active, talking to everyone and reading books when he gets home. I hope when I get old I will be just like him.

Mama told me in the morning that she had slept like a baby. It was the first time she woke up in the morning without pain all over her body. She feels that the sponge-like foam on top of her mattress was the cause of feeling so good.

Alice, my parent's employee, seemed to be a really decent person. She was very attentive to my parent's needs and told me how concerned she was with their health. She seemed to be a very decent and caring person towards my parents and all my previous negative feelings towards her seemed absurd once I met her.

She came to my bedroom the night I arrived and kept insisting that I should give her all my money so that she could put it somewhere safe. It sounded weird to me that she should have said that, but I figured that she was just being nice.

I told her that I only had a couple of dollars on me, and that I was not worried about getting robbed because I only use my charge card when I travel. We both hung out by the window in my bedroom talking about life in general. She told me that she was forty-five years old and had been working most of her life as a maid. She was in love, and counting on being married in about a year. The love of her life was in prison for some silly stuff he did, but he would be out next year. She had two grown daughters who lived on their own in Lisbon. Every weekend she looked forward to visiting her fiancé in prison.

I went looking for a motorized wheelchair for Mama to use. I was thinking that if I could get her out of the apartment she could drive her wheelchair around the block for some fresh air. I found out that if you are a handicapped person in Portugal, tough luck, you are stuck at home. There were no wheelchairs available, not for rent or for sale. I even called two hospitals, and they only had a few regular wheelchairs, but even then they weren't ready to rent them. They needed them for their own patients.

Three days after being with my parents their forty-year-old refrigerator went kaput. Mama was very distressed since they couldn't afford to buy another one. I found out that in Portugal, when it comes to electric appliances the price is prohibitive, about three times what it costs in America.

According to American standards, the new refrigerator I bought for my parents was a real piece of junk, more like a tin can. I could have carried it home on my back! I was also disappointed that after buying the refrigerator, which was overpriced to begin with, the storeowner, Mr. Silva, told me that I had to go somewhere else to buy a special adapter to connect it to the wall since they didn't carry those items. Why did I buy the refrigerator at that store? Because my parents knew Mr. Silva, and they felt he would give me a good deal since I was their daughter. What does that have to do with anything? I felt like I had been robbed when I put $850 on my charge card for a refrigerator that didn't even plug directly into the wall. I had to go to another appliance store and buy a plug adapter.

Before I went to the appliance store, however, Mama warned me about Mr. Silva, the owner.

"Swear on my head that you will not tell him your age. Mr. Silva is dying to know how old I am, and as long as he doesn't know how old you are, he won't be able to figure out my age. If he asks you, tell him that a man never asks a woman's age, because..."and after a split second thinking what to say next she added, "Because, it's sacrilegious!"

Mama was right.

After Mr. Silva asked me the usual polite question, "How are your parents doing?" he added quickly, "They are getting old, aren't they? And you, Miss Veronica tell me please, how old are you?"

I was ready as I said smiling, "If I told you how old I am, I would be betraying my mother and that would be… sacrilegious!"

When I got home I told Mama about it, and she laughed with tears, saying, "I'm proud of you. That bastard has been trying to find out my age for fifty years, but he will never know." She laughed heartily.

Okay, I thought, nobody including myself knows Mama's age, but being in school has got to make me a little smarter now. If I do the math correctly, fifty years she knows Mr. Silva plus about twenty-five to thirty years more — which is about the age she got married — Mama must be around 80 years old!

I didn't tell anyone, but someone went through my luggage and my clothes while I was out buying the refrigerator. I could tell because my things were not in the same manner I had left them, and my personal tweezers had been switched for a used one, which had no grip. Good thing that I have the good habit of always carrying my money, charges, and even the passport in my money belt, which is always under my underwear, even when I go to sleep. The only time I take it off is when I am taking a shower but even then it stays with me in the bathroom. The switching of my tweezers showed me that it was a woman that did it. May God forgive me if I am wrong, but it had to be my mother or Alice, since there are no other females in the apartment. I didn't mention anything because it was too petty, but I felt angry and somehow violated. I would gladly have given away my tweezers. All she had to do was ask.

I tried to convince Papa not to use Saccharin in his morning coffee, because of its cancer association.

"I'm not going to worry about that at my age."

He is so set in his own ways!

While Papa was taking a nap, Mama asked me to sit with her in the sunroom — as I used to call the pantry area when I was a kid. Mama wanted to have a woman-to-woman talk.

She asked me the dreadful question, "Verónica, are you happily married?"

I decided that I would not lie, and I told her that my life with Al was better when I wasn't near him. Al and I can't talk about anything without ending in an argument. But in all fairness to both of us, I was going to try my best to save my marriage.

Mama said she was glad that I had confided in her, and while holding my hands in hers she pleaded, "For me, for your Mama, please try being submissive to your husband and don't argue back. Don't give your opinion on anything. Whatever he says, just respond with a yes and then later you can do whatever you want. If you say yes and agree with everything he says, you are going to notice that your marriage will be a much happier one. I do the same with your father. Don't you think he drives me crazy? He is hardheaded and has to have his own way all the time, so I make believe that I agree and go along with whatever he says, that's why our marriage has lasted this long. He is a very difficult man to live with but our marriage is strong and we love each other." She then let out a deep sigh and added, "You were always such a good little girl when you were growing up."

I took that last remark as an encouragement to speak up. "Mama, if I was so good, why was I always getting beat up?"

"What are you saying? I never hit you, you were a perfect child."

"Mama, I remember the beatings, believe me when I say that you used to hit me a lot."

"No, I never, ever hit you. I don't remember ever hitting you. Veronica you are mistaken about that."

There was no point arguing over something that in her mind didn't exist. She obviously had forgotten the beatings that caused me to have so many bloody noses; not only from her, but also from Papa who was told as soon as he got home that I had been bad and deserved a good spanking. Oh, well; if she doesn't remember beating me, then she is to be forgiven for all the pain she caused me. Those must be the blessings of old age; you only recall the good old times.

I promised to follow her advice when Al arrives from America tomorrow morning.

After finding so much dirt in the water we drink, I bought a large bottle of water hoping to encourage both my parents to drink it instead of the water they get from the faucet, but it didn't go well.

During lunch, Papa raised his glass of water and said, pointing at the nasty water in his glass, "Look at all the nutrients in the water we drink, these particles at the bottom are the minerals we need. I'm sorry Veronica, I know you mean well, but I don't like the idea of drinking purified water. They take away all the good stuff. We are doing fine with the water we have from our old but faithful pipes in our apartment."

While everybody at home was having a siesta I decided to take a breather and go for a short walk to the Fonte Luminosa (Fountain of Lights) with my video camera. Some boys between the ages of eleven and thirteen years old were diving between the marble horses and naked statues when one of them saw that I was filming the fountain and, calling my attention with gestures, he pulled his shorts down and exhibited his penis, shaking it back at me. I was not shocked. What's wrong with me I thought, I am not even blinking! Instead I took that as an opportunity to film an unusual statement by a young punk. I remained calm and continued to film him, bringing the lenses up closer. Of course, when I got home I showed my film footage to Mama who got a real kick out of it and laughed with gusto. Papa, on the other hand, didn't find it funny and became saddened by what he saw. He called it a representation of a doomed world of lost morals and values.

Mama winked at me. "Your father has a gloomy personality and you shouldn't pay attention to him." Then she reprimanded him by saying, "Joachim, my love, it was just a young boy playing around. Stop depressing us with your negativity."

Papa has become very philosophical and sensitive. I don't recall him being this way when he was younger, if anything, he hardly spoke and showed little emotion. Mama is a lot more in control these days when examining situations that need to be addressed calmly. Papa cries easily and gets emotionally distressed over the news, like when they announced on television last night about a man that had suffered a stroke in bed and how his dog saved his life by keeping him from getting dehydrated with a wet towel. The dog would dip a small towel into the toilet and then bring it to the old man's mouth so that he could suck on it. This went on for three days until a neighbor noticed that the old man wasn't coming out of the house for a while and decided to see what was going on. She found the old man in bed, unable to move but alive because of the dog that took care of him.

Papa was crying as he said, "Imagine that, a dog with a heart and soul, caring for his master and keeping him alive with toilet water. We may feel sorry for the poor old man, but he was cared by the best friend anyone could ever wish for."

I got up before dawn and left my parents apartment to take the bus to the airport. Al was arriving that morning. I was so excited that I left without a coat. It was very cold and windy, and instead of walking I ran to the bus station trying to keep my blood flowing. Only one thing was going through my mind, Al and the re-start of our lives together.

I was disappointed that our reunion wasn't exciting and romantic like I had imagined it would be. He was tired and cranky from the long flight. When we got to my parents' house he went to sleep for the rest of the day. I took the opportunity to show Alice how to use the video camera I had brought along just for this special occasion. Then I went to the bakery and bought a really nice cake for us all to share the next day, after lunch.

The next morning I wore my favorite flower-print dress and put a piece of baby's breath in my hair for a touch of white. José, my brother, did a prayer at the table before our meal, and it felt perfect with Mama and Papa holding hands and looking joyously at Al and me. For lunch Mama had Alice prepare my favorite food, green soup and cod fish Gomes Sá style. We took our time eating, talking, and having a great time. Finally it was siesta time, so Al and I said goodbye to everybody and left to pick up the rental car at the airport. Al didn't like the idea of driving, so I gladly offered to do it since it would be safer anyway.

Before heading out to the famous Serra da Estrela, we stopped for a quick visit at Aunt Morena's apartment in Oeiras. I surprised her with the gift of three American lipsticks. She was very happy that I had not forgotten the promise I had made the last time I had seen her. Her husband had died two years before, and she was still having some difficulty living without him. After her husband's death she suffered a nervous breakdown and tried to kill herself by jumping out of the bedroom window, but she lost her balance and fell backwards into the bedroom breaking one of her legs. I was touched by her love story.

Half an hour after being with Aunt Morena, her son Leão showed up at her apartment. It was like seeing an ugly ghost from the past. I didn't like him when I was younger and my feelings had not changed towards him, I still hated him.

The first words out of his mouth were, "Verónica, you have not changed a bit since you got married. I thought that by now you would be looking older and as big as your mother."

I couldn't help thinking, Lousy pervert! It wasn't enough that you tried to molest me when I was a child, but you were successful with our little cousins Marcia and Lorraine, and as if that was not enough, you also tried to take advantage of my brother José. And there you are Leão, with stinking tobacco-smell coming out of your pores, a bald-headed toothless old man. You sure deserve to rot in Hell.

But I was good. I smiled back at him, hoping that he could read my mind, and quickly hugged Aunt Morena after waving good-by to him without a word. Al was glad to leave too since he doesn't understand Portuguese, but also because he knew all about Aunt Morena's depraved son, the child molester.

As I was driving to the Serra da Estrela, I felt I was going to go mad traveling with Al. It's not that he is a bad person and that he doesn't love me, or that he doesn't do everything under the sun to make me happy, it's simply that we have nothing in common. The trip was a reminder of why I had sold our motor-home after taking a few trips with just the two of us. I couldn't share my thoughts with him. Whenever I expressed an opinion it became a struggle between us, so I decided to follow Mama's advice and become a yes wife to everything he said. Talking to each other became a one-way conversation. Either he slept, made remarks that he thought were hilarious, or complained about our surroundings. That night we stayed at a pousada, and while he slept I stared at the ceiling waiting for the sandman.

We were back on the road after breakfast. Whenever I saw a castle or a panoramic view that I would like to have shared with him, like I had done with Ralph, I opted for not waking him up. I was by myself driving to a place that he could care less about. There was no enthusiasm, no passion, there was nothing left but sharing a honeymoon with a bored companion who would much rather be shopping at a mall or watching television. I stopped at a small village and called Mama on the phone to tell her the advice she had given me was not working. Mama told me that José was in the hospital again due to an overnight drug overdose. I had the perfect excuse to return to Lisbon. The truth is that I didn't want to continue our trip; if a marriage needs a second honeymoon in order to survive, then it's over. I had to accept the reality of our relationship and to stop fantasizing over something that didn't exist.

On the way back to Lisbon we saw a country fair and stopped to see the festivities. I was waiting on the side of the road for Al, who had gone to the bathroom, when a young guy came over to me and said in horrible English, "Give me that camera or I'll kill you!"

I didn't know that I could remember so many Portuguese curses, but all of a sudden I began to spray profanities out of my mouth like bullets from a machine gun as my hands went up towards his throat. The coward robber ran away. Eventually Al returned none the wiser.

That afternoon I went with Al to visit José at the hospital. Mama and Papa told us that every so many weeks José is taken to the emergency room because of a drug overdose. They are puzzled because José has no money to spend on such things; as a matter of fact, the only money he ever gets daily is a couple of quarters, just enough to go out and buy himself a cup of coffee in the morning. They think he might be selling something, like his personal books, to buy the drugs. But I didn't agree, his books would be gone, since drugs are expensive. It has to be something else he is selling, even though our parents don't seem to be missing anything from home. The only medicine José takes is what Alice and Mama put in his food to make sure he doesn't kill himself, and medical doctors are the ones prescribing those.

We found that José had recovered and was in good spirits, so I took a chance and asked him where he got the drugs. He said he couldn't tell me, because he had promised not to tell anyone.

Then he lowered his voice as if he was willing to cooperate and asked, "Verónica, my dear sister, if you promise to take me with you to America, I will tell you where I get the drugs from."

I didn't translate to Al what José was saying. "Okay, if you tell me where you get the drugs I will take you to America."

"I get the drugs from Alice, our employee. She is my friend."

I started to laugh. That was the most ridiculous thing I had ever heard. Alice knew better than to give my brother drugs that could kill him. That made no sense at all.

I was upset of course. "José, you are lying to me. If you don't tell me who is giving you the drugs I am not taking you to America with us."

José answered once again in the same convincing, almost child-like manner. "I swear to you that Alice gives me the drugs, but she asked me not to tell anyone."

When we got home I relayed to my parents what José had told me. They both agreed that José had to be lying. Alice was a dedicated kind woman, and they trusted her completely. I had to agree with them. Alice was a very compassionate and caring person.

During the last two days of our "honeymoon" I continued to be a good obedient wife by agreeing to everything that Al said and not saying much of anything. There were no arguments, and he was happy. I was miserable.

Mama kept telling me, "Don't be a fool, he loves you and takes good care of you. What more can you ask for? You must accept that you are married to Al for the rest of your life, for better or worse."

I didn't dare tell her that I don't agree with her philosophy on what marriage is supposed to be, and while she was talking I was thinking only about one thing, how to get a divorce from Al.

It was during this trip though that I realized how incredibly lucky I was to have grown up in Portugal with two wonderful friends: Aunt Heydee and Encarnação.

Aunt Heydee taught me to appreciate life's ups and downs and that problems are just fun challenges to keep us entertained. Encarnação was my loving childhood friend and a second mom to me as well as so many others lucky to be in her life. She is now eighty-eight years old. Al and I went to visit her the day before we left Lisbon. Her apartment house was exactly the same way as I remembered. Nothing had changed. She took me to her husband's study where I had spent many days reading his African books when I was a kid. "As you can see, my husband's office is exactly the same as when he was alive."

She had never stopped loving him.

Encarnação smiles a lot, and she never complains, but I remember her feeling sad when she would show me pictures of her first child, a little boy who had died when he was only two years old. Then Eduardo her older son, who used to let me play with his airplane toys, died when he was about twenty-seven years old while flying a small plane for the Portuguese Air Force. His plane crashed, killing him, and a friend.

Mama always said, "May God never show us how much suffering we can carry."

But Encarnação had so much love to give that after Eduardo died, God provided her with a baby to love. A few months after Eduardo died, Encarnação's maid, Maria, was close to having a baby of her own. Instead of firing her, Encarnação offered Maria, and her husband João, room and board in exchange for their services. Maria's baby was born with several birth defects on his hands and feet. That didn't stop Encarnação from loving the innocent child, and she offered to be his godmother, and that she was, to the full extent of the word. He received a proper education and lots of love, and he grew up to become a successful architect, thanks to Encarnação.

While visiting Encarnação, Maria and João her husband, came into the parlor and joyfully hugged us, saying they still remembered being at our wedding.

Maria asked Encarnação, "Would you like me to bring your guests some tea and cookies?"

Maria came back with a large silver tray with tea and home-made butter cookies. Maria takes care of all Encarnação's needs, and when Encarnação dies the apartment house will belong to Maria and her husband, and their son too. That is the law in Portugal, because they have lived with Encarnação for many years as family they are entitled to the apartment when she dies. I was very happy to see that Encarnação is well taken care of and most of all happy.

She grabbed my arm, and took me to see one of the bedrooms her godson uses as an office. She was very proud of him and what he had accomplished in life. I was sorry that we missed him. Before we left Encarnação's house she gave me a little silver box she had made just for me, out of aluminum foil.

After visiting Encarnação, Al and I went to downtown Lisbon to pick up some of Papa's favorite cookies. Mama makes sure she always has plenty of them at home. She feels that the cookies make Papa thirsty, which is good, because he was diagnosed with bad kidneys and was told that he has to drink a lot of water every day to cleanse the kidneys from disease. On the way back Al got robbed in the subway. I had told Al over and over again not to flash his wallet or money anywhere in public, principally in the subway. But he would not listen to me. We were waiting on the platform for the subway train when he decided to see how much money he had in his wallet. Of course that was not the real reason, he is always looking for the opportunity to flash his shiny silver First Aid emblem, which looks like a sheriff's badge, one that is attached to the inside of his wallet. It's been years since he last volunteered for the First Aid Squad.

I freaked out and said to him, "By flashing your wallet, you have just put us both into a dangerous situation when we get into the train."

"You are always imagining things. You are becoming psychotic in your old age." He remarked. Then, he laughed

I heard the bird whistle sound. The gypsies always whistle like that to each other when they have caught a "bird," otherwise known as sucker.

I immediately showed Al my empty coat pockets; I pulled them inside out, saying dramatically, "Oh! No, I forgot to bring my money with me. See, my pockets are empty!"

I was thinking, Thank God I've got all my valuables in my money belt, which is inside my underwear and nobody can get to it unless they make me strip down.

"You are so weird!" said Al convincingly. "What the heck are you doing that for?"

"I'm just making sure that they see that I don't have any money to steal."

Al hit his right backside pocket with his hand saying, "Yeah, yeah, tell them to try and get it from me."

Great, now they knew exactly in what pocket he had his wallet. A rush of people came along with us as we entered the train. It was crowded. A Portuguese man was aware of what was happening, and in his crude manner he stated, "Some idiot is getting robbed."

I didn't say anything to Al; he was being pushed in different directions. If he knew what was happening to him, he might have tried to defend himself. I felt it was better not to say anything. Male gypsies doing that kind of work are known for carrying thin blades on the side of their boots, and they have no problem using them if necessary.

When we got out of the train I waited until we were safe above ground, and then asked, "Why don't you check your wallet."

"Stop bugging me; it's right here," he said, as he reached for his empty back pocket. The wallet was gone with his $300, driver's license, charge cards, and of course his silver badge.

I left Portugal very sad since my intent to save my marriage had failed. I had followed my plan to the letter, including Mama's advice to be more submissive. But I can't live like a mute or a slave. It would be like going back to the way I was when I first got married, and I am not the same person anymore. Another reason I am sad is because I found José standing in front of his bedroom mirror and as I entered his room to say goodbye he remarked, "Look at me, my sister. Look at me in the mirror. I look like an ugly monster."

He was right. He was obese, and his face was enlarged as if every cell in his body had duplicated and gone crazy. He was no longer the handsome man he used to be, and he was aware of it. Mama told me that some of the side effects of the medication she gave him made him gain weight. It had to be emotionally devastating for a young man his age to see himself as a monster, and I wanted to cry. My brother was a wild kid when he was younger, but he had a heart of gold. I remember when he took the chickens and turkeys from our backyard, and hid them in the neighbors chicken coop, trying to save them from becoming our meal for the holidays. My poor brother José deserves more in life than being dependent on our parents for the rest of his life, spending the days eating, sleeping, and listening to the radio while working on his geometrical drawings.

Honestly, I just couldn't wait to go back to the US and return to school, back to my studies, and the theatre. I was dying to be with my friends, to laugh freely, and be in my own environment. I no longer belong in Portugal. The city of Lisbon is just a memory of times that no longer exist. I was a foreigner in my own country, and except for my parents and my brother José, I have no reason to be there except for a very short visit.

We got back from Portugal on the second of June, and things between Al and I have returned to the way they used to be. I spend my days away from home as much as possible, and when I get home I'm glad that Al is already asleep. I get up before he does. Going to school and the theatre is the only thing that gives my life balance and hope. I am making my wish here; I wish with all my heart for a divorce, soon.

Among all the mail waiting for me when we got back from Portugal was a letter from Michael's mom. She wanted me to know that they were doing well and was wondering how I'm doing. I wonder if Michael put her up to writing this letter because he is too much of a coward to do it himself. I didn't expect this letter, but since it is from his mom I'll answer it.

Ralph has come down to his final decision; he will be going to Chiropractic College with me. He has most of his pre-requisites completed and only needs a few more to be eligible to enter Chiropractic College. We are going to Pennsylvania tomorrow to check out a Chiropractic College that is about an hour and a half each way from our home.

Ralph and I drove to the school in Pennsylvania this morning. Coming home every day would save us room and board, but we came to the conclusion that we will be gambling like fools if we attend a school that is still waiting for accreditation. What if they never get accredited? The choice came down to Georgia or New York. We are both leaning towards Life College in Marietta, Georgia. We have not been there, but it is accredited, and Dr. Peruzzi said he heard it is a very good College. Putting things into perspective, Georgia is less expensive to live in, the weather is warmer even in the winter, and the tuition is less than the school in New York. Ralph and I voted on going to Georgia. Al wants to stay in New Jersey where he feels established. Now I have to contend with getting some kind of loan since neither Al nor I can afford the tuition to Chiropractic College.

I got a phone call from Aunt Coty in Lisbon. I knew she wouldn't call me unless it was bad news. In the thirty years that I have been in the US, she has never called me on the phone or even written. I held my breath as she told me that my brother José had died in the hospital on June 9th. Four days after Al and I had left Portugal Mama found José unconscious in his bed. Obviously he had bought some more drugs, most likely during the night because he seemed fine before he went to bed. I was taken aback, and called my parents immediately to find out what had happened. Mama was not available to talk. Papa told me that upon finding José unconscious in bed, he had been rushed by ambulance to the hospital and that he had recovered once again from the overdose. The day before José died, Dr. Silva called my parents to tell them that José was doing well, but that he wasn't going to release José to go home until he found out who was supplying my brother with the drugs. Early the next morning Alice offered to go and visit José, and when she came back from the hospital she told my parents that José looked good and in great spirits, and had told her that he actually liked where he was staying. A couple of hours later the doctor called Papa to tell him that José had lunch and about an hour later collapsed on the floor, dead. Supposedly the drugs he had been able to get that morning had done the job of killing him.

Al said, "They probably killed him in the hospital, with a beating, or by giving him the wrong medicine."

I felt sad because what Al said out loud was exactly what came through my head, but I was afraid to say it.

I pray to God to put his arms around my younger brother José and hold him like the child he was, an innocent victim of medicine and the society he lived in.

The whole time Al and I were in Portugal I barely saw José, except for meal times. May God forgive me, but José's appearance was so bad that I basically stayed away from him, except when we said goodbye and another time to watch him drawing geometric figures, his favorite pastime. Also, a few days before Al arrived in Lisbon I had gone into the dining room to help clean the table after breakfast, and as I reached for the sugar bowl on the table José put his hand over mine, smiled softly, and said, "I am happy that you are here, my sister Veronica. Thank you for coming to visit us."

I answered by saying that I was also happy to be home and to see him. This was the way I want to remember him, a gentle kind soul.

Ralph offered a great suggestion concerning financial aid to Chiropractic College. If I am divorced I will be able to receive financial aid. Of course Al didn't agree with that, but once Ralph explained to him the financial benefits — and where the heck are we going to get the money to pay for my tuition — Al agreed to start proceedings immediately.

We are not getting a lawyer for the divorce; Al got the documents to be filed, and we are doing everything ourselves. We will still have to appear before a judge, but that is just the preliminaries. I am getting divorced! This is what I call a miracle, even if it's only on paper.

Summer of 1992

I called Papa this weekend. Mama is still unable to come to the phone; I imagine that she is severely sedated.

I confided in Papa, "I have a gut-feeling, and I can't really explain exactly why, but in the last few days I have thought a lot about José's cause of death. I think that Alice had something to do with José's death. Call me crazy, call me whatever, but this is what I feel is true."

Papa was on the same track, when he said, "I have started to wonder that myself. Perhaps José was telling you the truth. I'm not stupid. Alice knew that the doctor at the hospital was keeping José under observation to find out who was supplying him with drugs. Weird that the day José died was the morning after Alice went to visit him at the hospital."

"I know, it's too much of a coincidence! Please be careful, she could be dangerous. She even fooled me into believing her instead of my own brother."

"I want José to have an autopsy, but your mother is adamant that she doesn't want José's body to be cut up. An autopsy is the only way to find out what killed him. I only want justice to be done. But I have to wait until your mother recovers from the loss of our son."

Papa told me not to worry about him, he was going to wait a few months and then proceed carefully. I know that Papa will be very tactful and he is not going to do anything to jeopardize his life or Mama's.

"Let your enemy talk, and then you will know what he is up to." That's one of Papa's favorite quotes.

When I got home from school today there was a message from Michael on my answering machine telling me that he needed to talk to me, but since I wasn't in, he would write instead. Thank God I wasn't home. I would not know what to say. I don't want his letters, his phone calls, or to see him again. My life and my future don't include him because nothing good can come of it.

Every time the phone rings, I am scared that it's him calling. What do I say, after all this time without seeing him? I don't care if he loves me, he can suffer all he wants. I don't care. Why is he going to write to me, why and what for?

Mama wrote saying that Alice, who is her confidant and best friend, is in agreement with her that nothing good can come from doing an autopsy; it is an unnecessary and cruel thing to do to José. He is dead and he should be left alone to rest. I don't agree with Mama, but one can't go against a mother's wishes.

I sat down next to Al, who was watching television, and decided that I would give him a kiss. As I reached for his lips he reached his hand for a bowl of peanuts and stuffed his mouth, and then, while chewing, he kissed me back. I got up and went back to our bedroom where I closed the door behind me and sat at my desk to study. I can't wait to leave for Georgia. I'm counting the days.

I received a letter from Michael saying that they finally found a family that's buying their house in New Jersey, but they want some work done before they sign the final papers. He said he misses me a lot, and with the letter he included a cassette tape he had done while driving to work. I had to smile, as I could hear in the background the familiar sound of his noisy pickup truck. He talked for a while about where he lives in South Carolina and how lonely it is out there in the boondocks, and then he sang along with the radio, "… I'll be your friend; I'll help you carry on. For it won't be long till I am going to need somebody to lean on."

I love the sound of Michael's voice; he could have been a blues singer. I wrote back, trying to be as witty as possible when I described in great detail the adventures that came along with driving my old jalopy green car, including other events that, at the moment, sounded funny to me. The only part that I was serious about was when I wrote that I also missed him.

He wrote back.

I answered his letter.

If I really want, I can stop writing to Michael, but I am scared that even though I don't love him anymore, there's a slight chance that I could be wrong. I spend the days in school, and the nights at the theatre, and in the morning I look forward to his mail.

What started as a bit of fun in the chemistry lab yesterday afternoon almost turned into a disaster later on. I was the only one in the lab, so I figured that would be the perfect opportunity to try to make glass sculptures out of the long glass test-tubes. It was going to be my first time at glass blowing. It was easy to heat up the glass with the small flame-blower we use in the lab. I thought I was up to some quality glasswork, but it wasn't simple to come up with anything recognizable. I played with a few glass tubes for a while, and after I messed up a bunch I gave up on the project and threw them into the trashcan worried that someone might see them.

I cautiously looked around to make sure no one was around. I was still by myself! I felt this was going to be the opportunity of a lifetime to mix chemicals and see the reactions produced without having anyone looking over my shoulder and telling me what to do. A little bit of this and a little bit of that went into two glass containers. One of them created soft low flames. I was enjoying myself as I picked it up, but I was nervous that someone would catch me doing stuff that had nothing to do with my regular lab work and I knocked the other glass over and the counter became covered by a flammable liquid that dripped to the floor. I immediately got rid of the glass in my hand by throwing it into the trashcan. The first thing that came to my mind was to rapidly fill one of the small containers with water from the sink and then throw the water on top of the counter and the rest into the trashcan. It got worse. The fire spread all over and the glass contents inside the garbage container came out flying in all directions. Whatever concoction I had created, water was obviously the wrong fluid to use. The good thing was that there was no smoke, and the liquid fire didn't spread out.

Thank God I didn't get hurt by the flying glass bits and that the fire stopped on its own but I had a serious mess in my hands to clean up. I cleaned everything the best I could with paper towels and I did use water again but the chemicals had burned out and there was no further reaction. The place looked good when I left, except for some brown stains on the off white tiled floor.

Rosanna invited me for lunch at her favorite seafood restaurant in Belmar. We are like sisters, and as such we share all our personal tribulations. I told her that I wanted to get a real divorce, not a temporary one just for financial reasons. I am afraid that if I tell Al that, he will get very angry and kill me.

"Don't be silly, financial reasons or not, according to the law you are divorced." Rosanna assured me.

But I know that I am not divorced until Al says we are. In his mind we are still married. What confusion! But God will guide me, I know, and when the time comes this mess will work itself out, as it always does. I only know that this is not fair to Al or me. For the last fifteen years our relationship has thinned out little by little, and going away to Georgia, not that I'm complaining, for the next four years, is going to separate us even further. Movie stars are a good example of what happens when two people are away from each other for long periods of time while filming for months at a time. Paul

Newman and his wife Joanne Woodward have the perfect formula for a happy marriage, because they always manage to work together.

Michael called me on the phone and said that he loved me and couldn't wait to see me. I told him the same. After I hung up I was angry with myself for telling him that I still love him. He is going to call me later with the details of his trip to New Jersey.

He called back and asked me if I would like to meet him Monday. It will be about two and a half hours to drive into Pennsylvania, but then we can hang out for a while together, and afterwards we could follow each other back to New Jersey.

I will go, but I'll be in control of my emotions. He can tell me how much he loves me and sweet talk to me all he wants, but I will take that as pretty words and empty promises.

Yes, I will meet him in Pennsylvania, but I have one purpose in mind, to prove that I am a grown woman and that I'm over and done with him. Nothing is going to allow me to deviate from this personal mission of self-accomplishment.

Poor Ronnie, poor naïve Ronnie, she forgot her mission once she saw him. That's all I can say.

We sat at a park bench talking, kissing, and being completely enwrapped in each other's words, just like in the old good days. We had a lot to catch up on. He told me about his lonely, boring life in South Carolina and I told him about my lonely but exciting plans of going back to school to be a chiropractor, and my work at Westwood Greens as activity director. We talked about theatre and some of the musicals I had produced lately and he mentioned that he had seen the musical play "Annie" ten times, this year and as a result of that he couldn't stand the music.

I told him, "I've never seen the show, but the thought of hearing the song 'Tomorrow' more than twice is more than I can bear."

I was thinking, Ten times? Hum, he doesn't do theatre anymore. There must have been someone in the cast that he was involved with, not that it is any of my business. We may kiss and exchange words of love, but we are only friends. I have no right to feel jealous about his personal life.

I decided to put these thoughts away and enjoy the moment without any personal questions.

There were too many people around us, and we decided that I would follow him with my car, as we would look for another park that was not so crowded. Somewhere in New Jersey there was a small park by a river where we stood silently holding on to each other until sunset. It was getting late, and he said he would have to stay at a motel for the night somewhere along the way. I told him that I would follow him to the motel and then be on my way home.

We stopped at a motel in Cherry Hill, but instead of saying goodbye I followed him silently as he opened the door to his room.

He sat on the bed, and when I sat next to him. He got up and lit a cigarette, saying, "It's better if we don't sit together on the bed."

"Don't worry; nothing is going to happen between us. I trust you."

"But I don't trust myself," he said, visibly nervous about the situation, and added, "It's really hot in here."

I told him if he was that hot he should take his shirt off.

We sat on the floor by the end of bed and talked some more. And then he said, "If you are not comfortable spending the night with me and want to leave, I will not hold that against you."

I immediately sat on his lap, since I know that's his favorite way of holding me closer, and I was very sure of myself when I responded, "I would like to spend the night with you. That is, if you want me to."

"I was hoping you would say that."

We kissed each other as if it was the last day of our lives together. We both got on top of the bed and we couldn't take our clothes off fast enough as we both rolled on the bed and fell on the floor, laughing. I pushed him on his back and proceeded to kiss him all over. Being that I've never been with anyone else but Al, I was assuming that was the way all men like to be loved. I wanted to please him more than anything else. But then, to my surprise, he got on top of me and began penetrating me. He moved very slowly with each movement, as if calculated to purposely bring me pleasure, and we both felt it together, like a multitude of fireworks exploding, followed by the delicious feeling of a calm ocean. We didn't pull away from each other; we stayed joined, like glue, for a long time. I was half dumbfounded by what had just happened. I had been able to express my satisfaction without being ridiculed. I didn't know that such feeling of fulfillment could ever become reality for me again.

I have been married to Al for close to thirty years and he had me convinced that intercourse was only good for one purpose, making babies, because real pleasure could only be achieved by oral sex. A few years into our marriage, Al and I were having intercourse when he suddenly stopped and laughed saying, "You are such a faker. You can't possibly be enjoying it. It's a known fact that women only get pleasure from oral sex. So stop acting!"

I was truly stunned by Al's remark, which felt more like a slap in the face than anything else. I felt so humiliated that at that very moment I felt my worth as a woman vanishing into thin air. I immediately closed myself from showing any further emotion as I held back my tears, feeling that it was a waste of time to defend myself or to even bother to argue the point. From that day on, when we had sex I began to fantasize that he was a woman and I was a lesbian.

Of course I didn't share these thoughts with Michael, I was scared of losing the magic of the moment; but I was saying to myself, thank you God for giving me this opportunity to learn that there's nothing wrong with me physically.

It was late in the evening and we were both hungry. I wasn't going home. On the way to the restaurant I called Al on the telephone, "I won't be home until tomorrow morning. Sorry, but it's late so I am spending the night with a friend." He didn't ask what friend, and I was thankful for that.

Going back to our room after dinner was like going back for dessert in Heaven. I was worried that I was going to wake up and find out that the whole thing was nothing but a dream. When he fell asleep I stayed awake smiling as I could hear his heart beat close to mine, and then I cried from the joy I felt and thanked God for everything. We held each other all night, and it was about seven in the morning when we both woke up to make love again. We took a shower together, got dressed and went out for breakfast. He told me that he would be working on his house for the next three days before heading back to South Carolina. At night he would be staying with his friend Morph. He promised to call me to let me know when he would be back to New Jersey.

I got into my car and, in an absolute daze, instead of driving home somehow I found myself in South Jersey, in Atlantic City, of all places. How did I get here I wondered since I didn't even have a recollection of driving. I had to pull into a gas station and get my mental abilities into gear so that I could drive north to Lakewood. When I got home I went to bed and didn't wake up until the next morning.

I know that I should feel some kind of guilt for spending the night with Michael but I don't. I know that in the eyes of society it's morally wrong what I've done, but I don't see it that way. I think the reason I feel this way is because I've loved Michael for many years, first as friends and now as lovers. Also, nothing exists that resembles a marriage between Al and me. We have been divorced both physically and emotionally for many years now. Still, in all honesty Al believes that the legality of our divorce is temporary, and as such we are still married. Yet I feel like God understands my dilemma, and has been very kind to grant my wish of being with the man I love.

Through the years I have learned so much about the performing arts that I can almost run each production with my eyes closed. But I'm no longer passionate about it. School has become my priority in life.

"The Owl and the Pussycat" was a hit with Robert Kras playing the main character. He also directed the show. It was very good, but to me it was missing the charm that Barbara Schiavonne had put into the same production, six years before.

The main chef at the Kobe Restaurant quit. It is a disastrous situation for all of us who love his salad dressing. The other cooks have tried and tried again to formulate the same salad dressing but it doesn't even get close. Ralph was very disappointed when he asked me to bring home a bottle of Kobe salad dressing. When the cook quit, he took his secret recipe with him.

Michael called me this morning saying that he misses me and that he was thinking about coming to New Jersey a day earlier so that we could spend it together. We will be meeting at his friend's house this Friday. When he said that he had to pay a visit to a barber for a haircut when he got here I told him not to bother, I would bring my scissors and a comb and I would be more than happy to cut his hair. I have years of experience cutting hair for Al, Ralph, and Steve.

We spent the day in a motel room making love, talking about the past and what the future held. Then we shared a platter of stewed mussels at a diner close by.

In my opinion, Michael looks good either with long or short hair. I must say that I never thought there was anything sexy about cutting someone's hair until I cut his hair. Michael makes me feel like a woman. While he was seated in a chair, I maneuvered my body around him like a professional barber, except that it was accented by the mutual pleasure of being so close. I purposely took my time cutting his hair.

On weekends I am still working mornings on and off at the Kobe answering phones and taking reservations. Mr. and Mrs. Ounuma can use the time off to recover from a long grueling week of work and catch up on their sleep. Having a restaurant has to be one of the most demanding jobs. I don't see any problem with helping them out, because I find it very rewarding to study in the soothing quiet atmosphere of the Kobe Japanese Restaurant when it's closed.

This Saturday morning I did my usual procedure before sitting behind the counter to study. I went into the kitchen to get a small bowl of pistachio ice cream. I didn't bother turning the light on in the kitchen, because by now I know exactly where the ice cream is even with my eyes closed. But something felt different that time, as if I was being watched and that gave me the creeps. I figured it was my imagination playing tricks in the dimly lit kitchen.

I got myself comfortably seated on the bar stool behind the counter. I opened my notebook and laid my pencil next to it. Then I put a spoonful of pistachio ice cream into my mouth. Once again I felt like someone was watching me. I looked up. It was Kuno, Kobe's guard dog!

Kuno was standing at the top of the steps by the front door, as if saying, "You are not getting out of here alive." Kuno hates Americans. A few years ago he attacked Tracey when she was innocently walking in the back of the restaurant's parking lot. She told me that she had to defend herself with the roll of posters she was carrying under her arm. They were chewed up to pieces when he attempted to go for her throat.

I tried not to move, and that meant not even breathing, while at the same time trying to remain calm. They say animals can tell when you are scared. There were no sharp objects for me to defend myself with, except for my pencil, and I couldn't find the darn piece of paper where I had written Mr. Ounuma's home phone number a few months ago.

On the first day I worked for them answering the phone, I had written Mr. Ounuma's home phone number on a small piece of paper and tucked it away under some papers behind the counter in case I had to call him. But I guess I have more brain memory cells than I give myself credit for, because I was able to recall and dial Mr. Ounuma's home phone number out of total panic.

I whispered into the phone, "Mr. Ounuma, please hurry and come to the restaurant. Kuno is not tied up; he is going to attack me anytime."

He started to laugh. "That's silly," he argued back. "Kuno likes you!"

I was crying, "Mr. Ounuma, he only likes me when I have my kimono on, right now I look like an American. I swear to you that he is looking straight at me in a very strange way, he is showing his teeth, and believe me when I say that he is not smiling."

"Okay, Okay," responded Mr. Ounuma in a condescending voice, "I'll be right over, just remain calm."

I stayed calm all right, more like frozen in time, until Mr. Ounuma showed up and took Kuno home with him, saying to me, "Kuno is a big dog it's true, but he is a nice doggie, he would not hurt you."

Yeah, I thought, doggie my foot. He loves Japanese, not Americans, and Portuguese people are most likely on his hate list too.

"The Murder Room" will be running from September eleventh through October seventeenth. This will be my last play at the Kobe Japanese Restaurant. Mr. Ounuma has given up trying to make me stay any longer; he knows that I have my mind made up and that theatre is no longer the most important part of my life.

Now that it is official that I am selling The Simy Dinner Theatre, I am getting several calls daily from various people that would like to buy my theatre. This is not an easy thing to do because I have to consider Mr. Ounuma's feelings in this matter, it is important that he likes the people I sell the theatre to.

Michael called me. He is coming to New Jersey, but his mom is coming along. His friends are also joining him. Michael and his mother are not going back until they finish fixing their house. The closing on his home is at the end of this month. He has to fix the roof, put on a new garage door, lay down some concrete, and re-do the wooden steps going into the house. The list is absolutely unreasonable. It would be easier to just level the house and then build a new one.

Autumn of 1992

The Chemistry teacher made an announcement on our first day of class. "Half the students in this class will drop out before the end of the quarter, and only a very small percentage of you will pass the course and "those" are the ones that already took my class before."

I came home completely discouraged, and told Ralph that I don't have a fighting chance at making it. He said the teacher sounds like a jerk and encouraged me to get a Chemistry tutor right away.

I drove to Michael's house prepared to give up everything in my life. All he had to do was ask me to move to South Carolina with him and I would quit school and go live with him in any hidden corner of the world away from civilization. He already knows how I feel, because the last time we were together I told him that my dream was to live with him and if all we had was an igloo that would be fine with me. On the way to his house I was thinking that when I am sixty years old he will be forty and most likely he will no longer think of me as attractive and he will see me instead as an old lady. He won't be running after me anymore, instead he will most likely be thinking about women his own age. Those were horrible thoughts, but I didn't care about the future, I would worry about that when the time came, the present was what was important.

When Michael saw me driving up his driveway he dropped his tools on the ground. I got out of my car and ran towards him, and we hugged each other with all our might. He held me for a long time and would not let go, saying, "I couldn't wait to see you. I've missed you so much."

His friends kept working, but his mom came over to hug me. I miss seeing her too. He told everyone that he was taking a break and then, putting his arm around my waist, he took me to the side of the house.

We sat on the grass and then he said the most horrible thing I could have wished for. "I want you to continue going to school. We must not see each other again until you finish what you have been working so hard for. If you still feel the same way about me when you graduate then we will make our future together."

I could hardly believe my ears. "You don't mind waiting five or six years without seeing each other?"

"Ronnie, I love you too much to destroy your future. It's the right thing that we both go our own way and meet again if it's meant to be, when you are done with school."

I immediately put on my clown face. The smile of everything is fine. "You are right. I don't know what's got into me. I've got to go now, it's getting late for my class. Goodbye, Michael, I'll see you when I graduate."

I hugged him briskly as I got into my car and drove off as fast as I could, waving back at him, his mom and friends.

Once on the highway on the way to school I threw the little brown teddy bear he had given me five years before out of my car window. It was easier than I thought. If I was going to continue to exist I had to break all my ties with him and leave no memories of any kind to come and haunt me.

When I got to school I took off the silver necklace he had given me when we spent the day at the Renaissance Fair in North Jersey, but instead of throwing it away, which was my first impulse, I left it on top of the school's bathroom counter. Let someone else have it, maybe she will have better luck with love.

I am finished with Michael forever. He was not strong enough to stand by my side. It's true, love conquers all, but what we had was never love, if it had been true love, it would still be alive.

I was walking through the College Campus and they were having a small jewelry fair in the cafeteria. I bought a necklace made of very small black stones shaped in the form of hearts. The stones felt as cold as ice and that brought me comfort. I'll wear this necklace every time I need to remind myself that I can be as cold as those stones, and still be happy without him.

I found an Asian student that tutors chemistry for $25 an hour. Mr. Huong is very impatient and I'm too embarrassed to say that I don't understand what he is saying because of his strong accent. Besides that, I am wasting precious time driving to his apartment in Red Bank when I could be studying on my own and getting a lot more done.

Talk about male chauvinism. The Chemistry teacher told Nancy, a girl in our class, that she was too pretty to waste her life in College and that she should be thinking instead about getting married and being a wife and mother. I couldn't believe my own ears.

We were in lab this afternoon when he started nagging Nancy again. She was crying.

"It just shows how sensitive you are that you can't even hear the truth without crying." He said mercilessly, "For your own good I'll say it again, you are a beautiful woman and school is a waste of time for someone like you."

Nancy dropped out of College. She told me that she couldn't take any more emotional abuse.

She is a weakling. If I was her I would not allow the chemistry teacher or anyone else to bully me on account of being a woman, and if anything I would work harder to prove myself.

After lunch today Al left to go do his rounds around our building complex, and I started cleaning the kitchen and putting the dishes into the dishwasher when I decided not to waste a small piece of the lasagna crust still attached to the side of the baking dish. It got stuck in my throat! It wouldn't go down or up, and worst of all I couldn't breathe with the darn thing stuck in the back of my throat. I went to the kitchen window to call for help, but I couldn't scream. Barely grasping for air I picked up the phone to call 911 but realized I couldn't speak either. I couldn't believe that I was going to choke to death like Mama Cass, the singer from The Mamas and the Papas band. I had no choice but to perform what I believed to be a self-imposed Heimlich maneuver. I positioned both my hands between my breasts and dropped as hard as I could several times against the kitchen sink. Just about when I was ready to say goodbye to life, the piece of crust popped out from the back of my throat. I was shaking and thought that I was going to pass out from exhaustion from the feeling of terror that I had never imagined could exist. I sat on the couch thanking God for helping me out, and realized how one day we are here laughing or crying whichever the case may be and then the next day — or even a few minutes later — a person can suddenly be gone for no darn good reason.

I quit seeing my chemistry tutor and came to the conclusion that I am better off using the brains that God gave me. When I get exasperated over something I don't understand, I put my question aside until I talk to Ralph on the phone or he comes to visit us; he is more than glad to explain it to me. At present, Ralph is taking biology at Ocean County College as one of the pre-requisites he needs to enter Chiropractic College with me next summer.

I was having fun with the Psychology class until the teacher told us to team up with another student and go into the library where we were to sit across from each other and one of us was to make something out of a small piece of soft clay. The idea was for the sculptor to create something, and while working at it, keep encouraging his or her partner to guess what was being created, while saying the same encouraging words over and over again. It sounded easy. It was decided that my partner would be the sculptor. It turned out to be the longest ten minutes of my life.

Marc started by slowly rolling the piece of clay on the table.

I was sure of myself when I said, "It's a hotdog!"

"You can do it, keep trying." He smiled.

"It's a small candlestick."

"You can do it, keep trying." He continued to smile at me, as he held it in his hands and it got a little longer.

"It's a sausage." I said doubtfully.

"You can do it, keep trying."

Shit! I thought, he has made a penis, and there's no way I'm going to say that word.

"It's a pickle." I said with my fingers crossed.

"You can do it, keep trying."

I no longer could look into his perverted eyes. Staring at his clay penis, I said," It's a cucumber."

"You can do it, keep trying."

"It's a carrot."

"You can do it, keep trying."

"It's a zucchini."

"It's not a vegetable, keep trying."

I had to rule out my intuition so I dared to ask, "Is it a body part?"

"Yes, that's all I can say."

I knew it! I thought. But there's no way in Heaven that he is going to make me say it. I said frustrated, "I give up."

"Do you want to know what it is?" He asked me obviously enjoying the psychological torture he was putting me through.

"Yeah, go ahead, tell me." I said daring him.

"It's a finger."

Yeah, some giant fat finger!

Ralph lent me his high-tech hand computer/calculator, which has a keyboard to enter data and a small screen to view. I can't believe that we are allowed to use calculators during tests. There are things about America and the level of freedom here that still throws me for a loop. Out of despair, I took a week entering everything I could find in the chemistry book that would help me with my final. I entered everything in alphabetical order and decided to take a chance in getting caught and thrown out of College. The way I figure, no matter how many times I take chemistry I have no chance of ever passing this darn class. Even the teacher said that.

I complained to Ralph, "What the heck am I going to do with chemistry? This is such a waste of my time."

"There is a reason for that," said Ralph, who has the wisdom of an older person, "They make you take all those unnecessary and difficult courses to see if you've got what it takes to be a doctor. It's their way of weeding out the weak that don't have what it takes to make it through a four-year degree. If you pass your pre-meds, you've got it made after that."

I am hoping that he is right, as a matter of fact I don't doubt that he knows what he is saying, but my brain hurts when I think about atoms, protons, or anything with numbers.

I sold the dinner theatre to Kyle and Gregg, who in my opinion are the best-qualified producers to keep the theatre alive. Over the years, they have worked for me as directors and actors and have proven their aptitude. They are completely passionate about theatre and they also work great as a team. They want to keep the theatre name, and that means The Simy Dinner Theatre will continue to live on. They gave me $5,000 and I signed the theatre over to them. Mr. Ounuma likes them and he approved of my choice.

Mr. Armstrong passed the final Chemistry tests around the classroom. I was ready with my sophisticated hand held calculator turned off and resting innocently on top of my table, close to my reach. First question, on the test I didn't even know what it was about, second question, I didn't know it either. After that everything became foggy. The teacher had his back to me and was looking at some papers on his desk. I was shaking from head to toe as I picked up the calculator and quickly started looking for anything that even resembled the testing questions. Nothing, there was nothing that even touched the subject.

I turned it off and started praying. "Dear God, please help me. As you know I have worked hard at this subject but I need a little help. I have to pass this test, but as you can see even my high tech instrument, where I entered most of the chemistry data, doesn't show anything that resembles the questions in this test. This teacher is a jerk and an egomaniac and he made the test impossible to pass on purpose. He wants us all to repeat the course so that he will never be out of a job."

Just as I was praying, Mr. Armstrong was standing in front of my table and facing me. He picked up my calculator and smiled as he said, with the look of I know what you are up to, but it isn't going to help you, "Nifty little thing. I bet it can store a lot of stuff."

I looked up and said daringly, "Yes it does, but oddly enough there's nothing in there that even comes close to the questions in this test."

He kept his obnoxious smile as he said back to me loud enough that everyone could hear him, "Like I said; nobody is going to pass my class unless they repeat the course."

Bastard, I thought. I am going to pass this test and answer every question. I took a deep breath and asked God to simply open my brain and let my knowledge out.

Psychology was very interesting to say the least. By learning about Ivan Pavlov and his dog's behavior associated with the sound of a bell with food, I learned something about myself. I recognize now that the reason I love chocolate is because, just like Pavlov's dog, I can recall vividly, at least in my case, the satisfaction of the taste, smell, and feel of chocolate melting in my mouth. My mother's chocolate pudding was a very rare and special treat, as she would say; "You were a very good girl today, so I made you chocolate pudding, just for you."

I may not physically salivate at the thought of chocolate, but mentally I am induced to longing for it. According to Pavlov's discovery on the science of behavior, my addiction for chocolate is called a conditional reflex, caused by me knowing that chocolate will give me emotional comfort. When I eat chocolate I am emotionally satisfied.

As tradition goes on, for closing night Mr. Ounuma offered the cast and crew of "The Murder Room" a free dinner at the hibachi table. It's his way of saying thanks to all of us. I was very sad as I sat quietly next to one of the male actors who decided to take advantage of the waiter because he was handsome. He kept asking him for a glass of water and would try to touch the young man's hand, making sexual innuendos towards him. Everybody was laughing, but I felt that even if the waiter had been a girl it's still in poor taste to be a male chauvinist. Be it gay or not, one should have respect for another human being.

I was glad it was my last night at The Simy Dinner Theatre where I no longer belong. That night was the closing chapter of my life in New Jersey. My next step is to go and find out what else is out there waiting to be discovered.

Rosanna has a good friend that works for the Holiday Inn, and she gave me four coupons that will allow me to stay free at any of their associated motels. The coupons are good for one year, and all I have to do if anyone asks is to say that I work as a housekeeper for the Holiday Inn in Lakewood. I'll be using the coupons for when I travel back and forth between Georgia and New Jersey.

I did it! Yahoo! I passed all my classes including the abominable Chemistry! But since my brain cells had to change gears from the arts to science courses, I went from being an A student with high honors, to a B which to me stands for, Best, Bingo, and Bravo!

I called Life Chiropractic College to confirm with them that I would be there in January to take the last two pre-requisites needed, Organic Chemistry II and Physics II. If I take those courses in New Jersey I will not be able to start Chiropractic College until the fall of next year. That's too long to wait. I want to get on with it. They offered two choices, and I chose the ten-week course instead of rushing through the shorter option of five weeks. They also told me not to worry about a place to stay, because there are plenty of students renting rooms around the campus.

I like the idea of finishing my last two pre-requisites at the College I will be attending for the next four years. It will give me a chance to get acquainted with the school. When I finish those two subjects I will come back to New Jersey and take a short break. Then Ralph and I will go together to Georgia for the more serious studies ahead of us and we will look for an apartment of our own to share.

Ralph encouraged me to keep my eyes open for scholarship offers while I'm at Life Chiropractic College.

I have no luck with used cars, so I asked Ralph his opinion on new ones. Those old jalopies that I have been driving around are not to be trusted even if they are free. I need a reliable car to drive to the college in Georgia. Ralph told me that he did some research by reading the Consumer's Report and the

Saturn brand had gotten raving reviews. My present junky car is not going to make it much longer on the road. I have never been to Georgia, but it's going to be a long trip by myself. I need a reliable, new car.

Passing all the tests at Ocean County College has given me a lot of self-confidence. It has proven to me that I can memorize anything if I study it hard enough every day — or in the case of being chewed up by Kuno the dog, panic can also work to my advantage. I am proud to say that I have memorized my social security number from repeating it over and over again when I would take out books from the College library. I can also brag that I still remember my home phone number in Portugal: 50164. This proves that I do have some reasonable amount of memory.

I am no longer scared of taking science courses, and besides, Ralph swore to me that from now on it's going to be even easier.

I took the $5,000 I made on the sale of the theatre and added the difference needed from what I had saved, and bought myself a brand new red Saturn. I left the rest of the money in the bank. Mama would be proud of me.

Winter of 1993

Steve's new girlfriend, Diane, is pregnant and it looks like they are staying together and possibly getting married. I'm keeping my fingers crossed. The baby is due around July. I'm finally going to be a grandmother! I was starting to worry that it was never going to happen.

I said goodbye to Dr. Peruzzi, and he made me swear that I would write to him. Then I went to see Dr. Holdman, and when I left his office he came to the front door as I was running down the steps and yelled at the top of his lungs, "Remember what I said, if you use intention with your patients you will be a very successful doctor!"

I love both Dr. Peruzzi and Dr. Holdman. They are a bit eccentric, but they have been a true inspiration. I like the idea that one day when I get very old I can still work. All I have to do is walk towards my patient and gently move their spine into place by "punching" them in the neck like Dr. Peruzzi does.

Papa called again. He is going to wait a few more months until things calm down with Mama. He is not giving up on the idea of having my brother's body autopsied. Like me, he believes there was foul play in my brother José's death and he is not ready to give up proving it. He told me that he is being careful not to let Alice know that he suspects her. He is not sharing his suspicions with Mama either. He is worried that anything he tells to Mama she will divulge to Alice. He intends to be very, very careful.

I waited until the day before leaving New Jersey to say good-bye to Mr. and Mrs. Ounuma, Jerry the bartender, the new chef, and the waitresses. Mrs. Ounuma handed me a large basket of goodies with all kinds of dried goods to take with me to school. We both cried as we said goodbye, and Mr. and Mrs. Ounuma hugged me instead of just bowing to me. I felt like I was leaving my family.

It was about six in the morning when I finished packing my Saturn with a pillow, a blanket, a set of bed sheets, my classical guitar, Mrs. Ounuma's gift, a small suitcase of clothes and toiletries, the two wood barrels used as props for "The

Playboy of the Western World," the dissection picture book, and a map with directions on how to get to Life Chiropractic College. After hugging Al, Ralph, and Steve, I got into my car and took a deep breath of its naturally delicious new car smell.

I felt light as a feather, as if floating across the highway empowered by the music on the radio. A classical radio station was playing a Bach piece. I was not surprised to find it befitting my newfound independence. I let myself be emotionally transported as if in a trance to the beat of what seemed to me a prolonged drum roll that kept on beating. No words were needed to express the fulfillment I felt. I was finally free.

I am spending the night at the Holiday Inn in North Carolina. It's January 3, 1993. It's the beginning of the New Year, and as Michael would say, the beginning of everything that I worked so hard for. I feel emotionally strong as if empowered by a new me that I was not aware existed.

Silly, but this is the second time that an eye specialist in Freehold has come to my mind. I went to see him about fifteen years ago when I was seeking some answers about getting contact lenses. He came into the room with his partially stained white shirt not quite tucked into his pants. He was out of shape and his disheveled unkempt look seemed to match his lack of knowledge. It wasn't until later on, when I was taking my pre-meds; that his image came to my mind. He was there to re-assure me I could do just as good if not better. Amazing how someone like him, among a few other people I have met, have made such an impact in my life. Characters like him have become my biggest source of self-confidence. I can do anything I put my mind to it. They did it.

I'm going to take a shower before going to bed.

I turned the hot shower on and went to get my pajamas from the bedroom. When I returned to the bathroom the smell of the hot water running made me gasp for air. I immediately turned the water off and closed the bathroom door so that the polluted fumes would stay away from the bedroom. I went downstairs to talk to the front desk personnel and told the desk lady that there was something wrong with their water because it smelled like sewage or some kind of nasty chemicals. She told me that was normal in North Carolina and they were used to it.

I'm not going to take a shower. I don't feel like having who-knows-what kind of chemicals penetrating my skin pores.

I'm going to sleep now.

Marietta, Georgia

I woke up about one minute before my alarm clock went off. I've come to the conclusion that over the years I have developed an internal clock, which is most likely due to constantly keeping track of time while I taught guitar for thirteen years. After a while I just knew when a half-hour private lesson or a one-hour group class was over without even checking my wristwatch. Still, I like the security of having an alarm clock.

Once I got on the highway I got myself comfortably situated behind a truck. The way I figured, if the truck driver was speeding I knew it was safe to speed too. Being up high in their cabin, they can see the highway police cars way ahead of them. In many ways I miss my old van where I was seated a lot higher than in my Saturn. The view now is a lot less panoramic. The other thing I have noticed is that my new car has no pick-up power, but it still drives great, and that is good enough for me.

I didn't know exactly what to expect as I drove through the southern states. But somehow I imagined that I would be driving on a narrow dusty road seeing a lot of small polluted lakes with at least one old farmer seated on a rock holding a fishing pole or Elly May and Granny from the show "The Beverly Hillbillies" standing by an old rundown wooden shack. Instead, I found the southern roads to be super comfortable, modern highways. The only thing I noticed to be different from the North were the trees along the road They appeared to have odd-shaped heads and long stretched-out arms that could be taken for green monsters out of a science fiction movie. If I were a child growing up in the south I would never look outside my bedroom window at night. Those tall, weeping cypress trees have got to be a scary sight for any child that is afraid of monsters.

I have driven through some major traffic jams in my life — like in New York City, the suicidal city traffic of Lisbon, and many highways, bridges, and tunnels — without any problem, but I was taken by surprise and definitely not prepared for it when I reached Atlanta and found myself in a super highway of five lanes that ended in a roundabout circle. I didn't want to get lost by taking the wrong exit, so I kept going around and around looking for some kind of sign that said north or even pointing to Marietta or Smyrna. Finally I decided to take a chance on one of the exits, but the other drivers would not give me the right to change lanes. I finally got my courage up and began cutting into one lane at a time until I was able to exit and look for a gas station. Now these are the prices I love paying for gas! I filled up my tank like a gas glutton and got directions to Cobb Parkway and the apartment where I would be living for the next ten weeks. Someone from the College's admission office had arranged for my stay with two other chiropractic students.

It was getting dark when I arrived at the apartment. To my astonishment, the room I was renting had no furnishings, not even a bed. I decided that for one night only I could sleep on the floor. But I didn't sleep much; my hips and shoulders were hurting, as a matter of fact after about two hours of rolling from one side to the other my whole body was sore. In order to sleep on a hard surface, fat is needed to compensate for having bones directly on the ground. And that was the night I wished I had a weight problem. The carpet on the floor had no rubber padding. It had been laid directly on the cement floor. I had two choices; lie on top of the thin blanket I had brought with me, or cover myself with it and cry from back and hip pain. I chose to freeze to death and to lie on top of the blanket. But it's hard to relax the muscles and fall asleep while shivering. It didn't last long before I stood up in the empty room. I wrapped myself in the blanket and, with my pillow under my butt; I sat against the corner wall waiting for the morning to come. I was born in Portugal it's true, but half of me is definitely German as I am not one to complain. The next morning I took it upon myself to go out looking for an army surplus store. Michael had told me several times how much he loved sleeping on an army cot when he was living in the attic of the Arnold Theatre. I figured it would be cheaper than buying a bed for the few months I would be renting the room.

I checked out the Chiropractic College, and it's about a ten-minute drive from the apartment where I'm staying. I got a really good feeling about the College. Everybody is very friendly, and it's fun to hear the southerners' accents, it makes me feel like I am in a different country. The only thing that has shocked me into disbelief is that in this day and age, the Ku Klux Klan members are still allowed to go on about their hate business in the town I am living in. I had seen them on television and in the movies, but it has a completely differ-ent impact when they are a few feet from me. Five of them, dressed in their customary white gowns and hoods, were standing by a traffic light. Then they came up to the cars and handed the motorists their propaganda pamphlets. One of them came walking in my direction and I rapidly closed my car window. The light turned green and I put my foot to the gas pedal.

Oh, my goodness! Between the freezing cold crawling up the cot's thin canvas material, and the thumping sound of drums in the room next to mine, it was another horrible night. Just my luck, one of my roommates likes loud rap music! I was getting nasty muscle spasms in my legs and feet, and to make things worse because of the position the cot held me in, there was no such thing as finding a comfortable position. I am going to try one more night sleeping on this cot, maybe I'll get used to it.

It was worse than I thought. I got out of the cot this morning holding on to my back, which felt weak and very sore. When my back starts to act up it scares me. I'm keeping my fingers crossed that the surplus store where I bought the cot will take it back, since I slept on it only for two nights.

They were very kind and exchanged the cot for a four-inch foam pad. From there I paid a visit to the Salvation Army and bought myself two thick blankets.

Wow! I found the foam pad to be better than a mattress. Monday is my first day at the College and I am very excited about starting classes.

It's so exciting to be here in Georgia, of all places. I have two roommates, Sally and Melinda. Sally is twenty-four years old. She is very shy, and when she speaks, the tone of her voice is that of an eight-year-old child. She is always smiling, but she has a look in her brown eyes that reads sadness. She is very sensitive and fragile, which fits her romantic personality. All she talks about is the boy at school who is two quarters ahead of her and how handsome he is. They had sex twice in his car, and then she made the mistake of confessing her crime to a church member. She was almost thrown out of the congregation. Her religion requires that she wear a chemise when she takes a shower so that she doesn't get sinful thoughts when bathing and she is to read the bible every night before going to bed.

Melinda is the boss in the apartment that three of us share. Melinda has red hair, the color my father refers to as tomato soup, one of the reasons why he will eat any soup except tomato soup. Melinda is quite obese and barely five feet tall, making her a real mean midget when she is angry. But she is twenty-two years old, which is what saves her from being ugly. Like Aunt Heydee used to say, "There's no such thing as an ugly young girl."

Melinda is also a control-freak, and we are reprimanded daily if things are not run her way. She sweats a lot and doesn't like heat, so neither Sally nor I are allowed to touch the thermostat even though it is winter. There's a heating system in the apartment but Melinda, the boss already warned us, "I don't like heat in my apartment and my bedroom is warm enough at night." Maybe because she is so obese, she probably has extra sweat glands.

One of the things that puzzles me about the South is that the highways going through Marietta and the other towns have a middle lane that nobody drives in. Even during traffic jams nobody uses that lane. What a waste of road space! Until someone tells me that lane is not to be used and it's there just for show, I am driving on it. I see the people in the other cars looking at me as if I am crazy, and sometimes they even shake one of their fingers in my direction as if I'm doing something illegal. I just wave back at the fools, and go on my merry way. It's their choice if they want to remain stuck in traffic.

Physics II is going well. I have a really good teacher and he doesn't mind helping out with questions and overseeing the lab experiments. But Organic Chemistry II is making me a nervous wreck from watching my classmates acting like spoiled children. These are the future doctors of chiropractic and their malice is the worst I have ever seen towards a teacher, our teacher, Dr. Gounder.

Poor Dr. Gounder, he used to teach at a medical school and was probably used to having some respect, but not here. Some of the wise-guys in class make him repeat the stuff over and over again, laughing at his Indian accent and then complain straight to his face that he is a lousy teacher. He definitely has the patience of a saint to put up with so much verbal abuse. I am lucky that I am able to follow what he writes on the board, most likely because he explains each problem, over and over again. I think that these students are vicious. This kind of stuff bothers me a lot. I don't like to see people being mistreated.

I finally got my courage up last night, and at about two in the morning I knocked at Melinda's bedroom door to ask her to lower the music on the radio just so that I could sleep.

"I like my music loud and I am not lowering it. Just keep your bedroom door closed." She yelled back from her bedroom.

I do have my bedroom door closed, but it doesn't help since the sound comes through the walls! Her bedroom is next to mine! She is freaking selfish!

I took a look at the scholarship opportunities posted on the wall of the financial aid department, and the one that made the most sense to apply for is the Harvey Lilliard Scholarship, which offers one full year of school tuition if I get accepted. They require three letters of recommendation, my own letter telling them why I deserve to get the scholarship, and also proof that I have done things for the betterment of my community.

I believe that I already have all the requirements that they are asking for. When I get back to New Jersey I will put everything together and send it to them. One free year of school will mean less money I have to pay the government when I graduate from Chiropractic College.

Leila is an older student who usually comes into the chemistry class wearing a black wide-brim hat, a long dark coat, a red scarf, and carrying more than she could handle, like a heavy backpack and two handbags full of books and papers. She always makes a grand entrance into the classroom as she arrives late every time. It's almost guaranteed that she will inadvertently drop something before reaching her seat. She sits in the very front and she is definitely hard to miss. She is constantly posing questions to the teacher who patiently goes over the same problem over and over again so that she and the rest of the class can comprehend what's going on. But Leila is not nasty like the others, she makes her questions politely and she is truly having a problem understanding what's going on.

One morning during a class break she sat next to me and said, "Hi, my name is Leila, would you help me with this class? Do you have any notes I can borrow?"

I wondered if I had a sign over my head saying, come get your chemistry notes here.

Of course I have notes, that's all I do in class is take notes. If I don't take notes I can't recall anything that happened in class, that's the kind of poor memory that I have to contend with. I take lots of notes and I study them every day when I get home. I have even created a log of questions and answers to help me pass the tests. I was more than glad to help Leila, and told her she could borrow everything I had.

The refrigerator is crammed with Melinda's food, leaving Sally and I barely any space available to store our stuff. Sally has a small spot on the upper shelf of the refrigerator door where her weekly ration of seven small veggie burritos are perfectly squeezed in as if saying sorry for taking so much space. I like to have fresh vegetables and fruit on hand, but because the refrigerator is tightly packed with Melinda's food I keep my fruit in a bowl on top of the dining room table and I only buy my veggies to last for two or three days.

I have started cooking. I divide the meals into three small plastic containers, but I could barely squeeze them into the freezer box. If I am not careful opening the freezer door, I am guaranteed to have a package of Melinda's frozen burgers or a frozen chicken fall out. Last night I injured my right toe when one of her frozen packages of meat fell out of the jammed freezer.

Leila is my only true friend at school. I don't mind helping her because as I am teaching her I am also reinforcing my own knowledge. She finds school to be a difficult endeavor and she has a hard time concentrating. She told me that she has been diagnosed as dyslexic and as such she needs extra help with her studies. I told her not to feel bad because I also have a learning problem. Most likely I am also dyslexic because sometimes I write things in reverse and I am also very slow at learning. Besides that, I'm allergic to formaldehyde, I am partially deaf, the English language is still hard for me even after all these years in America, and I have to use eyeglasses, otherwise I can't see well from far away. She agreed that we are both special. Our weaknesses have made us sisters under the skin.

Leila has been taking me in the evening to chiropractic adjusting clubs at the College. This is where chiropractic students that are eager to practice their adjusting technique offer free adjustments to other students. So far I have been to three adjusting clubs: Gonstead, Activator, and SOT which is short for Sacral Occipital Technique. I was a bit scared, but I did volunteer to be adjusted at each meeting by their members so they can practice and I can also experience how it feels to be adjusted by these so different techniques.

The Activator Technique is practiced with a hand held instruments that looks like a gun, and SOT, is practiced by using blocks under the hips, but it all seems very difficult to learn with so many detailed procedures that correspond to what step to follow before adjusting the spine. I am not sure that I can ever learn all those moves.

The Gonstead Technique, on the other side of the spectrum, is done manually and very harshly. From what I heard, it was discovered by a man, named Gonstead. He was a butcher in a meat store, prior to becoming a chiropractor. The problem is that he not only had arthritic hands, but he was also a tough heavyset guy, and when you add force with big fat crooked fingers they become a lethal weapon in my opinion. Of course, these students at the Gonstead club are fanatical about the Gonstead Technique, and they twist their fingers and make a fist and by the time they are finished they are like Gonstead clones. I went to the Gonstead club once with Leila and swore never to let them touch me again. They moved my neck and my lower back in both directions like a nutcracker, and I was so sore from their so-called spinal adjustments that when I left the room I couldn't walk straight for the rest of the night.

What I would like to learn is the Toggle Technique, which is what Dr. Peruzzi in New Jersey did to me. But that technique doesn't have a club, and I will have to wait to learn it when I am a regular chiropractic student.

The students go around the school roaring about their elected technique being better than all the rest. I am confused with so many choices. I thought there was only one-way of adjusting the spine and that would be it. But it looks like there's more to adjusting than I imagined possible. I told Leila that I'm not going to anymore adjusting clubs it takes too much of my time that I should be using for studying. I'm making my priority to concentrate only on what I came down here for, which is passing my two final pre-requisites to enter the chiropractic program this summer.

I was really surprised when Sally invited me Friday night to go with her to a party at the College's clubhouse. It was a small room packed with people standing, drinking, and talking to each other. Of course once I enter a place like that I am basically deaf with all the noise. There is a student at school who wears her hair really short and she seems to be proud of showing off her two hearing aids, one in each ear. I admire her self-esteem.

Sally wouldn't let go of my arm as we walked into the crowded room, and then she pulled me outside.

"I can't stand places like these," she said crying. "It's like a meat market, for men to pick up women."

I didn't see anything bad about the place except for being filled to capacity, but just to make her happy I agreed with her and drove her home. I believe that the reason Sally wanted to go to the party was because she was hoping to see the love of her life, her ex-boyfriend. Supposedly the clubhouse will be having another party next Friday. I'm going to check it out by myself.

Leila told me that Dr. Williams, the president of Life Chiropractic College, believes that it's not important how well we do scholastically, what's most important is how good we are at adjusting the spine. She encouraged me to take advantage of the once a week free morning lectures to learn more about chiropractic philosophy.

Dr. Williams is the one that started Life College and supposedly he is a great speaker. Leila is not only my friend but she is also teaching me the ropes around the College. I'm attending next week's chiropractic seminar.

I have been going by my real name. Signing it everyday and introducing myself as Veronica has given me a sense of who I really am. The name Ronnie belongs only in New Jersey. Thank you God, for giving me the opportunity to be me.

I am doing well both in physics and in chemistry, and my first tests were at my comfort level. No matter how much I study, I have come to terms with the fact that I am not a great test taker. I blame that on my language barrier. But I did feel confident that I had done reasonably well when I finished taking the first chemistry test. I came out of the classroom and noticed that some of the students taking the test with me were already hanging out in the hallway so I figured they must have done pretty good.

I said to Gary, one of the older students, "Not too bad, the chemistry test, right?"

He looked at me with fuming eyes and responded irritated, "Why do you say that?"

I knew I had made a mistake to voice my opinion, but it was too late to back out and I tried to fix what I had just said by adding, "You finished before I did, you must have done well." Then I took a deep breath and went on not knowing when to shut up. "Everything the teacher taught us in class was on the test."

He made a closed fist in my direction and said angrily, "Oh, I see! Miss Smarty Pants. You think you know everything don't you? How would you like me to punch you in the mouth?"

I felt like he was going to hit me, and I believe that the only reason he didn't was because there were other students around us. He must be in his mid fifties, but he is obviously mentally retarded.

I walked away shaking from the experience, and decided that from now on I'll go into class but I won't talk or mingle with anyone. Some of these people are scary!

Sally says she wishes I was her mother, and just about every night she comes to my bedroom to cry on my shoulder and talk about Larry, the boy from school. She told me that she didn't mean to sin, she just wanted to please Larry so that he would love her. But as it turned out, he doesn't want to marry her, he only wants to have sex with her. She wishes he would be serious and marry her, but she also realizes that would be impossible for two reasons; one, he would never be accepted by her church, and second, her church looks down on sex before marriage. Her only hope now is to find a boy from her congregation who will marry her and then she won't have to continue with chiropractic school. She wants to be happily married, and have lots and lots of children. She also feels very lonely and without a family because her brother is gay and her mother has a girlfriend she lives with. As far as the church she belongs to, both her mother and her brother are not welcome in it because of their so-called aberrant life styles. Sally cries a lot. I can hear her at night in the bedroom next to mine. Sally doesn't really want to be a chiropractor. She would rather work as a gardener until she gets married.

Sally told me that she believes that Melinda is a lesbian. She feels very uncomfortable when Melinda touches her, which is quite often; like when they pass each other in the hallway,

Melinda bumps her body into hers as if it was an accident, and also a day doesn't go by that Melinda doesn't touch Sally's shoulder or hands when talking to her.

I think that Sally is homophobic because of her family. If Sally were a glass vase, she would have been broken a long time ago. I don't know how she is going to survive with the ups and downs of normal life.

Friday night, I put my acoustic guitar in the trunk of my car and drove up to the clubhouse at the College. When I got there it was later than I thought, the crowd was dissipating. I was leaving the building and going through the foyer by the bathrooms when I saw two guitarists jamming-up on their acoustics. I stopped, and stood there watching while thinking about my old days of playing guitar. When they stopped, I asked the one smiling at me if he would let me play a tune just for fun. He handed me his Yamaha classical guitar and I sat down and played "Romance Antigua." I had hit gold! They absolutely loved it and wanted me to play it over and over again. One of them told me he was disappointed that I didn't have my own guitar since he would like me to join them. I smiled happily as I told him that I had a guitar in my car and would be right back. I tuned my guitar to one of theirs and I started playing "Romance Antigua" once again. Chris and Justin, the two guitarists, were addicted to the tune, and a couple of people were standing listening.

"I know this is going to sound odd, but do you mind if the three of us go play inside the men's bathroom? I bet the acoustics in there will make this song beyond anything one can imagine!" Chris suggested.

Who am I to question something out of the norm? We took our three metal chairs and got settled in the men's bathroom. Of course, the bathroom became a music studio in the sense that the acoustics were indeed the best I had ever heard. They

Porta-Stage

were phenomenal. Each time a guy would come in and wonder what the heck a woman was doing in there, we would just keep playing as Justin would yell out, "Don't worry, she is cool."

A musical bond had been created.

Students all over the world are this way, they are the first to fight for liberty and freedom of expression, it's a part of being young and I am definitely stagnant in the young mode. I love school; and the surrounding atmosphere of pure ideals where one can learn the secrets of the wise. Also, I must confess that this experience gave me extra inner strength, and while I was playing I was able to forget my loneliness without Michael.

Leila took me to hear a guest speaker, lecturing about chiropractic philosophy. It felt like the movie scene from Logan's Run, where all the young people hurried eagerly into the huge gym-like auditorium, rushing to get the best seat in the house. Then Dr. Strudel appeared center-stage, and put his hands up as everybody cheerfully clapped. He then went on to talk about the healing power of chiropractic, and how pathetic it was to waste so much time and money on education when all we needed was to learn to adjust the spine.

"Why are we here?" He asked everybody.

Someone yelled out of the crowd, "To be chiropractors."

Dr. Strudel pulled a twenty-dollar bill out of his pocket and waved it in the air so that no one could miss seeing it, and he yelled out to the crowd once more, "No. The truth is that we are here for the money."

He kept the twenty-dollar bill up in the air, chanting on, "Money, money, money, money! Everybody say it with me! Money, money, money, money!"

I looked around and saw a few students shaking their heads, as disappointed as I was, while others were laughing. But the majority was chanting along with Dr. Strudel.

I was so disillusioned with what I had seen and heard that I called Ralph to let him know that I had second thoughts about becoming a chiropractor. Of course, I want to get paid for my work when I become a chiropractor and I would be lying if I said no; I am not naïve, I know that I will need to pay my school loan back, and make a decent living, but money is not my only goal. My priority is to be a healer like Dr. Peruzzi and Dr. Holdman.

Ralph reasoned with me, reminding me about the crooked dentist in Freehold and that I shouldn't give up my dream because in every profession there's always someone spoiling it for everybody else. He is right. There are good and bad presidents, just like priests, lawyers, and so on. The more I thought about it, the stronger I felt that I have an obligation to pursue my career.

I did express my feelings to Leila, but she said that she admired Dr. Strudel as much as Dr. Williams. I decided not to say anything against either one of them. In her opinion Dr. Williams was a great man and he had accomplished many good things for the future of chiropractic. If it weren't for him, there would be no Life College. He had made our college a reality. In her opinion we must be more forgiving when a guest speaker is acting silly. I agreed with her; it makes sense.

Melinda's breasts are so humongous that they hang down to her waist. If I had breasts like that I would have a breast reduction. She likes to come out of her bedroom butt-naked, while patting her wet red hair with a towel. Poor Sally freaks out every time this happens as she runs to her bedroom and closes the door behind her. I just stay seated at the dining room table, looking down the best I can at my books or the letter I might be writing to Rosanna. She has become my pen pal, I write to her about my roommates and life in school. Melinda has got to know that she is a sight to behold when she sees Sally taking off in a frantic panic out of the living room, and me just staring down at my books as if ignorant of my surroundings. But she doesn't care, and if anything she is proud of creating turmoil, she will say stuff like, "This is the way I was born, and I have nothing to hide."

Okay, I agree with being proud of who we are, but does she see Sally or me flaunting our naked bodies around the house?

I spend the weekends studying, and whenever possible I reward myself by playing my acoustic guitar. I really came prepared when I brought a bunch of music books. I sit on my foam bed and play sad songs of love and some classical tunes and I save the popular tunes just to show off in case Melinda or Sally come home early. Every day I think about Michael. Sometimes after I play a love song I stop for a few seconds to think about him. I wonder how he is doing.

I have decided to go see a gynecologist and have my breasts examined. I have a very small blister on my right nipple, and that worries me. Twice I went to see a gynecologist in

Lakewood, New Jersey who told me not to worry, and that it would go away. But it's been three years and it's still there. It is the size of a pinhead but it leaks what looks like milk, and sometimes it even bleeds for no reason. I just want to make sure it's not cancer. I asked Leila if she knew a woman doctor. She recommended Dr. Lawoski.

I got good news and bad news from Dr. Lawoski. The good news is that my nipple is fine and she said that it looks like one of my milk ducts are leaking and I shouldn't worry about it, but I have trichomoniasis. I tried to remain calm as she said it is a common sexually transmitted disease, and the only way to get it is through intercourse. I took a deep breathe of relief. That meant that Al didn't have it since once a year I have a check up, and I had also gotten a clean bill of health before being with Michael. I told her about Michael and she said that I had most likely caught it from him. Dr. Lawoski said that I should let Michael know about it so that he can take care of it, and she gave me a prescription to send to him. Usually men don't have symptoms, but they keep spreading the infection to their partners. She gave me some medicine samples and told me that I would be fine afterwards.

Michael wrote back apologizing, and also thanking me for letting him know. He went to see a doctor and was told that he will be fine after taking the medication. He also wrote that if I wanted to finish our relationship he understood how I felt.

My first impulse was to write back and ask, "What relationship?" Instead I wrote back saying that I loved him too much to make such a decision. But during the night I couldn't sleep and wrote him another letter saying that since he was so understanding, I was taking upon myself to accept the responsibility of terminating our relationship forever.

Trying to make it easier for him, I also wrote that if I didn't get a letter back that meant he accepted my decision. Most likely this is the final chapter of our love for each other and we will never meet again.

Someone has been using my underarm deodorant! I found hairs on it. When I asked which one was using my deodorant, I found out that even though Melinda has her own bathroom she likes to snoop around the extra bathroom that Sally and I share.

"I ran out of deodorant," Said Melinda. "You don't mind, do you?"

"Oh, no; I don't mind."

I lied.

I bought myself a new deodorant, and now I keep all my toiletries along with my hairbrush and soap inside a small straw basket in my bedroom closet. After I take a shower I take all my toiletries and bath towel back to my bedroom, and storage them in my closet.

I got a letter from Rosanna telling me to take revenge on Melinda before I return to New Jersey. She instructed me to steal something from Melinda, something that she finds very dear to her heart, and then I can use it later to blackmail Melinda into giving me back my rent deposit. In Rosanna's opinion Melinda is going to find some kind of excuse not to give me my rent deposit. Rosanna even called me to tell me that I must be strong and do it. I didn't want to disappoint Rosanna by seeming to be a weakling, so I said, "Okay, I'll do it."

Even though the idea of revenge sounds like a great idea, just the thought of doing something like that makes me feel sick to my stomach.

I saw an old pick-up truck with a South Carolina's license plate in the school's parking lot. The first thought that came to my mind was that Michael had come to Georgia looking for me. Just in case it was true, I remained seated in my car waiting. About an hour later, two students got into the truck and took off.

Children have more brains than me. In my desire to conquer love, I imagine our life together being possible even though I know it is a hallucination that I created. It's all part of being in love and not knowing when to let go. Michael smokes and drinks too much, he has a depressive nature, and I have seen him lose his patience with other people. I know that with time it would be only natural that he would lose his patience with me too. We would never last long together.

Melinda and Sally were kidding, of course, when they said I had brought the snowstorm with me from the north. They couldn't even remember the last time snow had fallen in Georgia.

They tried to dissuade me from going out since everything was closed and the roads would be like ice. I went out anyway. I told them that in New Jersey five inches of snow is like drizzle for us Northerners. Snow doesn't scare me; if anything, I was looking forward to the excitement of having my car skid just a little.

It just happened that there was a gun show at the Convention Center, and I thought it would be a unique experience to check it out, since there was nothing else open. There were cars stranded all over the highway and the roads, and I was the only one that seemed to be driving without any tribulations. The problem began when I got to the Convention Center's parking lot. It was a sheet of slippery ice. But I wasn't going to acknowledge that I had made a mistake driving there, and, being stubborn, I decided to take my chances and walk across the parking lot. I must have an ice skating angel on my shoulder, because I made it safely across the slippery parking lot. I was done looking at the guns within forty-five minutes and came to the conclusion that I don't like guns and will never own one and took my time driving back to the apartment.

Waiting to take the Physics test, I sat cross-legged on the hallway's cold concrete floor and concentrated on breathing and relaxing. I thought about smiling, which helps me a lot before a test, but I didn't want anyone around me to think that I was weird. I figured that if I could relax by letting go of all thoughts, I could reach complete mental relaxation and be in control of my fears. I kept breathing deeply with my eyes closed. A few moments later they called everybody in to take the test. I was feeling so relaxed that when I sat down to take the exam I didn't feel like I had to rush about it. Instead I looked around the room watching everybody taking the test as if their life depended on it and then I stared into the air, maintaining my state of relaxation.

The teacher came up to my desk. "I have been watching you. Aren't you taking the exam? You've only got twenty minutes left to answer all the questions!"

I responded, still feeling peaceful, "Oh, okay. Thank you for telling me."

Like, big deal! What was the rush anyway?

I marked the answers feeling like I knew the answers, and in my head I was singing yeah, yeah, yeah! I was in good spirits as I finished the test along with everybody else. It wasn't until I got up from my desk that I realized that I must have hypnotized myself to a state of careless abandonment and that's when I got scared. What if I answered the questions wrong? That would mean that I would have to stay in Georgia, and continue to live in the apartment I was renting from Melinda. I promised never to relax like that again. I must stay focused and most of all alert!

I think about Michael every day, principally when I hear Whitney Houston singing "I will love you forever," but I have no hopes of ever seeing him again. I have to confess that I like the feeling that I am in love with somebody, even if nothing comes of it. It just means that I am alive. I am the loneliest person in the world.

I was in the school hallway waiting with a bunch of other students to enter the next classroom. I found a corner spot and was busy writing a letter to my friend Rosanna when a young man — blonde, blue eyes, and a smile that could sell any brand of toothpaste on television — sat next to me and introduced himself. Rick's interest in me took me by surprise. Instinctively I didn't inform him that I was either legally divorced or married. I answered his first questions with a lie. After the second question the lies flowed more easily. I became aware that I was purposely doing my best to attract him by giving him the answers he most likely wanted to hear from a sexy woman. Greek Gods are not supposed to bother with mere mortals like me, and he was the personification of Adonis. He was passionate, and his undivided attention made me feel as if I was the only woman in the hallway. Obviously he was fascinated by my mature looks and I felt the physical attraction growing with each second that ticked away. Reality hit me as we were being called back into our classes. Rick is twenty-five years old, half my age, and besides that, he only has one more semester 'til graduation. I was glad to say goodbye and leave things as they were, two ships passing in the hallway, that's the way I saw it.

After what happened today I've come to the conclusion that I don't love anyone. What I feel is more like an out-of-control sexual need, and I can no longer blame Al for our marriage falling apart; I only have myself to blame for being the way I am.

The Chemistry teacher didn't show up at the testing center. We were informed that he had suffered a stroke and was in the hospital. Gary and a few other students were celebrating Dr. Gounder's ill fate. Gary announced loudly that it was the best thing that could happen, and he hoped that our teacher wasn't going to make it. They were hoping that the chemistry test would be cancelled on account of the teacher dying! I was horrified; it's at times like these that I am ashamed of being part of the human race. Of course the test wasn't cancelled. God bless Dr. Gounder's soul, he had prepared the test the day before he went to the hospital. I have no doubt that these immature malicious students induced the professor's stroke from so much aggravation. I went home after the test and wrote Dr. Gounder an anonymous letter, telling him that I wished him health from the bottom of my heart and that I admired him for putting up with so many ignorant people in his class. In my opinion he is the best chemistry teacher I have ever had, and it was an honor to be in his class. I signed the bottom of the letter, "Please get well soon, from an anonymous student that cares."

The next morning I slipped the envelope into his office mailbox.

Melinda heard me playing the guitar in my bedroom and she shared with me how much she loves music and said she would do anything to sing in public. I got an idea, but I have not told her. Her birthday is this weekend. I am going to find a place where there is karaoke and take her there for her birthday.

I was studying at the school's library when suddenly I looked up and there was Rick standing in front of my table. Talk about magnetic energy! He sat down and we talked softly but enthusiastically. Then he asked if I would go out with him. I wanted to say yes, and why wait, let's go right now, but instead I said that I was too busy studying for finals.

"How about going to the movies with me Saturday night? You need to have a break from your studies."

But I was quick to answer, "Maybe another time. I really have to get back to my books, so please excuse me."

He gave me his phone number and left. I am not calling him. He is too young and too beautiful, and that scares me. Right now I only have one goal in my life, to do well with my finals.

Dr. Gounder is back to teaching, much to the disappointment of the majority of students in his class. Before he began today's lecture, he seemed to be visibly touched as he remarked to the class, "I want to say that the anonymous letter sent to me while I was in the hospital gave me the strength to get better faster." And he pointed to the row where two students were seated way in the back of the room and, taking a slight bow towards them, he added. "I know it was you who sent me that letter, thank you."

The two students had a dumbfound look on their faces since they had no idea what the teacher was talking about, I was the only one who knew. I had done well. It feels wonderful to do good deeds, and I thanked God for giving me the insight to write that letter.

Melinda was glowing with happiness when I told her that I was taking her out for her birthday. Once we got into the Karaoke bar she realized why I had taken her there. I bought her favorite drink, and to make her comfortable I asked her to join me singing one of my favorite songs, "Sweet Home Alabama."

Melinda proved that she could carry a tune. On the way home she demonstrated that she also had human qualities when she said, "I appreciate what you did for my birthday. Thank you for taking me out to sing, you made my wish come true on my birthday. That was very special, I didn't expect it."

The next day she was still in a pleasant mood, and she made dinner for Sally and me and the three of us had a good time talking about the man of our dreams. I don't believe that Melinda is a lesbian like Sally told me. I think that Melinda is just looking for attention.

After taking Melinda out for her birthday she has been more amicable towards me, so much so that she invited me to go out dancing to her favorite bar where she had met someone about two weeks ago. She wanted me to meet Tom and let her know what I thought of him. I felt like an experienced woman of the world. Of course Sally couldn't go out dancing with us, her Church would not approve.

Once again I found out that the bar scene is not for me. The music was too loud. Being half deaf made it difficult for me to hear Melinda. I yelled out to her that I would be on the dance floor and she yelled back, "You don't have to yell, I can hear you."

Neither Melinda nor Sally know that I'm partially deaf. I hear fine on a one-to-one basis, it only becomes difficult when there's a lot of noise around me; then I'm completely at a loss. I decided to spend the night dancing, that way I would not have to deal with trying to figure out what someone might say to me.

About twenty minutes later Melinda waved at me from the bar to come and join her, but I made believe that I didn't see her and kept dancing. Finally she came to the dance floor, grabbed my arm, and took me to the bar with her. She introduced me to Tom, and I did my usual thing when I don't hear; I smiled and nodded to everything he said. Tom was an average-looking guy, and I had to wonder what he saw in Melinda. She was wearing her lowest-cut blouse, so I figured that he liked short, red-haired women with huge breasts. I also noticed that Melinda was flirting more with him than he was with her. When Melinda excused herself to go to the bathroom he must have felt that I was in line for his affection. I could hardly hear anything he was saying with the loud music over our heads. I was nodding and saying the usual, "What? What?"

He got really close to me, and I felt his breathing on my face as he said in my ear, "I really like you."

"Thanks." I didn't know what else to say.

"Do you like big-band music?"

I hate big-band music but I couldn't bring myself to tell the truth. "Yes, it's very nice."

I stood up to go back to the dancing floor as I was feeling self-conscious not being able to hear anything he was saying unless he had his mouth by my ear. He stood up too, and put his arm around my waist just as Melinda was walking towards us.

"I was just going to ask Veronica to dance," he said, sheep-like.

"Can't wait for me to leave so that you can make out after my girlfriend, hum? Well, we are leaving."

Surprisingly enough she was not angry with me; instead she thanked me for going out with her to the bar, because it had helped her make up her mind about Tom. She knew now that he was the wrong man for her. Now she is sure that her best bet is the guy she met over the Internet a month ago. He meets her requirements when it comes to being her prince charming. She told me that she has this thing for tall, heavyset men, and a jelly-belly really turns her on. I don't know if she is saying that because the guy she met on the Internet is out of shape. Maybe she feels more secure with someone that is not attractive. Her Internet man is six feet tall and, according to his own description, he is quite large. He told her that he likes the idea that Melinda is short and also on the heavy side. If Melinda is happy, that's all that matters.

After thirty years of marriage, I finally had a regular conversation with Al on the phone that lasted five minutes, and when we hung up I was not angry with him. I believe this happened because we are away from each other. It's not that I'm a negative person, but this was definitely a fluke. Al never pays any attention to what anyone tells him, including myself of course. It's just the way he is, he doesn't do that on purpose, but if he pays attention he will respond by criticizing. If I really loved him I would be happy near him no matter how many faults he has. When a person is in love he or she is blind to their loved one's faults. I only know that the thought of going back to New Jersey makes me want to cry.

I stayed home Sunday, studying, and couldn't help noticing that Sally was seated quietly by the window twirling her chair slowly around and around. I was seated at the dining room table, which is where I always study since I don't have a table in my bedroom. Someone knocked at the front door and I opened it. It was two young men about Sally's age dressed in black suits, white shirts, and black ties. One of them carried a small attaché case. I thought they were insurance people selling something, but Sally was expecting them as she welcomed them to come in and sit down on the couch.

"Do you want me to leave?" I asked.

"No, I'd rather you stay." Her eyes were also asking me not to leave.

Sally sat in a regular chair across from them and was visibly uncomfortable as she wriggled her hands on her lap. I have to admit that I was a bit curious and I was paying more attention to what they were saying than my studies.

They talked about church matters and then one of them asked, "So tell me Sister Sally, have you had any sinful thoughts lately?"

I couldn't believe what I had heard, these two guys were as old as her and they were asking her very personal questions.

"Sometimes I do." She answered them honestly. "I think about a boy that I know in school."

One of them said, "You will need to repent to clean yourself from damnation."

I'd had enough. I got up and asked to be excused. I went into my bedroom and started playing my guitar softly. A while later I heard a knock on my bedroom door, it was Sally crying. "They left. You can come out if you want."

I decided to stay in my bedroom. I didn't want to ask why she was crying. I figured the two young men had made her feel like dirt and given her some kind of penance for having the normal feelings of a human being.

I am finally done with the finals in Chemistry and Physics. God willing, I have passed these classes.

Tomorrow morning I will be driving back to New Jersey. Rosanna called tonight to remind me to take something from Melinda's room so that she can suffer for what she did to me.

I am in North Carolina and I am using another free coupon to spend the night at the Holiday Inn. I have with me a large bottle of water for drinking, and I am not taking a shower tonight, not with the polluted water they have here.

I got here pretty quickly by following the truck drivers on the highway. Sometimes I pass them, other times I'll drive side-by-side flirting with the drivers and listening to the loud music on my radio. The idea is not to fall asleep behind the wheel and to have fun at the same time. "And I will always love you, I will always love you my darling…"

Both Melinda and Sally had already left for school when I left their apartment this morning. I had my car packed and ready to start my trip back to New Jersey within an hour and a half after I got up. Reluctantly, I went into Melinda's bedroom to take something that she would miss, like Rosanna had told me to do. I stood inside Melinda's bedroom for a few minutes hearing Rosanna's voice in back of my mind, "Go ahead Ronnie. Take Melinda's favorite jewelry. Take her favorite teddy bear; that will definitely break her heart."

But I don't want to steal anything, and I don't want to make Melinda suffer, I kept saying to myself. So what the heck am I doing standing in her bedroom against my will? I am almost forty-nine years old and I still have no backbone? I am still unable to stand up for what I believe in? Is this the way I will be going through life, like a good little girl, always doing what people tell me to do? Don't I have some form of self-respect?

I took a deep breath as I left her bedroom and closed the door behind me, saying to myself, I am who I am, and I choose not to do harm.

I walked out of the apartment feeling like I had finally grown up to stand on my own. When Rosanna asks me what I took with me, I will tell her the truth, nothing was taken because that was my choice. Like Papa used to say with pride before he retired from his job, "I will not even take a stamp out of my office unless I pay for it. When I sleep at night I have a clean conscience."

I confess that I am not as honest as my father. I have become aware of my large collection of pens and pencils taken from banks, stores, or anyplace they give me one to sign something or another. I also collect at least one towel from each hotel or motel where I stay overnight. It is a traditional practice that started when I came to the US in 1962. I don't want to blame anyone but the truth is that Nelly, my mother-in-law and Al, were the ones that told me that hotels expect their guests to leave with at least one or two towels and they are already included in the price of the room.

~ Chapter Six ~

College, Dating, and Sex

Lakewood, New Jersey

Spring of 1993

Having to live with Al until the summer is more than I can bear. I am irritable, I have no patience with anything he says, and I am not a pleasant person to live with. The divorce proceedings have been dealt with and now we are just waiting for the final papers from the judge. We are two strangers living together, and I believe that it's mostly my fault since I am the one that wants out.

After three days at home I was going batty, so I went looking for a temporary job that could keep me busy until I leave for Georgia with Ralph. I thought it would be a good idea to look for a position in a chiropractic office, that way I can get an idea of what to expect when I open my own practice.

I stopped at a chiropractic office in Lakewood and they hired me as a physical therapist. When I showed concern for not having any experience, Dr. Smith, the chiropractor, told me not to worry; they are going to train me on the job. I am starting this Monday, and I have to buy a white nurse's two-piece uniform, preferably with pants.

Steve got married to Diane. She is truly a dream come true. Like they say in Portugal, she is precious. I can't believe that Steve is finally settling down. I always thought Ralph would be the first one to get married, but I was wrong. I believe that Diane and Steve are truly in love; consequently they will be very happy. They are having a baby at the end of July, which is going to be a boy. Finally I will be a grandmother, and Steve will have a family of his own.

The wedding was very intimate, and I got a chance to meet her parents and family. Diane's mom prepared all the food that was served, including the delicious homemade chocolate cakes. I really like Diane's family, her parents and her sisters are very kind and straightforward people and I recognize a certain familiarity in their culture since both her parents are German just like Papa. The wedding was performed in North Jersey where most of Diane's family lives. May God bless their union.

My working experience in the chiropractic office is not going well. The chiropractor is a crook and so are the two girls that work for him. He is not even a nice crook; he has an attitude problem which is complimented by the two women that work for him and the talking parrot that he has in his office.

I already applied for a government loan to pay my tuition at the College, but with Ralph's encouragement I also got the three letters of recommendation from friends, and several copies of newspaper clippings, awards, and letters where it shows my community involvement with minority groups. Like Ralph said, I have nothing to lose by applying for the Harvey Lilliard Scholarship. He really believes that I deserve to get the award. After I wrote a long introduction letter, I had Ralph proofread it, and he helped me to cut it down to two pages.

Dr. Smith wants me to enter patient visits onto the charts so that he can collect money for visits that were never provided. I am working for a very dishonest person. This is not right, and I am not happy with what's going on.

A patient came in and asked angrily, at the front desk, "I got some papers from the insurance company and noticed that you are charging them for dates when I was not in this office. What's going on?"

Susie answered unsympathetically, "Do you want to collect a good compensation for what you suffered in the car accident? Because the more money we show in care provided to you, the more money you get. But if you don't like that, I'll take those charges off to make you happy."

"Oh no, if by doing that I get more money, you go right ahead and charge them whatever you want."

I was very disappointed with the patient's greed.

When I went looking for Dr. Holdman, I found out that he had sold his practice and moved to Florida. In the evenings I hang out with Dr. Peruzzi, who is very happy that I am following in his footsteps. I have not told him about the chiropractor I work for; I am too embarrassed to tell him what's going on. I know he would tell me to quit.

Dr. Peruzzi took me to a chiropractic social meeting last night. They get together once a week to talk about chiropractic philosophy. At the gathering he made his opinion heard loud and clear, "It's demeaning to our profession the way modern chiropractors dress in jeans and a short sleeve tee-shirt when treating their patients."

The other chiropractors said they were going to dress the way they wanted. Dr. Peruzzi was very upset that they would not listen to him. He is a bit of a dictator, and very old fashioned, but at the same time I can see his point. He did look a lot more refined than the chiropractors in t-shirts.

He is so adamant about it though that when I met with him to go to the meeting he came down on me for wearing jeans. "A woman should always look like a lady and wear a dress or a skirt, particularly when she is going to be a doctor."

I felt like a child being reprimanded. If I want to feel that way I'll hang out with Al. If Dr. Peruzzi keeps it up I am going to stop visiting him

I also had a horrible experience that night, actually two bad experiences. The first one happened at the meeting when a plate of fresh strawberries was passed around the room and, instead of taking a small bite, I put the whole strawberry in my mouth. It looked ripe, but I found out it wasn't, so I had to open my mouth wider than usual. I heard my jaw pop on the right side, followed by sharp jaw pain. I believe that I now have what everybody calls TMJ. When I chew I hear a clicking, and it hurts too. I used to love listening to Aunt Heydee's clicking jaw as she ate next to me. I guess I liked it so much that God has given it to me.

The second tragedy that night happened when I was driving home. By the time I dropped Dr. Peruzzi off at his house and stayed talking with him, it was almost two in the morning when I left him. On the way home I took a short cut on an isolated road. I hit a pothole on the road and the car dropped on its back right tire, and then the front left tire blew out almost immediately. The car went off the road and into a ditch. It was fairly dark except for a beam of light coming from a building in the distance. I was scared being alone, but I knew that I had to start walking towards the light or spend the night in the car. The building was a gas station, and luckily it was open. The garage man would not let me use the phone inside. I had to use the payphone outside. I called the Saturn road-help number and the lady on the other side asked me if I was alone. She insisted on staying on the phone with me until help got there. Speedier than lightning they sent a tow truck, and they changed the tires and I was back on the road in no time. I am glad that I bought a Saturn!

I was going from one patient's room to another at the chiropractic office, putting heat-pads and Interferential Therapy on their spines and getting other patients ready to be adjusted, when suddenly I heard a scream, which I was convinced was coming from the annoying parrot in the office yelling his usual, "Help! Help! Get me the hell out of here! Help!"

I told the girls at the office that the parrot was very annoying and they didn't even bother to answer me. The yelling kept going on and I decided to go tell the parrot to shut up or else. As I went by the treatment rooms, I noticed that the sound of the parrot screaming was actually coming from the last room in the back of the hallway and not the chiropractor's office where they keep the parrot. When I walked in I saw that the patient's table had come up, and two of the electrodes had gone flying into the air while the other two, still stuck to his mid-back seemed to be electrifying him.

He was the one screaming, "Help! Help! Get me the hell out of here! Help!"

I always forewarn the patients not to play with any of the buttons on the adjusting table, even if they get bored. But sometimes they don't listen.

I got a short letter in the mail from Melinda, saying that she was marrying Jason, the guy from the Internet. They finally met, and it was love at first sight. He is very nice to her, and on their second date surprised her with a pair of soft slippers because he knows how sensitive her tiny feet are. She enclosed my deposit check and wished me luck. I am glad I chose not to take anything from her.

This is the week of good letters in the mail. Ralph and I received a letter from Life College in Georgia, I passed my classes, all our pre-requisites have been met, and we have been accepted. We can make plans to start school together next month. We also got a letter from Judge Buczynski. My divorce is now final.

Dr. Smith tells all his patients that he is against drugs, but he is a hypocrite. He has me go to his red sports car parked in back of his building to get his prescription drugs, as he always forgets to bring them in with him. He is probably taking tranquilizers because he is extremely hyper and neurotic.

About twice a week he sends me out on a very specific errand. He gives me about three to four thousand dollars in cash, and I am to go to the post office or the bank and change it into cashier's checks. He is putting the cashier's checks in a security box in his office, and he hopes to get enough money together to open a restaurant. He said that he is sorry that he never became a surgeon, because then he would be making a lot more money. He is a disgrace to the human race!

The two girls in the office are snotty to me and so is Dr. Smith. Yesterday he threw his car keys at me, and when I didn't catch them in time he laughed along with Susie and Marcia, his workers, saying, "Look at those slow reflexes! You are definitely retarded."

I felt like I was being emotionally abused. Even if it is true that I am retarded as he says, he has no right to make fun of someone for his or her physical inabilities. If he doesn't like the way I am, he should fire me.

Dr. Smith yelled at me because I didn't enter into the charts that all the patients had come in for care that day. I don't like to be yelled at, and out of desperation for the way he treats me I wrote on the charts that those patients had been there every day of the week. Then I asked him sarcastically, "Is this what you want me to do?"

He looked at one of the charts and without blinking an eye, said, "Exactly. Now you are doing your job!"

I was angry when I heard him say that, and to make things worse, he told me that he wanted me to start doing patients X-rays that morning. I followed him into the X-ray room.

He placed the patient against the wall-plate and then grabbed my arm and took me behind a metal partition saying, "Go ahead press that button and then the other one."

"I have never done X-rays. Shouldn't I first learn what the buttons are for?"

"You ask too many questions. Just do what I am telling you."

I don't like X-rays; it's too medical and invasive in my opinion. Besides all that, I didn't feel safe being in his X-ray room. What if his old equipment was leaking radioactive material?

"Am I not supposed to have some kind of a license to do this type of work?" I was also curious.

He got angry and pushed me against the machine with his huge body as he pressed the buttons himself. Then he released me, saying, "Get out of here."

I was glad to get out of there.

Every morning Dr. Smith has daily staff meetings, and it's all about reinforcing his crooked business. I found out that all his present clientele are coming directly from referrals by a specific lawyer in Freehold. If anyone comes to our office without mentioning the lawyer in Freehold and asks if Dr. Smith is in, we are to say that, he doesn't work there. The building he owns has already been put under his mother's name so it can't be taken away from him. Whatever is going on, I don't want to be part of it. I want my paycheck that is due to me, and to quit this job.

Rosanna asked me to wait a week before I quit. She wants to do some investigating of her own. She is going to visit the lawyer that Dr. Smith is working with, and act as if she was in a car accident and see what he does.

Rosanna called me to tell me her experience with the lawyer was very interesting. He was very nice to her, and finished the meeting by handing her Dr. Smith's card and stating that he encouraged her to have regular chiropractic care with Dr. Smith. Rosanna said that the lawyer was very charismatic, and if she had been the victim of a real car accident most likely she would be seeing Dr. Smith.

She also asked me to allow her to write my letter of resignation to Dr. Smith and to his staff, since she is a writer by nature, she would get a lot of pleasure out of that. After she writes the letters, I can sign them.

I'd really rather write the letters myself, but I don't have the courage to say that. I am a lot more self-confident now than I have ever been, but I am still far from being assertive.

I wonder when I'm going to learn my lesson and stop going to medical doctors. I should know by now that they are going to hurt me one way or another. I consider myself lucky when everything goes without any tribulations. I just thought that it would be a good idea to see my regular gynecologist and get a clean bill of health.

"It looks good. You are in good shape, nice and clean," Commented Dr. Madison.

The next morning I woke up with a serious white vaginal discharge. How could I be perfectly healthy one evening and the next day I had what I believed to be a serious yeast infection?

I called Dr. Madison's office. He wasn't in, and I was told by his nurse to go to the hospital immediately. I walked into the emergency room like a cowboy, with my legs bowlegged. I was very sore and itching like crazy.

"I've never seen a yeast infection this bad!" said the emergency room doctor. "How long have you been this way?"

"I woke up this morning with it. I was fine yesterday. As a matter of fact, I saw the gynecologist yesterday, in the afternoon, and he even remarked how good everything was."

"Are you married?"

"If you are thinking that I got it from my husband, I can tell you that would be impossible. We have no sex."

"Well, if you were fine when you went to the gynecologist, that tells me that you got infected in his office."

"Maybe he forgot to clean the instruments used on the patient before me? Is that possible?"

"You didn't hear this from me, but that is most likely what happened to you."

I was very upset and when they asked me to pay for the hospital visit I called Dr. Madison's office right then and there and told his nurse what happened. I told her that I was putting the responsibility for paying for my hospital bill and the medicine I needed in Dr. Madison's hands. They were liable for all the bills I had incurred as a result of my visit to his office. She put me on hold for about five minutes and said that their office would take care of all the expenses. She was actually very nice about it.

The doctor at the hospital told me that if I use the vaginal cream he prescribed every night before going to bed, in a week it would all be gone.

Since my last experience at the gynecologist I have started thinking about the need for a Pap smear, once a year. If it's true that this test is done to rule out cancer of the cervix, why are they doing that to me? I don't have a cervix or a uterus!

This realization hit me today. Either they don't read the charts with my medical history where I put down that I had a partial hysterectomy — due to a medical error many years ago — or they are doing the procedure blindly without any idea of what they are doing. Maybe Al is right and I'm getting senile, because I'm starting to think that perhaps they do read my chart but are lying when they know well in advance that there's nothing to "smear" about.

What a jerk I have been, going for a Pap smear twice a year. Well, at least I've wised up.

Rosanna wrote what I consider three of the most hateful letters I've ever read. One was directed to Dr. Smith's dishonest conduct and his obnoxious parrot. The other two letters were very specifically addressed to each girl in his office. I have come to the conclusion that Rosanna has a lot of anger inside her. She doesn't get along with her family, and I believe that writing gives her the opportunity to air out her personnel frustrations. I took the three letters to the chiropractor's office and put them in his mailbox along with a note stating that I would be back after their lunchtime to pick up my paycheck and I had no intentions of returning to work. I was at their front door at two exactly, and one of the girls came out and handed me my paycheck without a word.

When I got home, there was a very disturbing message from Dr. Smith on our answering machine.

"This is Dr. Smith and I just called you Ronnie to wish you a happy, but short, life."

After that message I got on the phone and called a few insurance companies and also the New Jersey Board of Chiropractors and shared with them my experience as an employee of Dr. Smith.

Summer of 1993

I bought a really nice thick mattress from Crazy Joe's Furniture store to take with me to College. After so many years of borrowing his furniture for the productions at The Simy Dinner Theatre at no cost to us, it's only fair that any furnishings I need I should buy them from him. Ralph and I are leaving New Jersey next week, to be exact, on June twenty-fifth.

Al insists on driving with us to Georgia. He is staying until July second, and then he will take the train back to New Jersey. We will be staying in a hotel while looking for an apartment to rent, hopefully close to the College.

The day before leaving for Georgia, the delivery truck company picked up all our essentials, like Ralph's television and his computer, the new microwave, our mattresses and bed frames, the dining room table and chairs, kitchen stuff, clothing, and so on that we will need for the next four years while attending Chiropractic College. The dispatcher for the trucking company said they will have everything delivered to our door as early as June twenty-ninth. We only have to call them with our new address when we get to Smyrna, Georgia.

I went to the Kobe Japanese Restaurant to say goodbye to everyone, but I didn't go upstairs to the theatre. I didn't want to feel sad. I also didn't go to Westwood Greens where I used to work. I didn't want to say goodbye again. I did visit my closest friends Francis, Tracey, Rosanna, and Barbara. Tracey was upset with me for getting a divorce from Al, saying that he is a great guy and I am wrong to leave him after all the years of marriage. She has no idea of what it's like to live with someone that you have nothing in common with and I didn't bother to give her the details. Francis and Rosanna are the only ones that know and understand my dilemma.

We took turns driving. Ralph and I did a lot of talking and dreaming about our future together as students, and then as chiropractors. We plan to work together after we graduate. Al slept most of the time. We drove straight through to Georgia. When we got to Smyrna we were not only tired, but also hungry. We couldn't help notice a large sign on a building that read, "Go-Go Buffet Special."

It wasn't a family restaurant. The girls were naked except for the bottom of a very small bikini, and they were dancing around metal poles. Interesting though what hunger does to people, we didn't care that they were basically naked. All we wanted was food! We sat down to eat, and I couldn't help notice how one girl was dancing around a guy that I thought might be her boyfriend — since she was dancing almost on his lap — but he was more interested in looking at the other girls dancing on the platform than paying attention to her. What a horrible job; no matter how pretty you are, the men are still looking at the other girls. I felt sorry for the dancer.

As soon as we finished eating we left to go looking for a hotel for the night. Ralph commented that we must have looked like a typical family, because none of the dancers came by our table to have us put money in their little panties.

Marietta, Georgia

We spent the next day looking for an apartment without any luck. Al was bored and agreed with us that he was better off leaving the next morning, back to New Jersey.

As soon as Al left, Ralph and I went to the College admissions office to make sure everything was going well with our student loans. That's when I found out that I had been granted a full-year Scholarship. I remained seated, and reacted very properly as I smiled back at the lady in the admission's office.

When we left the building it finally hit me and I started jumping up and down cheerfully.

"Oh, my God!" I finally screamed out. "Oh, my, God! I can't believe it!"

Ralph was laughing. "I was starting to worry when you acted so calmly."

"Yeah, I was too dumfounded for any form of reaction." And I kept jumping and screaming until I ran out of breath.

We celebrated by going to a barbeque restaurant called Pig-n-Chik, where we had a delicious southern meal of pulled pork.

The first time I got sprayed with pesticides I was taking a walk at a bird refuge in south Jersey. A helicopter hovering over the area was crop-dusting the field where I was standing. I ran as fast as I could to get into my car, but no matter how much I held my breath I could still feel the taste in my mouth and the smell up my nostrils. The second time, just a few years later, I was walking in Lakewood, New Jersey and they were dropping the "stuff," also from a helicopter, but that time I saw the yellow dust coming down, and once I recognized the smell I ran into a shop in time to get away from the dusting. Why they do that when there are people on the ground I will never know, but it is to my benefit that now I recognize the odor. Now I'm an expert at recognizing the smell of insecticide spray in corn as well as in fruit and vegetables that have been sprayed for bugs. I always take a whiff first, before I buy anything from the fresh produce department in the food stores. Once again, this knowledge has been to my benefit when Ralph and I were checking for apartments around the College.

He was ready to take the last apartment we saw, but I told him, no way. It was below the ground floor, and the sunlight barely made it through the narrow windows. Along with the cold dampness inside the apartment, I could also smell the familiar smell of insecticide in the air. As if that was not enough, the apartment was cold, dark, and smelly. When I opened one of the kitchen drawers, I was horrified to find a mummified cockroach covered in white paint. That did it for me.

Ralph said I was too picky and it didn't matter what the apartment looked like, because we would be spending the days in school anyway.

I told him we had one more place to look at, and then I was willing to settle for whatever.

The next apartment complex was it for both of us. It had a swimming pool, hot tub, laundry room and beautiful garden surroundings. The apartment complex is less than one mile away from the college. What more can we ask for? We can walk to school if our cars break down, and the apartment is like new, fresh and clean. It is on the ground floor, and I know that Ralph would rather be on the second or third floor for safety, but it has sliding glass doors from the living room to a private patio, and I love the idea of sunshine at my doorstep. The kitchen is small but very modern with a counter peninsula big enough that we can use it to eat on. There's a dining room, one nice master bedroom with a private bathroom that Ralph immediately said was his, and another bedroom with a full bathroom across from it. There are windows everywhere and plenty of sunshine; I also like the modern white window shades, for privacy. The rent is $400 a month, that means $200 each and that includes all utilities.

I feel like I am in paradise, surrounded by beautiful flowers and tropical greens all around the grounds. We are very fortunate! Ralph called the moving company to give them our new address, and their secretary said that this Monday they would deliver all our things to our new residence.

We bought ourselves two high stools so that we can sit by the kitchen counter to eat and to study. Next, we went shopping for a few summer clothes at Goodwill, and while there we came across two thick foam pieces, for five bucks each, to sleep on until our mattresses arrive.

Thank God we were smart enough to bring with us some towels, blankets, and our pillows.

Ralph called the moving company on Tuesday and they apologized and promised that next week everything would be delivered to our apartment. We have no dishes, no pots to cook with, but it's sinful to buy anything when we know that next week we will have all our stuff. We did buy a large, deep, frying pan that we use for cooking just about everything.

Ralph bought his new car today. It's a red Plymouth Duster, not my favorite look for a car, but he is happy with it, and that's what counts. He likes the way it drives and also how much power it has on taking off. My Saturn is very nice, but when it comes to taking off it's a real stick-in-the-mud.

I found out why I couldn't find directions for driving north when I first got here. Ralph and I came to the conclusion that the word North doesn't exist here in the South.

Ralph and I have been studying together. Whenever I have a question, he is ready to help. He is even smarter than I thought, he can read something and he's got it. I am very blessed to have Ralph as my roommate and friend. We are taking the same classes. Our first quarter classes include Embryology, Osteology, Histology, Anatomy & Physiology and Lab., Public Health, Clinical Experience, Health Care Terminology, Introduction to Chiropractic Philosophy, and Introduction to Business Principles I. They don't teach the Toggle Adjusting Technique until I'm in the fourth quarter. I can't wait.

Besides being study buddies, Ralph and I have lots of good heart-to-heart talks about life.

"Ralph, I don't know how to go about it, but I don't want to go back to Dad. I want the divorce to be permanent."

"When I get back to New Jersey, during the next break, I'll talk to him about it."

"I am scared that he will come down to Georgia and kill me, but I am so miserable living with him that I am willing to take that chance."

"Mom, you are so dramatic. Dad is not going to kill you. Once I explain, he will understand that this is your decision, that's all."

"Tell your father that he can have the condo and all its contents."

"Stop worrying about it. I'll tell him you want the divorce to be final and that's all. Everything is going to be all right."

I am very lucky that both Ralph and Steve are aware of the situation between Al and me and understand how I feel.

I called Steve, and he promised to be with Ralph when they both convey my request to Al.

I hope Ralph is right that Al will not come down to Georgia and shoot me in the head. I sure don't want to gain my freedom and then die.

I have finally grown up and I need to go in a different direction by myself, that's all.

Ralph doesn't want to study with me anymore; he says that if he keeps tutoring me I'll never become independent.

I have accepted that I have to study on my own. I feel sad and kind of abandoned, but I also understand that he can learn things a lot faster than at my speed of learning. I am most likely dragging him down.

I bought myself a long folding table to use as my desk and a cheap metal chair and put them in the empty living room. Ralph got himself situated in his bedroom with a smaller table and a chair. We are both still sleeping on the foam pieces and waiting for our stuff to be delivered to us. The days go by in class and the evenings at home studying. If I have a question regarding something that I don't understand, Ralph is still willing to explain it to me, but he no longer holds my hand while I am studying, he wants me to figure things out by myself.

This week, Mitchell, one of the older students at school, dropped dead while walking to one of his classes. He was only fifty-nine years old. Everybody who knew Mitchell stated that he was always too stressed out and that was probably the reason he died. After that happened, Sarah, one of my classmates, who is sixty-two years old, told me she didn't care if the same happened to her because at least she is living her dream of being a chiropractor. And she was quick to add with a smile in her eyes, "If that happens to me, I won't have to pay my student loan!"

If I am not in school, I am at home studying into the wee hours of the night. With English being my second language, and my loss of hearing being a learning disability in a crowded classroom, I have to work harder than anyone else if I'm going to make it.

After studying all day Saturday I got up early Sunday morning to continue my studies, in preparation for a test early the next morning. It was about noon when I felt a strange fluttering of my heart. I checked my pulse and asked Ralph to check my pulse too.

He said it was wiser if he drove me to the emergency room. An exam was performed and then they asked me to stay in bed and wait for the results. While waiting I took the opportunity to go over the Embryology notes, which I had eagerly taken along. I had my notes all over the bed and was intensely looking them over. When I looked up, the doctor was standing by the doorway staring at me. He pulled up a chair and sat next to my bed.

"What are you doing?" He asked puzzled.

"I'm studying for tomorrow's test. I can't waste any time."

"How long have you been in school?" He gently took the book from my hand.

"Almost a month. I have a test next week…"

He interrupted me and said with a smile, "I have good news, and bad news. First let me tell you the good news. There's nothing wrong with your heart. Now for the bad news, you are suffering from stress, and you are not going to make it at the speed you are going."

Then he gave me the best advice any doctor can give their patient. "If you don't take care of yourself and take one day a week to rest, you will soon return to this hospital, and I can't promise in what state of health you will be. Take a walk in the park on Saturday or Sunday. Go out for dinner or to a movie. Do something else besides consuming yourself with studying. Get a life! You will do a lot better when you take a test."

I thought about what happened to Mitchell and decided to follow the doctor's advice. From now on, I'm taking a day off from studying and doing something special for myself.

Every weekend I take either Saturday or Sunday off from studying. I have started taking walks in the park next to a river not even half an hour drive from where we live. I like it there because it's got a lot of people hiking or walking their pets, and it's fun to watch the dogs swimming after the sticks their owners throw in the water. There are lots of kids playing and joggers all around including a guy who is proud of walking with his pet pig on a leash.

Monday night, Ralph and I are treating ourselves to a Middle Eastern restaurant in downtown Atlanta. We had never been to one, except for the one in North Africa — but that doesn't mean we're going to have the same experience. We are taking advantage of a coupon offer we got in the mail; buy one dinner and receive the second meal free.

There were no chairs or tables at the restaurant. They had us seated cross-legged on pillows around a small table where they put an array of exquisite food in small dishes for us to eat with our hands. That was the best part of it, to be able to eat without the conservative rules of table manners dictated by the society we live in which states what is proper or not. We were both laughing and having a good time using our fingers to pick up each delicious morsel, even the wet dripping ones. Putting our cares aside as to how messy it could get, we made use of the white towel on our shoulders, provided by our attentive waiter who encouraged us to use it to dry our hands on, after he poured rose water over our greasy hands. I had never seen belly-dancers performing, but they weren't going to start dancing until eleven at night, and sadly enough, we had to leave to go home since we both had early morning classes. I'll never forget this dinner. Being out with Ralph is always fun. I am a very lucky mother.

Ralph and I are taking turns calling the moving company every week, and their latest is that they will get back to us as soon as possible, as they are trying to find out what the delay is about. Then as they always do, they assured us that next week, most likely, they would be making the delivery.

Leila is in some of my classes, and since we are good friends I confided in her how much Ralph and I are upset at the poor quality of teachers at this College. We are very, very disillusioned. Russell, one of our classmates, who used to be an engineer, just like Ralph, is also very disappointed. They are always talking about how — if they had a chance — they would choose another college. But Russell is married and has a child. It would be very difficult for him to just pack and go. He has a house and a mortgage, and besides his roots are here, in Georgia with his family.

I'm starting to get worried that Ralph may want to quit school because he told me that he is starting to believe that he made a mistake wanting to be a chiropractor.

Ralph finally convinced me to go out with him to a bar. I was a nervous wreck, thinking about what to say if someone started talking to me, and what if it was too noisy. I would not be able to hear a thing.

The club was packed with people, the majority being students from the College. I was Ralph's partner in a game of pool against two other students. After the second game Ralph went to talk to some of the girls at the bar, and I was left walking around acting like I belonged.

There was no dancing floor, so I couldn't hide. The feeling of being alone in a crowd and having one drunken student trying to make-out with me was more than I could stand. I decided that nightclubs of that kind were not for me and I told Ralph afterwards what I thought of the place.

"Mom, you are single now, if you are going to meet someone you need to learn to be more forward. When you see somebody you like, just go up to that person and start a conversation."

"Ralph, I've never dated and I am not good at starting conversations with someone I've never met."

"You need to lose your fears. When we go out; start practicing."

Sure, that's easy for him to say. He is a guy. I can just see myself going up to someone seated at a bar and saying, "Hi, my name is Veronica. So, do you come here often? Oh yeah, I should also tell you that it's too noisy here, so don't bother talking to me because I can't hear you."

I am not going back to that club or any other club. I don't drink.

Leila is still struggling with the curriculum. We count on each other for moral support and it's always easy to talk to her but a week doesn't go by that she doesn't call on the phone to say that she would like to come over to talk. Of course she is always welcome to stop by. Ralph gets upset, saying that she is interrupting my studies, and he is right. Sometimes she is, but I don't have the courage to tell her not to bother me when I am studying. Friends are supposed to help each other. Knowing how nice she is, I know that she would do the same for me.

Ralph is absolutely amazing. He spends most of his free time talking on the phone to friends, goes out at night, sleeps during the boring classes in school, and then at twelve midnight he makes an announcement, "I have to study for the exam tomorrow, I am not to be bothered." Then he closes his bedroom door and studies through the night. In the morning we both go into the testing center, and he whizzes through the test. I, on the other hand, have to study daily like my life depended on it in order to pass my tests. The only class that I am a wiz in is Healthcare Terminology. Those three years of high school in Portugal learning Latin have paid off.

Mama is in the hospital once again. She is constantly going to the hospital and fighting between life and death. After she gets out of the hospital she sends me poems about kicking death in the butt. Personally, I think that if death wants someone it isn't going to ask permission, but if Mama believes that she has such power over death, then good for her, because it's working.

We finished our first quarter! Or I should say we survived our first quarter of neglectful teaching. We were basically on our own during those three months, since everything we learned was self taught from the books we bought. Some of the teachers wouldn't show up for classes, and others were right-out wackos on chiropractic philosophy. Ralph had a lot of trouble coping with such ignorant morons for teachers, because he is more intelligent than me. But once we got to the party at Sylvia's house — one of the students at the college — it was time to celebrate the end of the first quarter with glee.

I was on a natural high, everybody was having fun drinking, laughing, joking, and lots of good food was on hand since it was a potluck party. I had never been to a potluck party before, and I really liked the idea of everybody bringing their best homemade dish. I also noticed that everyone left their shoes in the hallway before entering Sylvia's house. My goodness, I had tried to implement that idea a few times at home, and Al wouldn't go for it. But it makes a lot of sense not to track in the dirt from outside onto the carpets. Ralph also liked the idea, keeping the carpet clean means less to worry about when we move out.

One girl at the party announced that she was using the next few days off to drive to one of the beaches along the coast and read a few novels. I couldn't believe it! Three months of reading has been enough for me! Nothing with letters is going to even come close to my eyes. I am going to clean up the apartment and do nothing, absolutely nothing, during school break. I need to rest my brain in preparation for the second quarter of hard work.

I was seated at a bench at one of Sylvia's back porch tables, munching away on a full plate of yummy food, when a slim, tall student, almost as old as me, with a pale face that was far from handsome, sat next to me. We started talking, and when we finished eating we sat on the cool grass and talked to each other for most of the night. Good thing that we were outside, otherwise I would not have heard a word Dexter spoke. The music was extremely loud, and so was the loud gabbing inside the house.

It was a really wonderful experience to talk to someone so interesting and of the opposite sex and yet feel so comfortable about it. I was wishing we could be friends forever while in school, but I accepted that most likely we would never see each other again. He will be starting first quarter next semester and the school is enormous. It was getting late, and Ralph had to get back home since he was leaving early in the morning to New Jersey. Dexter said it would be great if we could exchange phone numbers and stay in touch. I wrote my name and phone number on a napkin and gave it to him, He did the same and I slipped the napkin into my coat pocket.

When we got home I gave Ralph a letter asking Al to give me the divorce for real. Because Ralph would be leaving very early in the morning to New Jersey we said our goodbyes.

I got up late this morning to find that Ralph had already left for New Jersey. I paid a visit to our apartment's main office and asked them if they could give me some white paint so that I could touch up some of the walls in the apartment. They said they never had a renter offer to do such a thing, but they were more than glad to supply the paint and brush. I touched up some of the spots in the hallway with paint, cleaned the kitchen until everything was shiny, and then borrowed a vacuum cleaner from my neighbor. One day's work was all I needed to clean the apartment, which is still empty of furnishings.

Everybody from school is gone; it's like a ghost town, even Sarah and Leila left. After dinner I sat on my foam mattress staring at the bedroom walls, and then realized that I'm only half way down to Florida, and I would be a fool not to take advantage of this opportunity to enjoy some free time on my own. I called Steve and told him I was heading to Florida for the next four days.

He said I was nuts to go by myself because carjacking was rampant down south. I told him not to worry, because I will have my buddy Joe with me.

Joe is a stuffed male doll, I ordered last month from one of those crime safety magazines. It arrived at our apartment this morning like an omen telling me to go wherever I wish because I have protection. Joe has a rough young looking face, good strong neck, shoulders and torso like a body builder, but his legs and arms hang limp. That's fine though, in the passenger's seat he looks quite real with sunglasses, a blue cap hat, and a sailor's shirt I bought at Goodwill. Everything fits him like a glove. I paid one hundred dollars for Joe and he will be my bodyguard on the road to Florida.

Eight hours later I was in an Orlando hotel and on my way to Disney World. After apologizing to Joe for what I was about to do, I put him inside my car trunk. He will become my traveling companion once again when we both drive back to Georgia. The only nasty things I found driving to Florida were the little ugly black insects called love bugs. By the hundreds, they splashed against the front of my car, causing a sticky clogging mess.

I spent the next day at Universal Studios, which I had heard so much about. I particularly liked the ET ride, which I shamelessly went on three times. Between Disney World and Epcot, my favorite was Epcot, where I bought an Asian-style blue ring for five dollars at one of the stores in the Asian Pavilion. I took my time walking through Epcot's World Showcase and then settled down for dinner at a restaurant in the Norway Pavilion where their buffet included my very favorites, cold herring in vinaigrette and herring with raw sliced onions and cream sauce. For dessert I gorged myself on a large piece of dark chocolate cake because I had not eaten chocolate for a long time. I reasoned with myself that maybe, just maybe, I was no longer allergic to chocolate. Afterwards, I went back to the hotel to pick up a jacket since I wanted to spend the night at Pleasure Island. I didn't know what the weather was going to be like at night.

I was waiting for the elevator to take me up to my floor along with a man that looked like a young Robert Redford. He was obviously there for some kind of business meeting, as he was well dressed. He said hello to me I said hello back. When we entered the elevator he asked me where I was from and, like everybody else does, he mentioned how much he liked my accent. Robert was very charming, and in view of the fact that he showed an interest in me, I felt I could get away being a little flirtatious, besides I would be getting out on the next floor.

On the way to Pleasure Island I was wishing that the man in the elevator and I could meet again. I would not mind hanging out with him for a little while, that would prove to me that Michael was out of my life forever. I convinced myself that I was having lots of fun walking around Pleasure Island by myself, and it was late when I finally sat at one of their bars acting like a woman-of-the-world and asked for a light beer and corn on the cob. I knew that I was a fool to order a beer, when I can't handle alcohol of any kind, but I didn't care, I was alone and slightly gloomy. Even the bartender asked if I was okay. I ate the corn and drank half the beer. I got into my car wondering if I was going to find my way back to the hotel.

I was walking in the hotel lobby towards the elevator when a miracle happened. Out of the elevator came Robert, a very coincidental first name, I should say. He was on his way downstairs to get some soda. We started talking, and he said something like it was one thirty in the morning so why stand in the hallway when we could go to his room and talk there. I may be naïve, but I am not that dumb.

"I don't go into a strange man's room to talk. Besides, it's getting late; bye, bye." Then I waved goodbye and started walking away. But I didn't really want to say adieu so I turned around and said something foolish like, "On second thought, I'm going to get my bathing suit and take a swim in the pool, if it's still open. Would you like to join me?"

He seemed to be delighted with the idea and proposed that we meet each other by the pool within the next fifteen minutes.

When I got downstairs Robert was already in the lobby and was wearing a towel wrapped around his waist. I couldn't help noticing his physique, and had no question in my mind that he worked out on a daily basis. He said he'd had to convince the night manager to allow us to use the swimming pool, which was already closed.

The swimming pool was outside, but warm from the pounding heat of the sun all day. I felt like I was in a water paradise as I let myself submerge as far as the back of my head. He dove into the pool and swam across twice. When he started coming into my direction I got this weird feeling of Robert turning into a shark. He put his hands on my shoulders and started massaging my back. I had told him that I was a chiropractic student, so he used that information to ask me if I was also learning massage at school. I immediately defended my future profession by stating that chiropractic was a technique of adjusting the spine and not soothing the muscles by massaging them. Then I swam away.

Once again he came close to me, but this time I didn't fight much as he held me in his arms, and we kissed. I closed my eyes as we kissed passionately and I thought about Michael. I was finally with Michael.

Then I heard him saying, "Let's take our bathing suits off."

"I don't see any reason to take my bathing suit off." And I moved away from him.

"Okay, okay, just let me hold you a little longer." He started kissing the base of my neck and then my lips as his arms were holding my body tight against his. I closed my eyes once again, trying to hold on to that blissful moment, hoping it would last forever. He slowly pulled my bathing suit straps off my shoulders, but I honestly didn't mind.

He said, "You have the most beautiful breasts I've ever seen."

I was thinking, what a fool he is, any woman in water would have beautiful breasts, because they tend to float upwards. I said thank you for the compliment. Then I opened my eyes and saw his face, a stranger's face. It wasn't Michael; it was the man I had met in the elevator. The water suddenly felt cold, I was shivering. I ran out of the pool and, wrapping myself in my towel, I ran into the elevator. He caught up with me as I pushed myself into the corner of the elevator. He stayed on the opposite side, and then smiling at me he displayed himself like a little boy showing his trophy. I looked at him like, you have got to be kidding. He must have read my mind because he immediately covered himself. As the elevator door opened on my floor I ran out as fast as I could, and holding the key to my room I opened my door and quickly locked it. I waited a bit and when I didn't hear a knock I judged that I had lost Robert for good. I was wrong. Someone was knocking at my door. Shaking from head to toes I took a look through the peephole. It was Robert. He knocked a few more times, but I could tell by his face that he was not sure if he had the right room and I didn't open the door. Finally he walked away.

About half an hour later the phone rang; stupid me, I had to answer. Robert had gotten my room number from the manager downstairs, and he wanted us to spend the night together. I told him that I was sorry but it had been an error on my part to go swimming with him, and I didn't want to go any further. He wouldn't take no for an answer, so I told him my husband was sleeping in the room, and I couldn't talk.

"Are you kidding me?"

"No, I'm not." Then I lowered my voice as if I was afraid to be heard. "He is sleeping, but believe me when I say this, he is very mean when he is jealous. I have to go before he wakes up. I advise you not to call me again."

On the way to Georgia I thought about what happened in Florida, but I am not sorry for what I did. Now I understand completely what loneliness can do. Still, I consider myself lucky that I didn't fall in the hands of some crazy woman-hater. He could have squeezed my neck until I drowned. I could have joined the other poor lonely women of the world that have died; victims of the same circumstances. Just another newspaper headline, "Chiropractic student's body found floating in swimming pool in Florida." Or worse, "Mass pool-murderer kills his seventh victim."

A call was left on my answering machine at home. It was Dexter saying that he would call me again. I hope so, because the white paper napkin with his phone number is nowhere to be found, and I really need a friend more than ever.

I am paying dearly for the chocolate cake I ate in Florida and the two chocolate bars I munched on while driving back. I am a chocoholic. I will eat a little brownie and the next thing I know, I need more chocolate. I am aware of the consequences and yet I always find an excuse to eat it.

The pain is really, really bad today; it feels like knives stabbing both my legs. I am hoping that this horrible, excruciating pain will be ingrained deep into my brain so I will remember it when I want to eat chocolate in the future.

I'm very thankful to have a few more free days before classes start. It has given me the opportunity to get to know Dexter. He listens to what I have to say, and he responds enthusiastically to my ideas. On our first get-together he invited me to his apartment. He made dinner, and then we went to the movies. Not once did we even hold hands, but we talked a lot. I believe from the way he talks about himself not being like other guys that he might be gay, but that is fine with me if that's what he is. I find his personality irresistible. I have also come to the realization that I am not attracted to a man just because he is handsome, like the one I met in the elevator in Florida.

My parents are not doing well. Mama is back in the hospital. Papa came to the phone today, but he sounded very weak as he said that he barely had any strength for anything and did a lot of sleeping lately. He thinks that he may have some kind of virus.

Autumn of 1993

The first thing that Ralph said to me when he got back from New Jersey was that everything had been taken care of.

Steve and he took Al out for lunch, and together they told him that I wanted a bona fide divorce. He also gave Al the letter I had written explaining how I felt. Al was upset and hurt, but Ralph explained that it wasn't his fault. He told Al that when I got married I was very young and still inside a shell, but over the years I had grown out of it. I was no longer the same person he had married. Ralph couldn't have explained it better.

Al called me and said that he was still my friend and if I ever change my mind he will take me back. I am very lucky.

Ralph brought the official letter from Life Chiropractic College concerning my scholarship. It was dated June twenty-second. The mail must have arrived to New Jersey right after we left to Georgia on June twenty-fifth.

Dear Ms. Esagui:

The Scholarship Committee met today and reviewed your application for the Harvey Lilliard Scholarship. You have met all the criteria, and the Committee has voted to award you the Harvey Lilliard Scholarship, which is for tuition for four quarters (D.C. PROGRAM).

The Accounting Department will be notified to credit your account accordingly, and awards will be given out at an upcoming assembly.

Congratulations! Keep up the good work.

Sincerely,
Morris W. Lutes
Chairman, Scholarship Committee

I went to check out one of their meetings, and I was the only white woman.

My schoolmates Leila and Sarah believe that because Mr. Harvey Lilliard was black, and the committee members are black I'm going to stick out like a sore thumb. They say that between the two of them they can conceal my skin with a long dress and long sleeves, and all I have to do is darken my hands and face. I don't want to discourage them but that doesn't sound realistic to me.

Ralph told me not to worry; the award was not given to me because of my skin color but because of what I did with the minority groups in our community.

The tuition for the year has already been taken care by the Scholarship Committee, and I have their letter confirming the award. I don't see the necessity to personally meet them at an assembly gathering.

Our second quarter is going to be busier than the first quarter. We have Spinal Anatomy, Musculoskeletal Gross Anatomy, Motion Palpation & Static Palpation, Instrumentation, Spinal Biomechanics, Clinical Experience II, Chiropractic Assembly, History of Chiropractic, Cell & Neuromuscular Physiology, and Introduction to Business Principles II.

I asked Ralph as my friend to explain how a man can go out with a strange woman and not be bothered to have sex with her.

"The difference is that a man only needs a place and a woman needs a reason."

Wow! He is so smart. What an eye opener for me. That would explain to what happened in Florida.

I called my parents, but when I asked Alice to put my father on the phone, she said he was sleeping and shouldn't be disturbed. I told her that I insisted on talking to my father.

He came to the phone, but his words were hard to understand as he mumbled, "I don't know what's wrong with us, your mother and I, all we do is sleep. I can't even move my lips to speak to you. I feel like I'm drugged as if in a stupor."

I am worried about my parent's health and I don't know what to do about it. I called Aunt Coty and asked her to go see my parents and find out what's going on. She is going to call me back.

We have given up on calling the trucking company; they still have not delivered our stuff. Ralph decided to call the FBI.

They told him to wait a couple of days, they are already investigating this situation because there have been a lot of people calling them about the same problem.

Papa called very early this morning, his voice sounded normal again and he had a lot to tell me. I had been right about my brother's death, he said. Alice had murdered José with the drugs she gave him the morning he died. Of that Papa was now sure, and he was determined to prove it by having an autopsy done to José, even if Mama didn't approve of it.

He felt that if it weren't for Luisa, a new part time employee that my parents had hired a month ago to take care of them, they would have both been dead by now. Alice had been poisoning my parents just like she had my brother José. All those months that Papa was sleeping and feeling weak were the result of the drugs in his food. Alice was stealing from him by going to the German Embassy and telling them that Papa had given her authorization to pick up his monthly checks because he was too ill to get them himself. She was falsifying his signature and cashing the checks along with the checks in the mail sent by my cousins from England, and also stealing the cash I was sending to my parents inside my letters. Alice was robbing them of everything they had, as they were too frail and out of it to be aware of what was going on.

Luisa confided in Papa that she had witnessed Alice putting drugs in their food. She took Papa to the German Embassy, and that's how he found out that she was telling him the truth. Luisa and Papa came up with a plan on how to get rid of Alice.

Papa acted very nicely towards Alice and told her that she was to have a week off with vacation paid, because she deserved it after working so hard. Luisa would work that week and cover for Alice's absence. When Alice left, he immediately made arrangements with someone he knew and sold everything he and Mama owned inside the apartment, and then he called the landlord and told him that he would leave the apartment for a certain amount of cash. Everything got done within five days, and Papa got all the money together he made from selling everything, including his apartment, and put it in the bank. He is now happily living with Luisa and her family.

Alice's intention after getting rid of my parents was to keep their apartment for herself, her daughters, and her boyfriend who was coming out of prison at the end of this month. Supposedly, the law in Portugal is that when someone renting an apartment dies, the ones still living there can take over the place. Alice was going to use that law to her benefit once my parents were gone for good.

Mama is still in the hospital and has not been told what happened. Papa said that when she comes out of the hospital she would soon find out. According to Papa, Luisa has a heart of gold and has offered a room in her apartment — for a monthly fee, of course. She has three children. Her husband is a chauffeur and doesn't make much money so they could use Papa's financial help.

"Veronica, my daughter, Alice, was poisoning your mother and me. We owe our lives to Luisa. I already went to the police and they are looking for Alice, to put her behind bars. She killed my son." Papa was crying.

My reaction was, "Papa, why didn't you call the police and turn her in, instead of selling everything and moving out of the apartment?"

I doubted that he had gotten paid fairly, since he was in such a hurry.

"Luisa and I were afraid that Alice's boyfriend and daughters would come over and get revenge on both of us for turning Alice into the cops. This is better, no one will know were your mother and I will be living, and they can't get to us."

I didn't say much after that, but the whole thing sounds odd to me. I hope Papa knows what he is doing.

This is truly beyond a soap opera. It's a horror story. But one thing about my father is that he only tells the truth, that's the way he has always been. So I have to believe everything he tells me, and that moving in with Luisa is the best for both of my parents. Knowing that he is alive and well, and that my mother will also be safe brought me some form of relief. I can only hope that Mama will feel the same way. I can only imagine the shock she is going to suffer when she finds out.

I wonder how much of this happens all over the world where old people are killed for their money or property. I remember in New Jersey some woman getting caught and put in prison for keeping two old seniors imprisoned in her cellar while she was collecting their social security. She was beating them and starving them to death. I hope Alice pays dearly for her crime.

Aunt Coty called this evening and confirmed what Papa told me. She had also had a bad feeling about Alice for a long time, but Mama would not listen to her.

The federales, as Ralph refers to the FBI agents, called back. Our stuff will be delivered this week, and if anything is missing we are to call the FBI. The moving company is liable for it. Supposedly this moving company in New Jersey was not making any deliveries; they were only picking up and then keeping everything in a warehouse. The FBI had been getting calls from all over the US. I don't know how the FBI found the warehouse, but they did, and according to them it was a very successful bust.

The Spinal Biomechanics teacher is really pathetic. All he talks about is his car-racing, as if we gave a darn about it, and then on the way out of the class he will say, "By the way guys, next week there's an exam."

Ralph and I are angry that we have to pay a private tutor to help us with that class because we have no idea what it's about. Dr. Shtick has a really heavy southern accent, and when he explains biomechanics, which is rarely, neither Ralph nor

I know what the heck he is saying. Once again we have to prepare ourselves for exams all on our own, if we are going to pass them.

It took me a while but I finally found the same white plastic panel I used at the Howell Music Center for writing down the teachers schedules. I bought a full 4'x8' white-board piece, and with Ralph's help I nailed the board sideways to the living room wall. It works like a blackboard without the dust and mess of using chalk. I like the idea of using colorful dry markers and writing everything big enough to read from the kitchen while I'm cooking. As I turn around I can quiz myself that way. The whole board is presently being dedicated to Spinal Biomechanics.

Wednesday night, Ralph and I were sleeping when we heard someone knocking hard on our front door. It was two in the morning. A humongous super duper truck was parked in front of our apartment. Our stuff had arrived. I was so excited that I ran out of the house in my pajamas and no shoes.

They literally dropped all of our belongings on the sidewalk, but not too far from our sliding glass door, and that actually made it easier to take everything into the apartment. Supposedly they were only deliverymen, not movers so they couldn't help us move our things into the apartment. All the boxes were marked with numbers and a basic statement of what was inside, and we still had the list to match with so we knew what was ours, a lot of the boxes were seriously damaged. My dresser was badly broken, my mattress was bent out of shape, but the metal bed frames were intact. Ralph's computer and stereo were still inside the dented boxes, so we wouldn't know their condition until we could open the boxes in the morning. My two small wood barrels from "The Playboy of The Western World" were falling apart at the seams. It was dark outside except for the streetlight, but we could see that there was a lot of property damage. We were just glad to finally get our belongings.

Ralph and I climbed inside the truck to make sure nothing was left behind. The truck was packed tight with stuff that was still to be delivered to other customers like us, all over the United States, as far as California. I was delighted when I found the old antique umbrella that Katherine, the costume designer for The Playboy of the Western World had given me when I helped her move out of New Jersey. Once we put everything inside the living room, all that was left to bring in was my dresser. There wasn't much left except for the drawers, which we carried two at a time. Suddenly I knew that I had stepped on a fire ant mound. They must have needles for teeth, because that's how it felt, sharp burning bites that really stung. I was crying in pain as I ran into the bathroom and into the tub to run cold water over my feet. Those red ants are nasty, but on the other hand they were probably pretty angry when I stepped on them.

The next day when we got home from school Ralph put the bed frames together. My new mattress was damaged beyond repair. Wherever they had stored it all those months had made the middle of the mattress collapse into a deep large hole. Ralph's computer had been smashed on one side, and the microwave was cracked on the outside. I threw away what was left of the dresser and stacked the six drawers on top of each other to use them as a bookcase next to my study table. The dining room table is missing one leg, so we couldn't put it up on three legs. What broke my heart were the wood barrels. I barely touched them and the old metal rings that held them together fell off, and so did all the wood pieces like a jigsaw puzzle. Ralph saw that I was sad and promised that when he has some free time he will help me to put them together with glue. They remind me of the old, Portuguese wine barrels, and that makes them very dear to me. I can't throw them out. The boxes with clothing and kitchen and bathroom stuff we will open when we have some free time.

Things are not going well in Portugal. I can just imagine the shock that Mama suffered when she was told that her home was gone and she was going to live in a room in someone else's apartment. When I called, Papa came to the phone and said that Mama was making everything very difficult, and he just went on about how she had written a letter to me, but Luisa had got hold of it. I wondered what right Luisa has to read my mother's letters to me. Supposedly Mama had written that Luisa had the disposition of an explosive bomb when it come to being impatient, and that she was quite aware that Luisa was a flirt and had Papa in the palm of her hands. Meanwhile, Luisa was so angry that she told them that if Mama was not happy they should get out of her house and go live in an old-folks home, because no matter how much money Papa was giving her, it wasn't enough to pay her for the aggravation she was going through with them.

I have three exams to study for, and I wish I had not called them; it's very hard for me to see a situation like this and not be able to do anything about it.

I called them back two hours later and they had made peace with each other and they were staying with Luisa and her family. Thank God for that, but I can't help wondering how long it will last.

Every once in a while a student will say something really dumb to Ralph and me like, "You are lucky that your mother is your roommate, I bet she is a great cook."

They don't understand that Ralph and I are living together, but we don't cook for each other. This is something we talked about when we became roommates. Ralph is actually the one that made it clear that he liked it that way. I accepted, because it's only fair that neither one is burdened by the other. We are both on equal terms now. We are students. Once in a blue moon Ralph and I will dabble together on some cooking experience, but it is rare. He likes adding hot spicy sauces to the food and I don't. One thing is for sure, it's nice to have all my cooking pots back, even though both of us were getting to be masters at preparing just about anything in the large frying pan we both shared through the months we didn't have our kitchen wares. There's nothing like a regular sized cooking pot and cooking utensils to make life easier.

My mattress had such a deep hole in the middle of it that in order for me to get out of bed in the morning I had to call Ralph to come pull me out of it. After one week of bothering him, and because I didn't think it was fair to make him get up during the night just to pull me up from the crater, I went back to sleeping on my foam piece on the floor and we threw the mattress into the dumpster. I believe that the reason my mattress is a lot worse than Ralph's is because Crazy Joe sold me his thickest mattress and while in storage they must have kept it flat on the floor and probably had put a refrigerator standing on top of it. That is the only reasonable explanation to cause such a serious cavity on a new mattress. Ralph and I have gathered all the bills showing what it's going to cost to replace everything that came to us damaged, and we sent it to the moving company just like the FBI advised us to do. We also enclosed the cost of getting a new dining room set, since the table only has three legs.

Dexter came over for dinner and then he asked me if I minded that he looked into the kitchen cupboards and the refrigerator.

He was obviously impressed as he remarked, "You really live by what you believe! Somehow I am not surprised. You follow a very healthy lifestyle. I never met anyone like you. You don't have a single can of food or sugary cereal stuff. All your food is fresh!"

I was glad that he was so impressed, but I was also wondering what the big deal was.

Dexter loved my cooking until he took a bite of my very favorite grapefruit salad.

"My God," he said twisting his face, "I have never tasted anything so sour in my life! Please, don't take this personally but…I can't eat it."

I had to control myself from laughing, and promised never to give him grapefruit salad again.

Grapefruit or orange salad is the most delicious salad I can wish for when I have a desire for some cool thirst quencher chunky fruit with fresh minced garlic, olive oil, and just a touch of rice vinegar. Aunt Heydee always made orange salad as a refreshing side-salad in the summer time. The grapefruit is my own invention; I figured that if oranges were good, grapefruit had to be even better.

What one learns in school goes beyond the classroom, as you tend to survive in a world of personal choices! Sunday morning is my shopping day for general groceries, and I always have the list of items needed for making the meals for the week. After my hospital experience, I realize how important it is that I have healthy meals ready to eat when I get home so that I have no excuse not to stay healthy and strong. School is very demanding both on the brain and the body. As one of the girls in one of our classes told me, she can't wait to graduate and be finished with school because she is losing a lot of hair on her head due to stress. Since the apartment is less than a ten-minute drive, I go home for lunch. It's also a great savings because I am being very careful with what is being spent. Just because I am on a scholarship doesn't mean that I can live as I want and be a spendthrift. Even though I was granted a scholarship, every month I pride myself on saving some of the money I receive as a loan from the government to pay for my living expenses. The government loan is not free money; I have to pay it back when I graduate. Every penny I save is for one thing only, to open our chiropractic office. Ralph and I are looking forward to working together when we graduate, and I believe in being prepared.

Ralph and I have discovered an incredible supermarket not far from our apartment that welcomes shoppers to sample their food. This is something I never knew could exist. About two to three times a week we are there for lunch. I have eaten fruit and vegetables that I didn't even know existed. By offering their customers a bite of their fresh unique items, it brings a lot of people in to buy them. I only shop there now. I get fish heads for free; if I don't take them they are thrown out. With the fish heads I make the best soup ever imaginable. Also, Ralph found out that in the freezer they have odds and ends from cold-cuts and they sell it at one quarter of the cost. He likes sandwiches, and I don't mind eating them too. I like corned beef and roast beef, but I'd rather have an egg or a tuna sandwich.

The latest thing in food, which has been introduced in our school cafeteria this month, is a vegetarian hamburger. I like the idea that I can eat a tasty hamburger without meat.

I got a letter from Papa complaining about all the wrong doings that Mama put him through while married to her for fifty years. Then I got a phone call from Mama telling me that Luisa confiscates her letters to me and if they don't meet her approval they get thrown away. She was also heart-broken to see that Papa is always on Luisa's side. Mama was calling me to let me know how unhappy she was being married to Papa. Then she hung up after saying that she had heard Luisa coming home.

I feel so sad knowing that my parents have arrived at the end of their lives not liking each other. I feel very lucky to be divorced. I thank God for that. I'm thinking about going to Portugal during my December school break, to visit my parents.

Each meal I make is made with one goal in mind, how many meals can I make out of a single large one? How many meals can I make out of the vegetable stew, the lasagna, or the large pot of vegetable soup? I purposely bought plastic containers that are the perfect size for a single serving. Ralph does the same and the freezer is well stocked. Sometimes the Sundays go by and, except for some fresh veggies and fruit, I have no need to shop or cook for several weeks. I always make sure that I have a small bowl of fresh green salad with dinner. It's not my purpose to become a vegetarian; I simply let my inner intelligence dictate what's good for me. I eat fish or meat about once or twice a month.

Dexter and I see each other every weekend, and during the week we talk on the phone. Last night he came over for dinner, and afterwards we laid down on the living room floor talking to each other. It was three-thirty in the morning when he left. He said he didn't want to go home because he knew his roommate had a bunch of women over for a meeting that night, and she would try to connect him with one of her friends. Dexter keeps repeating to me that he is not like other men. I really don't care, I enjoy his company, and I feel very relaxed with him as I can express my thoughts without holding back. He is the opposite of Al. I never thought it could be possible to spend so many hours with someone and never run out of good conversation. Now I realize that Michael and I were more like kids together. Our talks were a lot simpler, like how we felt about each other, the theatre, music, and daily events. Being with Dexter is more like an intellectual exchange of ideas. Dexter is very educated, yet he is very big into spirituality and that's something that I enjoy discussing.

Ralph asked me how I can be attracted to Dexter when his face looks like a turtle. Yes, it's true he is not handsome. His face is far from it, but I only noticed that the first time I met him. Since we became friends, I no longer see him that way. He is eight years younger than me, but he looks more like my age. He is very tall and has a very nice slim physique. But his exterior is not important to me, I enjoy listening to him, and when I am talking, he knows how to inspire me to think freely. That is something I've never had in my life. I am not attracted to Dexter the way Ralph thinks. He would probably laugh at me if I told him that I am seriously attracted to Dexter's intellect. He is a dream come true.

Dexter is definitely the adventurous type. He loves Brazil even after he got robbed while taking a nap on the beach of Rio de Janeiro a few years ago. He said he wasn't even aware of the robber taking his wallet. I told him about my cousins who lived in São Paulo and Rio de Janeiro. They had told my mother thirty years ago that those cities were infested with criminals. If it was bad then, it has got to be even worse now. Dexter says he doesn't care. He is actually thinking about practicing in Rio when he becomes a chiropractor. Not me. I want to be able to walk the streets where I live without having to look over my shoulder wonderingr if I'm going to be robbed or kidnapped. I want adventure, but not at gunpoint, unless of course I am with the man I love and he can keep me safe even when we are in a dangerous situation.

Sylvia, the girl that invited Ralph and me to her end-of-the-first quarter party, stopped me in the hallway in school and accused me of stealing Dexter from her. I was shocked and hurt. I told her that she was wrong because Dexter was the one who called me after we met at the party at her house.

"Dexter and I were dating each other until you showed up."

"Like I told you, he called me. You are making a big mistake. Dexter and I are only friends, and there's nothing, absolutely nothing between the two of us."

"When I called him last week, he told me that he was seeing you. You should be going out with men your own age. Besides that, you have already been married. I would like to be married too, you know." She began crying.

"My goodness! Go ahead and marry Dexter! You have my blessings. I swear to you that Dexter and I are only friends." But no matter what I said it didn't do any good.

She had two girlfriends to console her as she turned her back on me. I was proud for not allowing myself to cry in front of her.

I told Leila about it, and she tried to comfort me, saying that Sylvia was a jerk, and that was the reason she never goes to her parties. I am still sad about what happened. I don't like when people accuse me of things that are not true, and I don't like being hated either. I won't be telling Dexter about what happened between Sylvia and me on campus. The whole thing is too dumb to even talk about.

Al calls every week to see how I'm doing. He called this week and said that he is taking special classes to become a detective, as this is something he always wanted to do. He also got himself some modern eyeglasses and a new wardrobe. That gives me hope that maybe he will start having a normal life and meet someone. I called Steve and asked if he would mind introducing his father to other women. He said he knows a really nice lady a bit young, but she is looking for a serious relationship so it might work. According to Steve she is a real knockout. She is a teacher and he's known her for a long time. He is going to invite Al and her to his house for dinner.

I am keeping my fingers crossed.

We got a package in the mail from the delivery trucking company. It was the missing wood leg to our dining room table. They had found it after all this time! They had also enclosed a check covering all the items damaged. I am going to look for a new mattress this weekend.

Ralph fixed one of my wooden barrels, and Dexter helped me put the other barrel together. I am happy.

After we had dinner last night in my apartment, Dexter and I went for a walk to the park by the College. We sat on some rocks and talked. The topic was religion and what we believe in. I don't like to talk about religion, but with Dexter it's easy because he is very spiritual. He is not trying to convince me to be this or that, and he doesn't push his beliefs on me. If anything, he told me I should be sharing my philosophy with other people. He tried to convince me to be a guest speaker at a spiritual religious group he belongs to, saying that they could benefit from my perspective.

I told him that I was Jewish, and he didn't even blink an eye. He said "So what?" He likes what he hears and is inspired by my insight. I felt very flattered, but there's no way in heaven that I am going to talk to a group of people. I would be embarrassed to talk to a bunch of people staring at me. I can only express my feelings on a one-to-one basis. More than two people around me becomes a crowd.

Dexter speaks fluent Spanish, French, Italian, Dutch and Brazilian which is just like Portuguese with an added flare. He has traveled to exotic-far-away places all over the world, and he tells me wonderful stories. But what I like mostly about him is his mysticism, which is ingrained in everything he says. Sometimes he goes a bit too far with it, but I keep an open mind about what he says. He respects my point of view even when I feel that some of the things I come up with are pretty much off the wall. This is the first time in my life that I am encouraged to dig into my thoughts and be outspoken. He doesn't criticize me. He is a lot like Michael used to be, except that he goes a lot further in the thought process. That encourages me to branch out even further. I can truly say that he feeds the fire of my views about life. When I'm with him I feel complete.

In the spine analysis class called Instrumentation, we get to use a small hand-held instrument that is rolled along the spine, supposedly measuring the heat from one side of the spine to the other via a unique, non-contact, infrared sensor. It let's us know where the subluxations are. Subluxation is a chiropractic word used to describe a misalignment of the spine. The College staff said that we had to buy the instrument, and it was automatically added into our tuition. Whether we like it or not, we are charged $350, even though after we graduate it doesn't do us any good unless we purchase the machine that puts out the reading and that costs a couple of thousand dollars. Like me, Ralph is very upset about it and feels like the whole thing is a joke and just an excuse to make more money off the students.

I was studying for heavy-duty exams when I got a phone call from Leila. She was distressed and said she needed to come over.

"I am in the middle of studying for exams. How about you call me tomorrow?" I said, feeling a bit frustrated.

"Oh, Okay. I'll call you tomorrow."

After I hung up I was terrified.

"What the heck did I just do? Ralph, I just hung up on Leila after she said that she was feeling down. I told her I was too busy studying to see her. What if she kills herself?"

Ralph shrugged his shoulders as he walked away into his bedroom. "Don't worry!" he said. "Trust me when I say that you will see her in school tomorrow."

"What if she does kill herself, then what?" I asked.

"If she is that nuts, then you couldn't save her anyway," and he closed his bedroom door.

Ralph was right. The next day I saw Leila in school going about as if everything was fine. She introduced me to Howard, who is known for being the best hugger in college. Students, principally females, look forward to Howard's embrace.

He asked me politely, "Would you like a hug?"

His big eyeglasses were thicker than the ones worn by the albino student in one of my classes. But Howard did have a nice friendly smile, and I figured a friend of Leila was a friend of mine.

This was no simple hug as I found out. First he wrapped his arms around my whole back as if his arms were two large wings, then, slowly but firmly, he shelled his body around mine like some kind of plastic molding. He was the reincarnation of what a mother's hug must feel like to a soldier that just returned from the war after being tortured in prison. When he let go he was still smiling at me. He knew he was good!

Dexter called. He sounded really bad on the phone. He has the flu. I told him that I would stop by his apartment and give him a healing massage to help clear his chest.

Huggin' Ya

On the way to his place I picked up a small container of Vicks VapoRub at the pharmacy. I had him sit on the only chair in his bedroom and started by gently massaging his head and neck and then did a few trigger points to release the sinus pressure as I had learned in school from another student. Quietly I surveyed his bedroom and its contents. A person's possessions, and even how clean they are, give me a detailed image of who is living there, very much like a fingerprint of their personality. Everybody lives in a homemade stage set and being a stage set designer for so many years, I automatically tend to study my surroundings whenever I visit someone's house for the first time. I had not yet seen Dexter's bedroom. His bedroom's main focus, was a full-size almost wall-to-wall bookcase. The majority of the books were about self-improvement, finding yourself, reaching within, and the joy of being better than you are. That told me exactly what was wrong with him. Dexter has been trying to find himself.

Of course, I didn't say anything. I had to admire him for not giving up. I applied some of the Vicks on his chest and back and after washing my hands, I left his apartment, but not before I told him to get some sleep, and get better soon.

What a freak-out bug experience I had this morning while seated on the toilet in my bathroom! As I pulled some toilet paper from the roll, a huge, round, humungous, black cock-roach came out from inside the toilet paper roll and fell on the floor. How could something so gigantic be so fast at running? I will never know. I came out of the bathroom screaming and Ralph didn't believe me when I told him how large the roach was. He made fun of me!

I could understand a roach showing up in the kitchen looking for something to munch on, but hanging inside a toilet paper roll is just too much for me to accept. Since the proof had run away, I decided that I am not taking any chances. Maybe Georgia's roaches also like to hang out between bed sheets, and with that in mind, during my lunch break at school, I went to the mall and bought myself a set of white bed sheets.

When I got home I threw away my flowery pattern bed sheets. Before I get into bed every night my covers will get lifted to make sure no roaches are sleeping in my bed.

I think that spiders are cute, principally the little ones that according to Portuguese folklore are supposed to bring good luck, but I can't stand roaches.

Over the weekend, Ralph and I attended a birthday party at Russell's house. He lives far away, forty-five minutes from school to be exact. I am so spoiled being ten minutes away from our campus; I can go home for lunch. Lucy, one of the girls in second quarter, was also at Russell's party and shared nonchalantly that she was a witch. I always thought that witches were characters in children's books, made up to scare kids into behaving. Lucy's announcement took me for a loop, but I acted like so, what else is new. When we left the party, Ralph and I came to the conclusion that there are a lot of odd people in our school and we should ignore them by not mingling with them. Ralph's best friend Russell and his wife Margie are normal, so we should be thankful for that.

Ralph told me he has proof that one of our teachers is a fake. He caught him in a few discrepancies, which proves without a doubt that he is not a medical doctor as he pretends to be. When Ralph asked him a few questions about the differences between female and male pelvis, he gave the wrong answers. The teacher doesn't even know the basic bone anatomy!

I trust Ralph if he says our teacher is a fake, because Ralph never makes accusations unless he has proof.

There's a student in our motion palpation class called Harold. Both Ralph and I have named him Harold the Hateful, because he has a hateful attitude towards the whole world. Harold's hands are cold and hard just like metal. Inflicting pain seems to be his only objective when he is palpating somebody's spine. I was teamed with him to do palpation on each other's spine. I told him to take it easy when he was palpating me, but he took offense. After the class I had to run into the bathroom because I wanted to throw up from the effect of his hands upon my back. At the next class the girl that Harold was teamed up with couldn't take it either. I found her cursing in the hallway from the discomfort inflicted on her back. Ralph had the same experience as I did, and agreed that Harold has too much hate when he palpates people's backs and necks.

I asked the teacher not to match me with him any more, because, he is too rough.

The teacher was a real jerk. "That's the way it is. You have to learn to work with whoever your partner is each week."

So, what did the teacher do? He asked Harold not to be so harsh with palpation, because I had complained.

Harold got upset and told me I had no right to whine to the instructor. I should have told him that he was hurting me. I defended myself saying that I had tried, but he would not listen, so what was I supposed to do? Then, feeling sorry for hurting his feelings, I told him that he could practice on me but he would have to remember that I was made of skin, flesh, and bone, not wood.

Thank God that Harold got teamed with a male student until the end of this quarter. Next quarter if he is in the same class with me I am putting my foot down, he is not touching me.

This is so embarrassing, but except for a few kitchen items and clothes, I have not opened all the boxes after they were delivered. I plan to do that when the semester is over, which will be in a couple of more weeks. It's amazing how little one needs to live with when it comes to stuff. Being in school all day I really don't have time to waste decorating our apartment.

Dexter took me to a small house-party over the weekend where I met Donna and Cody, the hosts, who are also chiropractic students.

I was introduced to meditation at the party. Basically, one sits cross-legged on the floor, puts the palms of their hands up so the energy flows through them, and with a slow rhythmic breathing and eyes closed, you are supposed to relax. I couldn't relax. Sitting on the hardwood floor was painful to my tailbone, but of course I didn't say anything. I opened my eyes slightly, to see what everybody else was doing, and everybody seemed to be relaxed and in their own mental space. I couldn't believe that they call that meditation. I had to smirk as I realized that as a kid I was proficient at meditating, but I didn't know it at the time. I prefer my own old meditation style when I used to sit on the soft sand above a small cliff with my eyes open staring at the ocean in front of me, listening to the waves hitting the rocks below my feet, and smelling the salty spray of the waves. To me, meditation means blending oneself into the universe. This thing about group meditation on a hard floor trying to disconnect from the world around was to me aberrant and very uncomfortable.

Afterwards, Donna and Cody served a delicious green salad with every conceivable raw vegetable known to man and warm Italian bread, for dinner. Loretta, one of the guests, mentioned a ghost that was putting a negative force inside her apartment. Donna offered to get rid of the ghost for her and the event was open to anyone that wanted to watch. Donna will be at Loretta's apartment next Saturday night. Dexter offered to pick me up if I would like to go with him. I am curious to see how Donna is going to play exorcist.

I love my student's life style; I have very good friends and a lot of fun with them. I feel like I'm never going to forget these life experiences. Papa always talked about his days as a student in Berlin, Germany. I wonder if he had as much fun as I'm having.

I showed my friend Laurie from school a special slow dance that I do when I want to relax at home. She said it's called Tai Chi and wouldn't believe me when I told her that I made it up. I love dancing, and I'm always trying to make up new movements to go with the music I am hearing. If I had a clone of myself I would be a dancer. Gosh there's so much I would like to do, but I can only carry out one or two things at a time, and becoming a chiropractor is now my biggest challenge.

We were in anatomy lab, which is next to the dissection lab, when we got a ten-minute break. I stayed seated trying to use every second available to memorize each bone detail in front of me. Ralph got up to explore around the room. When he came back a few minutes later, he was noticeably disturbed, "Whatever you do, Mom, do not go into the dissection lab and open the white buckets standing against the back of the room."

I had no intentions of looking around the dissection lab, but I had to ask him, "Why?"

"They keep the cadaver's heads inside the buckets."

Dexter and I got to Loretta's house ahead of everybody else. She was in the kitchen making spaghetti sauce and adding some fresh basil. She remarked that a lot of cooks use oregano instead of basil, and in her opinion that was a gastronomic crime. She knew that because she was Italian and so was her mother who is still living in Italy. I always thought that oregano was the key ingredient to spaghetti sauce. I had just learned something new.

Soon everybody started arriving, including Donna and Cody. She said she could feel the spirit of a young black man who needed a little help to move on. She went around the rooms lighting candles as she held in front of her, like a protective shield, a three by five inch carved-glass figure of a Jesus head with a crown of thorns. When I saw the Jesus' head I was very disappointed because Leila had confided to me awhile back that both Donna and Cody were Jewish. I had just lost my confidence in Donna's clairvoyance. Why she didn't use David's star was a puzzle to me, and somehow I felt that what she was doing was a mockery to someone else's religion. Donna returned to the living room and had us turn off all the lights in the apartment. We all followed her quietly as she went from one room to another doing what sounded like some incantation while holding Jesus' head in one hand and a lit candle in the other. Then she went back into the living room, blew the candle out, and put both items on the fireplace mantel.

She solemnly announced, "Loretta, you can blow the candles out in the other rooms. The young man is gone. Loretta, from now on, you can relax and enjoy your apartment."

As we all sat down to eat the spaghetti, I looked at Donna and wondered if she was smarter than she looked. Was she using psychology to free Loretta of what she believed to be a spirit in her apartment? Of course I didn't share my thoughts with anyone, not even Dexter. Maybe there had been a spirit imprisoned in the apartment after all. I sure wasn't going to question its validity.

I was studying at the College's library when Leila showed up and sat next to me complaining that she could hardly walk. When I asked her what was wrong, she told me that she had attended a weekend seminar that specialized in instilling self-confidence into people like her who are insecure. They had her and a few others walk on hot stones. She was told that she lacked self-confidence, that's why she had burned her feet! I couldn't believe my ears that she was so naïve as to believe such nonsense. Then she said that prior to that they convinced her to climb a telephone pole and stand up on top of it.

In my opinion, Leila is the kindest, most giving person I have ever met, and I feel that she is going to be an awesome chiropractor because she's got what it takes. She doesn't need anything more than what she already possesses. She spends a fortune going from one seminar to another looking for answers when she already has the answers. If she were to put more time into studying she would not be doing so bad scholastically. I wish I could rub off some of my self-confidence, onto her but all I can do every time we meet is use my own form of psychology to give her self-esteem. That lasts a couple of days, and then she is back to feeling down again.

I have had it with Dr. Shtick. When I finished taking the test, I knew I had done poorly even after paying a tutor to teach me. Ralph felt the same way, but he went home. I stayed at the school. Outside, Leila was sitting by a flowerbed, and she had a chance to see the worst side of me.

"Leila, I want to blow this college to kingdom come!"

"Now, take a deep breath; relax and tell me what's happening," she said sympathetically, trying to appease my anger. Leila was a psychotherapist before she decided to become a chiropractor.

One thing about being Portuguese, we tend to talk too fast when we are angry, and usually we add bad words to give it more impact. That is what I did when I described how I wanted to blow up all the buildings on the campus at the same time.

"Veronica, what you are saying makes no sense; you are far from being a terrorist. You can't blow up a college. Think of something a little more reasonable in its place. What would you like to do besides that to help with your frustration?"

"I want to step on all the flowerbeds and kill all the pretty plants around here. Instead of spending money to make this place look beautiful, they should be spending the money on qualified teachers."

"Now, Veronica. Why would you want to hurt the flowers? Can't you think of something more productive?"

"Yes, you are right Leila. I'm going to stay with my original plan, and you are going to help me because I know you agree that the academics here suck!"

I felt better after that remark, and then she had me laughing as she told me some stories about the students that, like me, were also upset about some of the teaching staff. She had heard from other students that the manly statue outside the gym — which has an interesting resemblance to Dr. Williams according to many people — had been found one glorious morning without its penis. The body part had been sent anonymously to his office. The story goes that Dr. Williams was using it as a paperweight on his desk.

Dexter called me. He heard from Lisa, a student in one of my classes at school, that I have a cold. He wanted to come over and do Reiki on me to help me get better. I've never heard of Reiki, except that it has something to do with using the energy in the hands to help people with health problems. He was at my apartment within a half an hour. Ralph was out with a friend for the evening.

Dexter put one of the dining room chairs in the living room, and asked me to sit down, close my eyes, and relax. I could tell that he was behind me, and his hands were around my head, not that he was touching me, but I could feel the heat of his hands on top of my head, and then around my face, and then my neck. It felt that he might be working his way down. When I took a very quick peek out of curiosity it confirmed my suspicion. His hands were facing my chest. A while later it was easy to tell that he was on his knees because he was holding my feet firmly in both his hands. That was the only time he actually touched me.

When he told me I could open my eyes and asked how I felt, I lied by saying, "A lot better!"

Still, I wanted to know everything about it "So, what were you doing? Can you show me what you did?"

"I cannot teach you. You need to learn it from a Reiki master like I did. But I can tell you this much, I covered you with gold-dustings from above."

He left, after telling me to get to bed and get some rest. While I was heating the chicken broth I had made the night before, I thought how nice Dexter was to choose imaginary gold-dustings to cover me, instead of silver or even plain dust. I poured the hot chicken broth into a cup and rested it on the old wooden barrel next to my bed. I ran the hot water in the bathroom shower until the bathroom was steaming hot. After I finished taking a very hot shower, I put on my flannel pajamas and went quickly into my bedroom. I sat on my bed, drank the hot chicken broth, and covered myself nice and warm. I fell asleep like a rock with one thought in my mind: getting well so that the next morning I could go back to school. Fever or not, I don't miss a class. Just my luck, the day I miss a class will be the day they are passing around the "underground" copies of the exams.

I woke up in the middle of the night with Dexter's slim naked body against mine. His warm hands held me tight against him. We were having intercourse, plain and simple. I freaked out! That wasn't a dream! It felt very real! How dare he take advantage of me being sick? Did he ask my permission, or did he just sneak back into the apartment and into my bed? What kind of a friend was he? I turned on the light switch next to my bed and came to the conclusion that what I had just experienced was nothing but voodoo, witchcraft or Reiki as he called it. I had no doubt in my mind that Dexter had put a spell on me, by projecting himself into my bed, like a hologram!

When Dexter called this evening to see how I was doing, I told him that Reiki had worked like magic, no pun intended, and I was feeling a lot better. He said he was done with classes for the evening and didn't mind stopping by the apartment and check on his patient. He cares!

Ralph was busy in the kitchen making his dinner when Dexter arrived at our apartment. I told him we probably should hang out in my bedroom. We talked, and then he offered to give me a massage. We took turns massaging each other. Then we started kissing, and one movement led to the next, and soon we were kissing passionately and our clothes went flying off. I was not thinking about Michael when I gave myself completely to Dexter. I took the experience as a sign that I was finally free to love whoever I wanted. Afterwards, I felt that the occasion required a demonstration of my womanhood, so I got up and put on my pink silk bathrobe.

He commented, "You are in such good shape. You must exercise a lot!"

I took that as a compliment since I don't even know the first thing about exercising. But when I lay back next to him I could sense that he was no longer my lover but had returned to being my friend. I took a chance and asked him if he would rather leave, and he said it was a good idea.

The next day he didn't call. He just showed up at the apartment with a heavy look on his face and said that we needed to talk. He was cold towards me, and seemed stressed out when I tried hugging him. Ralph was close by, cooking in the kitchen, and my instinct warned me not to invite Dexter to my bedroom. He said that since tomorrow was Saturday, he would like to take me to the movies in the evening. He left quickly after waving goodbye. He could have called me to say what he wanted to say, but obviously he wanted to talk on a more personal basis, and since Ralph was around it wasn't going to happen.

While watching the movie Dexter didn't hold my hand. I tried reaching for him, but he squeezed my hand lightly and said, "I don't like holding hands in public, and definitely not while watching a movie."

What could I have done wrong, I kept asking myself. I know that I am not as experienced in the matters of the heart as I wish I could be, but I always thought that after making love that feeling should remain between two lovers at least a day or two. When we got back to my apartment we talked about antiques. I told him about my grandmother's dress, which is over 100 years old, and asked, "Would you like to see it? I keep it in my bedroom closet."

He followed me quietly to my bedroom. When I closed the door behind me, he stood against the wall looking as if he was about to be sacrificed to some angry God. I became conscious that he was having some kind of emotional problem, and without saying a word I went directly to my closet and removed the small box where I kept the dress inside of a plastic bag. I sat on my bed and laid the box next to me and began taking the cover off.

"Stop right there," he said in an almost angry voice. "We need to talk about our relationship."

I remained seated, listening, and I was thinking, my goodness, he hasn't even seen the dress, isn't he the least curious?

"Veronica, I know what you are doing. You are trying to seduce me by bringing me into your bedroom."

I stared at him, and turning my head from side to side several times, I lied, "That was not my intention."

"The night we had sex was simply that. We are mutually attracted to each other, and our hormones acted upon that, that's all it was. But I don't want to lose you. Your friendship is very important to me. I need you to understand that I don't deal well with any kind of affection; things like kissing, hugging, or holding hands, make me feel as if someone is choking me and I can't help going into an uncontrollable panic attack. It doesn't matter if it's in private or in public, I can't handle amorous behavior."

I was thinking how sad it was that someone so intelligent was so mentally defective. I kept nodding as he continued to speak.

"Trust me when I say it's not your fault. You are the best thing that has happened in my life. Over the years I've been to several psychiatrists and other forms of therapies and nothing seems to help. I'm aware that the way I am is the reason all my relationships end quickly. But I can't help myself. According to my latest psychologist, all my emotional inadequacies are the result of something that my mother may have done to me when I was a child. My last psychologist has come to the conclusion that I was probably sexually abused, even though I don't recall anything out of the normal. I only know that I don't like my mother."

I have no experience with psychologists, but from all the stories I have heard it sounds to me like psychologists tend to put dumb stuff into the heads of their patients. Instead of teaching them to get over it and go on with life, they'd rather link their patients' emotional problems with the past by putting them into a stagnant repetitive mental disorder of victimized lost souls. I had just become aware that Dexter was one of those victims.

"If you just want to be friends, that's fine." Then, to prove that I meant it, I added "Would you like to join me for dinner since it's late?" And I said that as naturally as I could.

Dexter was surprised that I didn't get angry or accuse him of something or another. Through dinner we talked easily as if everything was perfectly normal between us. He left with a smile, as I was very careful to give him a very brief hug when he left the apartment.

And then I cried. It serves me right for leaving Al. God is punishing me for wanting too much out of life. Al was always expressive when it came to showing that he cared, but we lacked any form of intellectual communication. Isn't it ironic that Dexter is just the opposite of Al? This is just too much of a coincidence. I am being punished, that's all I can say. Dexter doesn't realize that after being married for thirty years, a serious relationship is the furthest thing from my mind. True, I am attracted by a man's intellect, but that's not enough to balance it with sex, afterwards there's got to be some kind of human touch, a kiss or even a hug is needed to establish a close and loving relationship. I learned about balance from producing the musical "Godspell."

Sex and love go hand in hand with me. Unless it's the case of a casual encounter with the stranger in the elevator. Love and sex cannot be separated when it's between two people that care for each other. If the years that Dexter had therapy didn't help him, I definitely don't have the wisdom to help him either. One thing is for sure, he doesn't realize that he wiped Michael's memory from my heart, and for that I am thankful. Now that I know that life will go on without Michael and Dexter, I only pray that God will continue to guide my steps so that I can make the right decisions when it comes to future matters of the heart.

When Ralph got his mid-term grades he was upset that he got a B and I had gotten an A in Dr. Frickenson's class. He said he wasn't angry that I had gotten an A, but he was ready to bet his life that Dr. Frickenson, who is a total moron, had switched our grades by accident because of our last name being the same.

Together we went to pay a visit to Dr. Frickenson, who is a very tall and extremely large man with a prominent buffalo hump in his upper back. According to what we are learning, that is a possible sign that he has hypothyroidism. His looks are matched by his nasty attitude, and everybody hates him. Dr. Frickenson was annoyed when Ralph requested to see his test.

"Why don't you be a good boy, and let your mother have the A? Don't be so greedy!"

Ralph argued back, "If my grade is a C then I deserve that C, just like it's only fair that if I have an A, I deserve that A. I want to see my exam, and I want my A back."

Dr. Frickenson looked at me and asked me in his usual sarcastic way, "What do you say, Mom. Should I give him the A and you the B instead?"

I hate when people call me Mom when we are not even related. Nasty bastard was all I could think, but instead I said, "What is fair is fair, if I deserve a B that's what I should get."

Dr. Frickenson went over the tests and found that Ralph was right.

On the way out, Ralph reminded him again, "I expect you to give me the grade I deserve."

Dr. Frickenson gives me the willies.

There are a few other teachers in this school that both Ralph and I despise, but the one on top of our list is Dr. Shuck. Grrrr that's all I can write down about him.

Ralph had his head on the desk, trying to stay awake listening to Dr. Shuck as he was rampaging on, "How despicably low can some chiropractic colleges go? There is a college in Oregon called Western States Chiropractic College which is promising their chiropractic students a medical degree along with their chiropractic degree. This is an abominable offense towards our profession. We must do everything we can to shut them down. This is nothing but another medical attempt to corrupt our profession!"

Ralph was now paying a lot of attention.

After class, Ralph told me that he is going to look further into the college in Oregon. If he has to attend another semester in this College he is tempted to quit.

Ralph didn't lose any time. The next day he called the Dean at Western States Chiropractic College in Oregon, and after talking to him he made up his mind to transfer to their College as soon as possible. Ralph has been on the dean's list since his first quarter at Life College. He is extremely intelligent and without a challenge he tends to get bored.

Dexter saw me in school and was excited when he asked me to follow him to the cafeteria. He wanted me to meet Cida, a new chiropractic student from Brazil. Cida had put him in contact with someone that offered a unique deep breathing technique. The breathing procedure was so profound that many people had been helped with emotional problems after experiencing their own birth process.

Who the heck wants to go through such trauma again and have their head squeezed out of a vagina while being yanked out by their head? It's not that I object to growing and enriching our lives with knowledge, it's just that some of this stuff can get completely out of common sense, like what they did to Leila by having her climb a telephone pole and walk on fire to prove that she had self-confidence.

Once Dexter left for a class, Cida told me that the therapy she was encouraging him to try was something she had found very useful for herself. She had tried it several times now and with each time she had gone further and further back in her life to almost the point of her own birth process.

No wonder I have no interest in taking recreational drugs; it's trips like those that turn me off. Cida told me that Dexter had shared with her his personal problems with intimacy, and she believed that the breathing therapy might help him to find out what happened between him and his mother that messed him up so badly.

Dexter will be seeing the breathing therapist in two weeks in the hopes of saving our relationship, since he likes everything about it except the affection part. Of course I didn't say anything to Dexter, but in my humble opinion breathing deep is not the solution.

I found Cida a little on the odd side, but at the same time a very cool person to listen to. Well, if anything I have a new friend at school that I can practice my native language with.

Ralph says that I would make a great psychiatrist, but what he doesn't know is that I actually have no patience for people like Dexter. With patients like him, I would probably slap them across the face and tell them to shut up and get with it. Not a very cool thing to do, but that is exactly what I feel like doing when Dexter sits all curled up in a corner if I dare to show him any form of affection. But I can't help it. He comes over to talk and just hang out, and then suddenly out of nowhere he becomes an ardent passionate lover, in bed only of course, where he puts me into a stage of euphoria. And then I'm supposed to stay away from him, as if nothing happened. Dating is not as great as I thought it would be. I'm starting to wonder if all men have emotional problems.

Lucy saw me in class and asked, "So, tell me Veronica, are you a witch too?"

"Of course I am a witch." I said, joking with her and not knowing what else to say. But then, reconsidering my words— like, what if she started asking me witch questions—I added convincingly, "I am just not as experienced as you." Then, keeping my fingers crossed that she would not ask me anything else, I smiled at her and quickly walked away.

I will have to be more careful from now on and exit the classroom through the other door. If she found out I am lying, she might get angry and put a spell on me. I wonder if Lucy is her real name. Either way I have no interest in finding out.

Rosanna called me on the phone to remind me that she is going to Florida. She is expecting me to meet her during my Christmas school break like we had talked about a month ago. After we hang up I thought about it and shortly afterwards I decided not to go. I decided not to go to Portugal either. I am staying in Georgia for my Christmas break. I called her back and said that I wasn't able to go because I wanted to put my energy into my relationship with Dexter and the school break was ideal for that.

She got very angry, "You lied to me! You said that you would meet me in Florida, and now you are backing out of it."

She already knows the problems I have been experiencing with Dexter's mood swings, so I tried appealing to her, "Yes, I said I would meet you in Florida, but things have changed. I am asking you as my friend to be more understanding about my situation. This is my only opportunity to get to know Dexter better, and see if it's going to work out between him and me."

"I totally understand, and you go ahead and have fun with your new boyfriend."

I had a feeling that she was being sarcastic but I thanked her for being understanding. I told her I would definitely stay in touch with her.

I rarely do anything in my life for one reason; it has to be multiple ones. But this time I have only one motive. Dexter is staying in Georgia, and he asked me to stay.

Leila invited me to go hiking with her last Saturday. I cut my hair as short as I could that morning just because it felt right and I put on an old tee-shirt from my theatre days, and then just for the fun of it, I wore Dexter's red shorts, because they are very short and perfect for a hot day in the woods.

What an awe-inspiring experience it was! First of all, I had never hiked before except for one time with Aunt Heydee, when I was a kid, so that doesn't really count.

Half way up the mountain there is a historical park, and Leila took my picture seated on an old cannon. When we got to the top of the mountain, I was feeling high, and that was not from the altitude. I was jumping around and singing and poured half of my water bottle over my head to cool off. Leila was laughing too and took several pictures of me along the way. I gladly posed for her with my arms wide open as I felt like I was hugging the whole world.

I sent the pictures to my parents.

Since first quarter, both Ralph and I have become aware of some illegal exam copies, which give the questions and answers to midterms and finals. Who puts these tests out we have no idea, but when a student in class was passing one of the so-called finals around, I took it home.

I asked Ralph what he thought of the copy I had gotten in class. Ralph said, "I don't believe that's going to be the test. We can't rely on that. We need to be prepared by studying for our exams."

When we sat down at the testing center, the final exam they gave us matched our exam copy word for word. I was ashamed and angry, which is weird because I should have been glad that I knew all the answers, but I felt like I was being dishonest. On the way out I couldn't help telling the teacher standing at the door, "Why even bother collecting them when you already know we passed?"

"You must have done well!" He said smiling.

Yes. I did really well. How about you as an educator? You must know that everybody is doing great, no thanks to your teachings, which suck. Of course, I didn't express to him what was on my mind. Ralph felt the same way and said he couldn't wait to attend the College in Oregon. He is done with this school and I don't blame him. He went back to New Jersey, for the Christmas break.

Dexter called. He wanted to know if he could spend the night with me. I was surprised, but I wasn't going to ask questions. We went for a short walk and talked a lot like we usually do, and when we got back to my apartment, we started kissing and then he whispered, "Let's go to your bedroom."

He closed the bedroom door and proceeded to pull the blankets and the pillows off my bed, making the bed on the floor. Then he asked me to lay down naked on the bed he had just made and whispered, "Please do not do anything in return for the love I want to give you. I am not here tonight to satisfy myself but instead to provide you pleasure."

I looked at him wondering what had gotten into him. He must have read my thoughts because he said, "This is my present to you. After all the bullshit you had to go through to finish second quarter, relax and enjoy the night."

Wow, what a guy, that's all I can say. I didn't ask if the breathing therapy had helped, but I took it that it had and we were on our way to living happily ever after. Either way, I would soon find out; if he stayed until the morning. He did sleep over, but in the morning I knew better than to get close to him.

My parents seem to be adapting to living in Luisa's house, and I am thankful that I was able to stay in Georgia for the Christmas break. I used some of the paint left from last quarter to do a few more touch ups. I enjoy having the apartment looking fresh. It makes me happy, when at the end of the semester I can finally clean my desk of all the book clutter and masses of notes gathered from each subject. The idea of clearing my desk is like a confirmation of my success. My second quarter is visibly done!

Except for dating Dexter, I am using these days off from school to relax. This morning I mailed out all my handmade Christmas cards. I actually bought a paper cutter to make the cards. On some of them I drew a few bones, and wrote, "I make no bones about it when I say, have a Merry Christmas and a Happy New Year."

To my parents and some friends I cut out little heart shapes of colored paper to make the cards a little more sentimental. For others I cut out odd shapes pieces of colored paper and glued them together to make them look modern.

I got a horrible Christmas card from Rosanna stating, "From now on I will not trust anyone because of what you did to me. I have lost my best friend, YOU!"

I immediately wrote back and asked her to forgive me. I didn't mean to hurt her feelings. As a friend, I would have understood if she had met someone special. I added that I was looking forward to seeing her again. I promised that I would call her when I went to New Jersey on my next break.

I also got a card from Dr. Peruzzi. "You promised to be my slave, so what are you doing so far away? Love, Francesco."

At first I wondered who Francesco was, until I read the return address from his office and realized that Francesco was Dr. Peruzzi's first name. It's true that I said to him that I would be his slave, but that was due to the elation of being out of pain. I didn't mean it literally. I sent back a simple hand-made card with a small origami bird glued to it, and I wrote, "Dear Dr. Peruzzi, I am not that far away. Love, Ronnie."

When I used to live in New Jersey, I introduced Rosanna to Dr. Peruzzi, thinking that since they were both single and about the same age they might make a good match. They hated each other at first sight, and I decided to stop being a matchmaker from that day on.

The relationship between Dexter and me during this break didn't improve as I had hoped; as a matter of fact, it isn't any different from before. We watch movies, go for walks, eat at home, and as always we share precious moments of laughter and meaningful conversations. Even sex has not lost its spar-kling blissful quality; but, very much like before, it is all or nothing. If Dexter had been a bricklayer I doubt anyone could beat him at building the wall he puts up so rapidly around him, like the one after we have sex. He will stay away for a day, and then he calls as if we are good buddies and nothing else.

Yesterday he came over, and without a word got into my bed and covered himself with a bunch of blankets. He remained distant and quiet, reminding me of a terrified child afraid of the boogey man under the bed. I lay next to him, talking, but I was very careful not to touch him. When he fell asleep I cried from within, feeling sorry for the broken-down human being next to me. I would like to help him, but I don't know how. I have already started distancing myself emotionally. This way I won't get hurt when we finally break up.

Winter of 1994

Third quarter classes are keeping me busy with exciting new subjects like Visceral Gross Anatomy, Bacteriology & Virology, Visceral Physiology, Basic Nutrition, and Anatomy/ Anomalies I, including more advanced classes in Motion & Static Palpation, Clinical Observation, Chiropractic Principles, and Business Principles, and the customary Chiropractic Assembly, with some inspiring guests speakers. Somehow, schoolwork no longer overwhelms me like it used to do. I have gotten so used to studying on my own that I could skip classes and just study at home.

Ralph finally believes me. I told him how big the cockroach was that fell out of the toilet paper a few months ago; I don't know if it was the same one, but this roach was as big as the old one. She was hanging out on the corner wall of the living room, close to the ceiling. They must have some powerful sucking feet ability to withstand the weight of their humongous bodies plus gravity. Thank God that Ralph was home and got rid of the pest for me. I can't believe that I used to play with cockroaches, smaller than these of course, when I was a kid.

Friday night Ralph came home quite touched by what happened to him when he went to a Jewish Temple in Atlanta.

Supposedly the Rabbi asked Ralph to carry the Torah scrolls during the religious ceremony at the Temple, and Ralph said something like, "I don't feel I have the right to hold in my hands something as sacred as God's words. I don't deserve that honor since I don't know much about our religion."

And the Rabbi responded, "Of all the people here, I chose you to carry the Torah because you are honest about your feelings. God wants his people to be Jewish by choice, from the heart, and not because they have to do it."

Ralph felt like it was such a great experience for him to be allowed to carry the Torah scrolls that he is going to do further research into our religion. Then he will decide for himself if he wants to be a Jew or not. I am very proud of Ralph for taking on such an endeavor.

Ralph has been busy transferring his credits and other necessary paperwork for admission to the college in Oregon. He hopes to leave as soon as he gets the word that he has been accepted at Western States Chiropractic College. He is planning to drive up to New Jersey first, visit the family and his friends, and then drive on to Oregon.

We have been very sad about parting. We are family, and most of all good friends. We have talked about it, but we have come to the conclusion that it makes sense for me to stay. I have a half a year more of free tuition, and even though some of the teachers' qualifications leave much to be desired, I would be a fool to leave. It's not just losing my tuition; it's that I am actually doing well studying on my own. Also, from what I heard, the academics at Western States College are outstanding, and that to me means more difficult than here. I'm scared of having to bite off more than I can chew. I am staying in Georgia.

I got a strange phone call from Donna. "Would you mind if I stop over this evening after school? It won't take more than a few minutes of your time."

"Anything special?" I asked her curiously since we don't really talk much to each other.

"I had a dream about you and I need to be in your presence."

I said fine and wondered why she had to be in my presence. It sure sounded heavy! But I didn't ask. I know Donna has a link with the occult, and that is good enough for me. She always comes across as a gentle yet very intelligent young girl, but there's something about dealing with ghosts that I find a little hard to accept. This is probably one of the reasons that Mama and I don't see eye to eye, because she is also into the paranormal stuff.

We sat on two chairs really close to each other. Donna had asked this when she came in.

Holding my hands in hers, she closed her eyes, and asked, "How are you doing?"

"Fine."

"I admire you, Veronica. You are a real inspiration to me."

"Thank you." I was too nervous to ask her why.

Neither of us was talking while she held my hands for a while longer.

I felt a bit overwhelmed — and even uncomfortable — by her behavior. I instinctively didn't want to know what her visit was about. Because she is into interpreting dreams, the thought crossed my mind that maybe she was saying goodbye as she had seen me die or something horrible like that. Then she hugged me and said that she was happy to have seen me and left.

Dexter has become a big disappointment to me for more than one reason. I guess that nobody is perfect, and he is no exception. But at his age I figured he would have outgrown the drug scene, and that his chiropractic philosophy would be strong enough to make him say no to drugs or surgery. I am tired of listening to Dexter constantly bringing up a certain drug which he would do anything to get his hands on, because, according to him, it can provide the exhilarating experience of seeing paintings melt. What the heck is the big deal about seeing anything melt at the possible cost of melting your own brain? It doesn't make any sense to me.

Dexter was visiting me this Sunday afternoon when once again he mentioned his peculiar desire. I got so upset that I called Ralph, who was in his bedroom, to come out, and then I asked him if he would mind taking Dexter for a drive around the block.

Ralph wanted to know what for. So I told him that Dexter was looking for a thrilling, mind bogging, melting experience, and I figured that after the drive Dexter would be satisfied.

Dexter was laughing and so was Ralph, but I was very serious. Ralph drives very fast. When we go out and he insists on driving, I do a mental prayer that we will both survive the crash in one piece. I always offer to drive, but he actually believes that I drive worse than him.

I will never forget the time that Ralph drove his car from New Jersey to Long Island and I was the front seat passenger. Seeing melting paintings compares nothing to seeing my whole life melting in front of me. Just a couple of weeks ago Ralph was driving home after being at a club not too far from where we live, and when he went around a corner he lost control of his car and drove off into a small abyss. Now that has got to be better than watching a stupid painting melting on the wall. At least it's a real experience!

Ralph has been busy on the phone making arrangements to have a trailer hitch attachment put on the back of his car. The dealership said his Plymouth Duster will do fine pulling a small storage trailer. He is relieved that when he moves to Oregon he can take all his belongings with him and not depend on a moving company.

Lucy came by my desk during Visceral Gross Anatomy class and handed me a medium sized pink paper bag, saying, "This is a little gift for you. Don't look inside until you get home. Enjoy it."

Of course, as soon as I got into my car I looked into the bag and was horrified to find a witchcraft book and four white candles. The card read, "To Veronica, from one witch to another, my very best, Lucy."

When I got home I showed the contents to Ralph and he remarked, "Great, all you need now is a witch's incantation book! Just throw that garbage away!"

I sat at my desk reading the book just to see what it was about, and after a couple of pages here and there I'd had enough of it. It was nothing but mumbo jumbo, and I decided that it belonged in the garbage just like Ralph said. I threw it into the small, plastic grocery bag at the front door where I keep my daily garbage to dispose of on the way to school.

I didn't throw away the candles! I put them in the kitchen drawer in case we lose electricity one night.

On the way out of the house this morning I reconsidered throwing away the book. I will never invite Lucy over, but with my luck she could show up at our apartment unexpectedly and ask to borrow the book. It's called Murphy's Law when things like that happen, and I can't take a chance. I put the book at the bottom of the homemade bookcase by my desk, and asked God to forgive me.

I was starting to be concerned that no one was going to call to rent the extra bedroom in the apartment once Ralph leaves next month. But I got a call today from a young guy in New York. I had forgotten how far in the country the ads in school go. He will be starting first quarter at our college in the spring. I told him how spacious the apartment was and that for $200 per month he would have a nice-size bedroom and his own bathroom across the hallway.

I am moving into Ralph's bedroom when he leaves; as he said, I would be a fool if I didn't.

Once I close my bedroom door I will have complete privacy with my own personal bathroom. With the other bedroom I don't have that luxury and I would have to walk across the hallway.

Sam, my future renting-buddy, asked me on the phone how old I am.

"How old are you?" I answered back, having a feeling that he was very young.

"I'm twenty four years old and single."

I remarked sassily, "I am older than you, and let's leave it at that."

Mama would be proud of me.

For the last five days I have been in excruciating pain with my legs, and Ralph shows no sympathy.

"Don't complain around me," he said coldly. "I don't feel sorry for you. You know better than to eat chocolate. You know how it affects you, but you keep eating it anyway."

"I swear that this was the last time." I said crying while hoping he would feel sorry for me "I will never eat chocolate again. I promise!"

"Yeah, yeah right; like the last time you said that too. You are addicted to chocolate, just like an alcoholic to liquor." Then he went into his bedroom and closed the door.

Oh my God, the pain is so horrible. I can't even sleep at night. I don't know how I'm going to survive for another week this way. That's how long the knife-like pain usually lasts. I am very sure of myself this time; I have no intention of eating another piece of chocolate for the rest of my life.

Three students I know from the forth quarter asked me if they could come to our apartment so that they can practice the Toughness Adjusting Technique on me. They even brought a portable adjusting table. Next semester I will need to buy myself an adjusting table too, so that I can practice adjusting on my buddy Joe at home.

When Ralph found out about the three students coming over, he announced flatly that he was staying in his bedroom and I was not to bother him. He says he can't stomach any more of the stupid nonsense being taught at school as proper techniques to adjusting the spine. He can't wait to leave for Western States Chiropractic College.

I understand how he feels, but I like staying open minded even if some of the outlandish techniques are hard to grasp. First I watched how it was done on one of the other students, and once I saw that it was completely harmless I willingly laid face down on their adjusting table. The patient doesn't have to take their clothes off. The doctor rubs his fingers on what looks like a small tambourine about ten inches from the patient's back until the tambourine starts to make a high pitched squeaky sound. That sound indicates where to adjust the spine. Incredibly enough it squeaked right over my L4-L5, which is where my back is the weakest. With the Toughness Adjusting Technique, kind of an ironic name for something so gentle, the doctor of chiropractic doesn't have to do spinal motion or palpation to find the subluxation, the little tambourine does all the work by squeaking like a fire alarm at the spinal level that needs to be adjusted.

I was sold on the power of the tambourine until I was adjusted by one of the students. He barely touched my back, and in my opinion nothing had been moved into place. I didn't say anything because I didn't want him to feel bad, but from laying face down for so long, my back was hurting like it always does if I stay in that position for a long time. I used to love sleeping face down, but once I found out how much more pain I was getting from extending my spine, I started acclimatizing my brain not to allow me to sleep on my stomach. It took me years to adapt to that, but I did it. If I have to lay face down, I have to put a pillow under my pelvis so that I don't extend backwards. When I become a chiropractor this is something that I will pass on to my patients who might have the same condition as me. After my clinician here at school took X-rays of my neck and back, I was diagnosed with lower back facet syndrome, and that explains why I can't sleep face down. When the facets in my spine get jammed, it puts pressure on the nerves causing sharp pain in that area.

Anyway, I was not impressed with the Toughness Technique, and I don't intend to learn it.

Ralph is leaving for Oregon on February second, which is next week. I made a dinner fit for a Portuguese king. I invited Dexter of course, Ralph's best friend Russell and his wife, and also Sarah, our mutual friend from school.

In Ralph's honor, and to wish him good luck, Russell brought along a very special gift, a rare and extremely expensive bottle of wine. Ralph was quite touched by Russell's show of friendship. A bottle of wine like that was like opening a one-of-a-kind national treasure, and we all savored it to the very last drop. Everything went well except for when I put my hand on Dexter's shoulder saying, "I am very happy that you are here to share this meal with us."

He went into his non-expression mood, and everyone became aware of his emotional problems as he got very quiet and sat on the floor in the corner of the living room not talking to anyone. He really needs professional help.

I admire Leila, how she keeps repeating some classes and, no matter how tough it gets, she doesn't give up. She doesn't even realize that in many ways I look up to her for her determination in becoming a chiropractor. She is falling behind, and I share with her most of my notes including the exam copies whenever they come my way. I encourage her to come over to my apartment to study with me, even if it slows me down a lot — because when she comes over she brings her whole household effects which include a boom box, a stack of books, enough food not to starve for a week, and lots and lots of giggling conversation. She is not able to concentrate on one single subject. I got my camera out and took her picture so that she could see what she looks like surrounded by an immensity of books and papers, and who knows what more. She should be concentrating on one topic at a time. I believe that she spends too much time on chiropractic philosophy seminars when she should be concentrating on academics instead.

Ironically, last quarter Leila was studying in the library for chiropractic philosophy finals and forgot that was the time she was supposed to be getting tested. She ran out of the library and into the testing center, but it was already too late and the teacher would not allow her in. That is so ridiculous because if anybody should win an A for chiropractic philosophy it would be Leila. She is the epitome of commitment and knowledge when it comes to being eloquent about chiropractic. Now she is repeating the course this quarter because she has a prick for a teacher. Interestingly enough, there are no illegal tests going around when it comes to chiropractic philosophy, only about science.

Leila told me that in her younger days she smoked pot, but she had also experimented with some hard drugs. That could explain why she is such a space cadet, unless she was already that way before she did the mushrooms. Dexter also did a lot of drugs in his younger days. I wonder if the drugs they used are the cause of their emotional inadequacy.

Ralph and I hugged each other this morning before he left for Oregon. Thank you dear God, for putting Ralph into my life as my son and my best friend, I am going to miss him terribly. I admire how unselfish he is, leaving by himself even though he would rather I went with him as we always have a great time together. He did ask politely one more time if I would consider going with him, but he understands that I am more comfortable with the curriculum here where I know what to expect, and that it would be silly to waste my free tuition. Like he said, if I change my mind after my scholarship is over, I can always transfer to the College in Oregon.

When I got home from school I began moving my personal stuff into my new bedroom. Good thing that Ralph helped me carry my bed to his bedroom prior to leaving.

Dexter and I are still seeing each other, but each time I keep distancing myself emotionally. Like Dexter described our relationship a long time ago, our sexual encounters are just hormones doing what they know best. I am writing this with a sarcastic feeling because it helps me to deal with our odd relationship.

My new bedroom is slowly turning into a dream room. I have been opening the boxes that were delivered a while ago but had remained untouched. I had forgotten what I brought along. I'm delighted to have found my favorite cream-color lace curtains and matching bedspread that were used as stage props for "Veronica's Room," a murder mystery I produced some years ago. It couldn't be more befitting.

On the left corner of my bedroom, between the two shaded large windows, I placed a beat-up round table I found for two dollars at Goodwill and covered it with the Japanese silk cloth that Katherine, my costume designer at The Simy Dinner Theatre, had given me. On top of the table I placed Mrs. Ounuma's maroon flowers, appropriately arranged inside a tall crystal glass jar I bought at the local flea market. It matches Grandmother Mutter's crystals, which I purposely used to decorate the table.

Next to my bed I put my old fashioned black telephone, an old prop I kept from my theatre days; and a small dainty lamp I found at a garage sale around here. The lamp caught my eye because the shade matched the bedspread and curtains. Now I only need to get an extension cord for the light switch next to my bed and I will have the control of turning the main bedroom light on and off while I'm still in bed.

The bathroom has been a pleasure to decorate. It is a nice sized bathroom, so I was able to embellish it with all my duck paraphernalia including the matching duck towels, dish soap, and tissue duck box just to mention a few collectable treasures. Thanks to Katherine's more than kind handouts from a few years ago, I have a very warm and luxurious bathroom.

The bathroom is so comfy and so inviting that when Leila saw it she fell in love with it and asked me if she could take a shower right then and there. That's how impressed she was. Afterwards she asked me if I minded that she come over once in awhile and treat herself to using it. Of course I told her that my bathroom is her bathroom, just like, mi casa es su casa, in Spanish.

In my opinion, Dr. Frickenson should be turned in for an attitude problem besides being a crummy teacher.

He came into class, and instead of teaching, which is what he is supposed to, he began attacking us with verbal abuse.

"You, young men in this classroom, you better enjoy it while you are young, because you are all going to wind up with prostate cancer sooner or later, and then croak." And he was laughing disdainfully as he continued on, "Read chapters five through nine for the test next week. Just so you know it, I won't be here Thursday because I have better things to do."

Then, he left the classroom.

We were dumbfounded. No one got up; we just looked at each other. Then I heard a student behind me saying, "Let's lynch the bastard."

Another voice was heard, "I'm with you man."

I added to it, "Count me in as a look-out."

It felt good to imagine Dr. Frickenson on his knees begging for mercy.

Part of me tells me that I made a mistake not going to Oregon with Ralph. Some of the teachers this quarter are really good, but there are still a few that come into class, at least the ones that do show up for classes, ill prepared and all they do is talk about their hobbies. Dr. Frickenson is the worst of them. This week he came into class, said a few more insults, towards the students and then proceeded to describe his latest criminal case. Supposedly he is also a lawyer.

Susan, one of the students, was late coming into the classroom and was walking quietly through the back door.

He pointed a finger at her and yelled, "You, loser, get the hell out of my class."

"I am sorry Dr. Frickenson, but it took me a while to find a parking space." She said flustered.

"Are you deaf? Didn't you hear me? I said get the hell out of this class if you know what's good for you!"

Susan left crying, and he went on with his story, which had nothing to do with why we all pay tuition. There's one more thing he does and we don't know what to do about it because if we complain, we are afraid he will flunk us. He opens the lab room and says, "You guys have fun. I'll be back in an hour."

We sit talking about what the heck he wants us to do in there since he gives us no instructions except for a print- out that we don't understand.

When he comes back he will say something like, "Please don't ask me anything. Just go home and read your book as-signments. I have work to do myself."

What a horrible nightmare I experienced last night. This was the kind of thing you can only share with a good friend, so I called Leila on the phone and told her all about it.

"That is gross!" she said audibly disgusted.

"Trust me. I feel the same way. Having sex with Dr. Frick-enson is not a pretty picture."

"You must be attracted to him to even come up with some-thing that gross into your dreams."

"Leila it wasn't a dream, believe me! I woke up sick to my stomach. It was a disgusting experience! A real nightmare!"

She was laughing hard and then, as she always says to me when I tell her anything that makes her laugh, "Veronica, my dear, you always make me laugh with your stories. Thank you."

"Please, don't mention it. It's my pleasure to make you laugh."

I have never told Leila this, but she laughs exactly like the famous old cartoon Muttley the dog. Sometimes I tell her something outrageous just because I love to hear the sound of her laughter. It takes away my anger and it makes me smile.

I took a drive to the large hardware store down the street to pick up an extension cord. But when I stepped out of my car I got a feeling, a very strange feeling, that I was being watched. A dubious looking character was walking towards me. He was a skinny white man, with a stubbly looking face that matched his unkempt clothing. I was alone in the parking lot, but I should not have worried about it since it was something like three in the afternoon, except that my instinct told me that I was in danger. That had never happened to me before, and without even thinking I nervously reached into the bottom of my pocketbook looking for the pepper sprayer that Al had given to me before I left New Jersey the first time I came to Georgia.

The man kept coming in my direction, grinning while saying, "Your plate says New Jersey, is that where you're from, honey?"

I froze in place and didn't answer. I was shaking while holding on tight to the pepper sprayer; I was ready to spray him if he came any closer. Suddenly he looked straight at me as if I had turned into some scary monster and, making a sudden turn about, he ran away. I thought I had scared him away when he saw the pepper sprayer in my hand, just then a heavy man's hand came down on my right shoulder, from behind me.

I was freaking out even when he said, nurturing, "Miss, don't worry about him. He won't bother you anymore."

I took off running into the store and asked to speak to the manager. I told him what had happened in the parking lot and he said casually, "Yes, that's our store detective. We pay him to be outside protecting our customers."

Al still calls me once a week. I feel obliged to listen and not to argue back while listening to his usual pessimistic opinions. I feel angry and frustrated afterwards, but at the same time relieved that I am no longer married to him. Besides that, I feel uncomfortable as he keeps sending me money every month though we are no longer married. I've told him over and over again not to do it. He says he accepts the way I am, and all he wants is for me to be happy. I hope he finds someone soon. Steve told me that he tried twice to connect Al with a woman, but he has given up. The teacher Steve invited for dinner at his house to meet Al didn't work out; Al ignored her. As for the other one, who was a real knock out according to Steve, Al had been very rude towards her.

Our teacher, Dr. Boyle, told us some interesting facts concerning the water we drink. I was so grossed out by the data he brought to our attention that over the weekend I bought myself a water purifier machine from Sears. It boils a gallon of water overnight and puts out a clean sparkling gallon of water by the next day.

This morning Dr. Boyle showed the class a video on nutrition facts, but first he shared with us a homemade videotape of his family, which seriously offended Doug, one of my classmates. Doug said that he didn't appreciate being forced to see two kids naked. He felt it was obscene and we shouldn't have to be put through such an emotional ordeal! I couldn't believe what he was saying. How can a three-year-old boy and his baby brother probably one or two years old, running around naked on the front lawn of Dr. Boyle's garden while being sprayed with the garden hose is considered an obscenity?

Before Ralph left for Oregon we both used to refer to Doug as "Doug the Degenerate" because everything that came out of his mouth was sexual and obscene. Doug is always very respectful towards me. He sees me as Ralph's mother, but he has a distorted way of analyzing situations that are perfectly normal. He is so weird!

I got myself a very small trampoline. I put it close to my desk along with my radio tape recorder. It's my modus operandi for taking a mental and physical break during the long hours of studying while getting ready for final exams. Every hour on the hour I have a timer going off. I get up from my seat and dance around the room to the tune on the radio. Then I get on the trampoline and jump up and down until I feel re-energized enough to go back to sitting at my desk.

Dexter was in the kitchen making tea right after we had some steamy sex in the living room floor. Without even giving it a second thought, I went from behind him and hugged him.

He pushed me away gently, remarking, "Why do you always have to do that? We had great sex, so why do you still need to hug me?"

I started to cry, first softly, and then out of despair I yelled angrily, "Our relationship is not normal, it's incomplete. Our relationship is like a really nicely wrapped gift box with all the trimmings, but when I open the box it's empty inside. Don't you get it? You are empty of human feelings. You are ice that never melts, because you don't have a heart. I curse you for not allowing us to be happy together and putting me through these emotions of anger."

I went crying into my bedroom and locked the door. When he knocked I didn't open. I heard the front door closing, and when I opened my bedroom door I found on the floor a cup of tea on one of my duck trays.

At moments like these I think about Michael. He is way in back of my mind, an almost vanished shapeless shadow, but thanks to my minds eye I can recover him any time I need him to lay down next to me and hold me the way he used to. Those few hours I had with Michael are kept dormant, burrowed deep into every part of my being. When I summon his presence he comes to me, like glistening snow covering the earth in white and breathing life back into me.

I write this from the heart; I wish for Dexter to go away, far away. Not dead, just gone. Dexter, go away!

Now I'll go to sleep. I have to be ready for my tests tomorrow morning.

Dexter called to say he had something important to talk to me about, and needed to come over at the end of the day. I was cold and reserved when I opened my apartment door. I knew he would be pleased with that.

"Veronica, I know that you are not going to believe this, but last night around ten I actually heard a voice telling me, 'Dexter, go away.' I'm taking that as a sign that I must leave Georgia. I'm going to transfer to the Chiropractic College in California, and I want you to come with me."

I almost freaked out when I heard that, I mean about the voice. Good thing he didn't recognize the voice as mine, maybe because I had written my wish, instead of saying it? This was too eerie for me to even care to understand. But it was good, very good news. He was leaving, I was thinking. Oh happiness, I must control myself from singing with joy.

Keeping my emotions in pretty good control I said, "You know that I can't just leave. I'm on a scholarship. But tell me more"

"A few weeks ago Donna and Cody and four other students invited me to go with them to Life West Chiropractic College in California. I wasn't quite sure if I wanted to go, but once I heard that voice last night telling me to leave, this is it. I'm going."

"Why bother to go from one Life College to another Life College, aren't they all the same?"

"No. I found out that the reason the College in California has the name Life is because Dr. Williams made a handsome contribution to them in exchange for adding the word Life to its name. At least this is what I heard. Also, when Dr. Williams was visiting Life College in California and spoke at the school's assembly, he made the mistake of saying some derogatory comments like he's used to doing here at our school. The students there didn't like what they heard and he had to leave after being booed out of the assembly."

"Wow! That is really fantastic!"

"Yes, I know. I have heard nothing but good things about the teachers in California. Yet I was not sure if I should go or not, but once I heard the voice last night that, to me, is a good sign. Now I am definitely going. Are you sure you can't go with me? Veronica, if you come along, I promise to see a psychiatrist in California that was highly recommended. I know that if I get the right help, we can make it together."

I was shocked when he held my hands in his. That actually gave me courage to say, "No, I can't go with you. Please don't ask me any more. But you should see the psychiatrist anyway; it would be good for you. Of course we'll stay in touch, we will always be friends, right?"

"Veronica, you know that we are more than friends. I love you."

"I love you too. But I really can't deal with our relationship the way it is. Dexter, let's just stay in touch."

"Then promise me that if I get help over there and it works that you will give me another chance."

I seldom say no to anyone, so I said OK.

The caravan, as he calls it, is leaving the end of this quarter and he needs to get rid of everything he owns. It's easier to travel that way, he told me, and also he wants to start fresh when he gets to California. When he said he was renting a truck this weekend so that he could dump all his stuff at the Salvation Army, I almost passed out since I know that he is not rich. I suggested he sell his belongings at the Farmers Market and make some cash from it.

He said he didn't think he could do that on his own. I told him I would help. All he has to do is pick me up early on Saturday.

I was talking on the phone to Leila, trying to lift her spirits and telling her not to give up, because when you least expect it that's when your wishes come true.

And she remarked in her psychotherapist tone, "And what is it that you wish for right now, Veronica?" She always tends to see more meaning in what I am saying than what I really mean.

"A couch. I need a couch badly!" I said very sure of myself. "Every time I have company they have to sit at the dinning room table. A nice comfortable couch would be great!"

Just then I saw through the open glass doors of the living room a couch on the lawn very close to my patio window. No, I was not surprised.

"Leila, I hate to hang up, but guess what? My couch just arrived and it is waiting outside for me."

"You didn't tell me that you bought a couch?"

"I didn't buy it. I wished for one, and there it is! Bye, bye."

Of course she was doing her Muttley the dog laugh, when I hanged up.

The couch was bigger than I expected. It was a soiled, brown, corduroy, beat up, huge couch. I was disappointed with the style and color but...it was a couch. I stood there looking at it, trying to figure out how to move it by myself into my apartment. Then I heard my two new neighbors coming down the steps from the first floor. They were smiling as one of them said to the other, "Just one more piece of furniture and we are done moving in."

This taught me a big lesson when wishing for a couch. I must visualize the size, because it has to be light enough so that I can move it by myself around the living room without hurting my back. I would also like my couch to have an exotic Asian flare.

Dexter picked me up at the apartment very early Saturday morning. His rented pickup truck was packed full with his possessions. He encouraged me to take anything I wanted for myself before we left for the Farmers Market.

I told him our mission was to sell his stuff, not give it to me. But he insisted. "I'd rather you have it than sell it at the market for nothing or donating it at the end of the day."

I took three huge creamed color pillows that I figured would be good to sit on the floor, and four very beautiful 25" by 20" ink hand painted Chinese drawings already framed and under glass. I love Asian stuff! I was also attracted to a 3' by 6' framed Batik cloth painted deer with a variety of maroon and gold shades. I picked the deer painting because it reminded me of Dexter, innocently standing at a cross road looking at the headlights coming towards him. I intend to hang all the framed artwork on my bare bedroom walls.

I can't believe how much money Dexter made at the market. He said that it was going to cover his traveling expenses to California, and he would still have plenty left over. He was amazed as to how well we did, and said that only proved we made a good team.

No way am I going to California. My mother already warned me not to go west, she has a bad premonition about the deadly earthquakes all along the coast.

It was about two in the afternoon when we packed what little we had not sold at the Farmers Market and put it into the pickup truck. He drove directly to the Salvation Army. There it had been patiently waiting, my like-new, silky cotton, red with white crane birds and golden flowers, medium sized Asian couch, with matching pillows. Special that day: $15!

Dexter wanted to pay for the couch, but there was no way I would allow that. In order to be truly mine I would have to pay for it; that's how I felt it should be. But I did take advantage of his offer to use the rented pickup truck to deliver the couch to my apartment. That itself was a miracle.

I told Leila about the couch, and she said it's called Karma. You do something good for someone and it bounces back. I don't know how much I really believe in Karma. If that were true, everybody would be nice to each other.

Steve and I were talking on the phone and then he said hurriedly, "Mom, I'll call you right back. Jacob needs to have his diapers changed."

Wow! My son is changing his son's diapers! Now that's really profound. My son is a caring father!

The phone rang again.

It was Steve, and he was a lot calmer.

"Mom, I am so lucky to have Jacob. I was changing his diapers and he smiled back at me when I cleaned his poop. He can't talk yet, so he smiled at me as if he was saying, 'thank you dad for cleaning me up.' Can you imagine that?"

"I bet his poop smelled pretty bad…"

I was immediately interrupted. "Mom, you've got to be kidding. Jacob's poop is never stinky. Everything about him is perfect, even his poop."

Now that, was a truly inconceivable statement that only a loving parent could say wholeheartedly.

Steve continued, "Mom, you were a good example to me of what a parent should be. I hope to be as good father to my children, as you were a mother to Ralph and me. I could not have wished for a better mom than you. We sure had some great times together, didn't we?"

I was not an expert mom like he makes me sound. I was just doing my best. "Thank you, Steve. Guess what? After my finals next week, I'll be coming up to New Jersey during my school break."

Leila believes that the reason Al sends me money every month is because I tell him not to do it. She also feels that I'm a fool for wanting to give it back, which is my intention when I get to New Jersey. She has decided that she is going to use psychology on her ex-husband and instead of pleading for her monthly alimony she is going to tell him not to send her any more money. She wants to see if it works for her the same way as it does for me.

I believe that the real reason Al sends me money is because he feels like we are still married. I have to face him when I get to New Jersey and make him understand that he doesn't owe me anything. I don't deserve alimony because I don't have small children; and besides that, I am the one that asked for the divorce, so why should he compensate me for the rest of his life? I don't feel that would be fair. Between the government loan and my tuition being paid for the year, I'm doing great at saving my money.

Except for two more exams, I am almost done with all my finals. I am a little nervous going to New Jersey and meeting Al. This is the first time we will see each other since I asked for our separation to be permanent.

While in New Jersey I will be staying with Steve and Diane. My grandson, Jacob, is now six months old. He is my main reason for going to New Jersey. I can't wait to meet him.

The next break I will definitely be going to Portugal with Sarah, Russell, his wife Cathy, and their three-year old girl.

They've heard me telling them so many interesting stories about Portugal that they are dying to see what it is all about. Russell's wife works for the airlines, and she gets discount airline tickets for her family.

I am going to take the train to New Jersey, but I remember my experience sleeping seated on a train to Florida, so I got a private cabin with a bed. I am looking forward to the train ride.

While waiting to go back into the testing center to take my final test on Visceral Physiology, I met Robert, a black student, who is going to be in second quarter next semester. Robert is probably in his mid thirties. He is very athletic and definitely very good-looking. His eyes are light green, and his voice is smooth and deep like that of a blues singer. He asked me all kinds of questions about second quarter and what he should expect since I have already experienced going through it. He wanted to know what my secret was for memorizing so much information. I told him that doodling and taking notes while studying helps me a lot, and I have also made cards with questions on one side and answers on backs. That helped too. He asked me if he could borrow the cards, and we exchanged phone numbers.

Robert called me on the phone last night, and I found out that he is divorced and has two small children. He said he would stop by my apartment this morning to pick up the cards.

Dexter left early yesterday for California with the other students. We said goodbye over the phone. It is better this way. I wished him and the others good luck, and even though I am a bit sad to see them leave, I wish them the best. They've done what they felt they should do, just like Ralph. I am doing the same, which is the reason why I am staying.

Robert came by the apartment and I handed him the cards. He wanted to know what I was doing during the next ten days that we were off from school. "I'm staying in town during the break and I would love to spend time with you." He couldn't be more direct, that's for sure.

"I am going to be in New Jersey visiting family, now if you'll excuse me, Robert, I really need to start packing as I'm leaving today."

We hugged each other as is customary between students, but when he left I couldn't help feeling confused because when we hugged each other, I didn't really want to let go. I liked being in his arms, and it had nothing to do with love. Plain and simple, I am sexually attracted to him even though I would like to rationalize that such a feeling was most likely due to being alone, and as a human being I need human contact. This part of me that I discovered today, after hugging Robert, has made me wonder if perhaps I never loved Dexter, and was just having a good time. Can it be that sex can be just as fulfilling without love? That would mean that I'm just as cold as Dexter. What a horrible thought!

Cida took me to the train station, and I was relieved when we said goodbye. The ride to the station was beyond my endurance as she is the perfect example of a one-way conversation. We are friends, but there's only so much I can take of listening to a person speaking Portuguese without ever taking a breath.

I'm finally seated in my private train cabin. It's smaller than I thought. In the James Bond movies, the train cabins seem to be a lot bigger. It's very hot in here, and when I complained to the conductor he told me that, as soon as the train starts to move, my cabin would get cooler.

I didn't bring any books to read, but I brought my journal, which is begging me to fill in the white empty pages of my next diary. I am looking forward to the journey ahead and what life will bring my way.

A READING GROUP GUIDE

The questions provided in this guide
are intended to enhance your group's reading of

Veronica's Diary III
Awakening the Woman Within

Veronica Esagui, DC

To schedule a meeting with the author,
please email: handson13@hotmail.com.

Questions for Discussion

1. Veronica begins her diary by writing about her pre-arranged marriage. She is frustrated and angry toward her mother yet, takes her time to write a long letter about the dinner theatre she named after her mom in the hopes of giving her, emotional comfort. Veronica describes her mother as a little bird living in a gilded cage. Considering Veronica's personal success, do you believe that she is also a prisoner of her own environment?

2. How do you feel about Veronica falling in love with Michael? Can you think of anything that might have prevented it?

3. Veronica considers the possibility of having lived a life previous to this one, and to her amazement she is able to travel back in time, to Egypt. Do you believe in reincarnation? Have you ever had a Déjà vu experience, or a dream that seemed vivid and real upon waking up?

4. What do you believe was Veronica's motivation to drive off on her own from New Jersey through Connecticut and Massachusetts, to spend a week alone? Being such a sociable person, why do you think she enjoyed being by herself so much? Given the chance, do you feel you would not mind doing the same?

5. The author believes that every American child should be given the opportunity to experience a trip to a third world country. Are you in agreement? If so, what might be learned from traveling abroad?

6. What are your thoughts about Veronica and Al's experience with the Welfare Department? If you were to lose everything you had, would you seek help from the Welfare Department?

7. Veronica decided to return to college at the age of 42. If you had a chance to change your profession, what would you do and why?

8. Veronica thinks that rekindling the romance between her and Al in Portugal will save their marriage. Why didn't it work? How would you advise a friend that is in the same predicament?

9. Concerning Veronica's parents and their situation in Portugal, do you believe this type of abuse against the elderly, does not happen in the US? Considering that today's baby boomers are now in the senior category, what do you think everyone should do while young, to make sure this type of situation doesn't happen to them too?

10. Many small miracles seem to happen to Veronica and she is always aware and grateful for those moments. What has been the biggest miracle in your life?

11. Being single again and free to date whomever she wants is something that Veronica never experienced before she married Al. It seems to have opened the floodgates of her sexuality. Do you believe that if she had dated prior to getting married, she might have been more cautious about whom she went out with?

12. Making wishes come true seems to be part of Veronica's daily life. Veronica makes her wishes come true not realizing that she works at making them happen. How do you feel about wishes? If you had one wish that you know could come true, what would it be?

13. What can be learned from reading this book?

If you were to ask Veronica any questions about her diary, what would they be?

If your book club would like to arrange a meeting with the author, please contact her at: Handson13@hotmail.com

About the Author

Dr. Veronica Esagui is a chiropractic physician and the internationally and critically acclaimed author of *The Scoliosis Self-Help Resource Book.* In addition to maintaining a successful practice in West Linn, Oregon, she hosts The Author's Forum, a television talk show featuring authors, publishers, editors, and others involved in the production of books. She is a member of The Northwest Association of Book Publishers, Pacific Northwest Literacy Alliance and the recipient of the NABP Member of the Year Award. She is the Chief Executive Officer of the Northwest Annual Book Festival, The Northwest Writers and Publishers Association, (NWPA) and Papyrus Press LLC, Publishing Company.

For information on upcoming events, interview requests, and comments about *Veronica's Diary III—Awakening the Woman Within,* or to find out more about the availability of other published works, please visit the author at: www. veronicaesagui.net or www.nwbookfestival.com.

About the Artists

Derrick Freeland – when not engaged in the fine and subtle art of Tom Foolery, Derrick can be found illustrating the lives of others, and those who never existed in the first place. His work can be found here in this volume and with Common Ties Publishing.
Derrickfreeland.blogpspot.com

Jean Sheldon is a graphic artist and the owner of Wellworth Publishing and the fiction imprint, Bast Press that has published her mysteries *The Woman in the Wing, Seven Cities of Greed,* and *Flowers for Her Grave.*
www.jeansheldon.com

Other books by Dr. Veronica Esagui:

The Scoliosis Self-Help Resource Book
This resource includes the illustrated step-by-step approach to TESP (The Esagui Scoliosis Protocol), a very specific group of exercises for the spine. Through this book, a person with scoliosis will discover that they may have options other than drugs or surgery. As Dr. Esagui says, "If by writing this book, I can shed some light onto scoliosis management that is more proactive than waiting under observation, then people will understand their options and I will have done my best as a chiropractor and educator."

Verónica's Diary—The Journey of Innocence (1944-1962)
Describes in the most candid manner the first eighteen years of Veronica's life growing up in Portugal, until a pre arranged marriage with her cousin, brings her to the USA in 1962.

Veronica's Diary II—Braving the New World (1962-1988)
Follows her trail blazing accomplishments as a music teacher, performer, news reporter, owner of three music centers, playwright, theatre director, producer and owner of the only American dinner theatre in the world in a Japanese Restaurant.

Coming soon...

Veronica's Diary IV—Angels Among Us (1994-1996)

Experiencing the darkest days of her life, Veronica is thankful for the angels along her path, some of who were still exorcising their ghostly past as they strived to earn their wings.

Veronica's Diary V—The Gift (1996-2003)

A stranger follows Veronica into a supermarket and hands her a small piece of pottery, insisting that the gift is meant only for her. She accepts it. Veronica's rich life experiences as a time traveler have taught her to recognize that her quest for happiness has finally been granted.

Request for Pre-Publication Notice

If you would like to receive notice of the publication dates of *Veronica's Diary sequels, Angels Among Us,* and *The Gift,* please complete and return the form below or contact the author at www.veronicaesagui.net.

Name: _____

Address: _____

City: _____ State: _____ Zip: _____

E-mail Address: _____

Postal: Papyrus Press LLC
       21860 Willamette Drive,
       West Linn, OR 97068

CPSIA information can be obtained at www.ICGtesting.com
Printed in the USA
BVOW020153080312

284706BV00001B/3/P